PROFESSIONAL ETHICS IN EDUCATION SERIES

Kenneth A. Strike, Editor

The Ethics of School Administration
Kenneth A. Strike, Emil J. Haller, and Jonas F. Soltis

Classroom Life as Civic Education: Individual
Achievement and Student Cooperation in Schools
David C. Bricker

The Ethics of Special Education
Kenneth R. Howe and Ofelia B. Miramontes

The Ethics of Multicultural and Bilingual Education
Barry L. Bull, Royal T. Fruehling, and Virgie Chattergy

THE ETHICS OF
Multicultural and Bilingual
EDUCATION

Barry L. Bull
Royal T. Fruehling
Virgie Chattergy

TEACHERS
COLLEGE
PRESS

Teachers College, Columbia University
New York and London

Published by Teachers College Press, 1234 Amsterdam Avenue
New York, NY 10027

Library of Congress Cataloging-in-Publication Data

Bull, Barry L.
    The ethics of multicultural and bilingual education / Barry L. Bull, Royal T. Fruehling, Vir-
gie Chattergy.
        p.   cm.—(Professional ethics in education series)
    Includes bibliographical references (p.   ) and index.
    ISBN 0-8077-3187-0 (alk. paper)
    1. Intercultural education—United States—Moral and ethical aspects—Case studies.   2.
Education, Bilingual—United States—Moral and ethical aspects—Case studies.   I. Fruehling, Royal T.   II. Chattergy, Virgie. 1938–   .   III. Title.   IV. Series.
LC1099.3.B85   1992
370.19'341—dc20   92-15962

Printed on acid-free paper
Manufactured in the United States of America
98 97 96 95 94 93 92   9 8 7 6 5 4 3 2 1

For
Arthur C. and Marjorie F. Bull
Aurora Fruehling
Rahul, V. Paul, and David Vikram

Contents

Acknowledgments

We are grateful to many individuals for their assistance in preparing this book. We thank Dr. Marie Wunsch and Dr. Ann Bayer for encouragement and support. We are especially indebted to Amanda So Young Chang, Dr. Reynaldo Contreras, Dr. Jesus Garcia, Angela Lee, S. Lee, Dr. Howard P. McKaughan, and Dr. Cheong Nguyen for information, advice, and critical commentary on several of the chapters and cases. Any remaining errors and infelicities are the result of our own inability to benefit from their wise counsel.

THE ETHICS OF
Multicultural and Bilingual
EDUCATION

CHAPTER 1

The Nature and Complexity of Issues in Multicultural and Bilingual Education

Cultural and linguistic differences have been a source of strength and controversy in the United States since its founding. Indeed, this country's founding and much subsequent U.S. history can be seen as a continuing search for unity in diversity, for *e pluribus unum*, especially among its residents of European extraction. What could unite the New York Dutch, the Pennsylvania German, and the Virginia English; the Massachusetts Puritan, the Pennsylvania Quaker, the Maryland Catholic, and the Virginia Anglican; the Yankee trader, the northern farmer, and the southern plantation owner? How could the United States assimilate and capitalize upon its Norwegian, Irish, Russian, Italian, Polish, and Jewish immigrants? And more recently, what relationship could white Anglo majorities establish with formerly disenfranchised and economically marginalized African-American, Chinese, Japanese, Native American, and Latino minorities?

The terms in which this nation has asked these questions and many of the answers that have been attempted—discrimination, exploitation, Americanization, civil war, segregation—suggest that, at best, our quest for unity in diversity is still significantly unfulfilled. And the recent arrival of new immigrants, even denser concentrations of new and old minorities in urban ghettos, and major contemporary shifts in the racial and ethnic composition of our population imply that the fulfillment of this quest is more pressing and problematic than ever.

The purpose of this book is to enable professional educators to confront and to think carefully, sensitively, and systematically about the educational and ethical dimensions of this quest. Of course, it cannot and does not pretend to resolve in any final way the thorny problems of cultural contact and conflict that have plagued not just the United States but most of humanity for millennia. But it will introduce readers to the variety and complexity of those problems and to some of the most well-developed and serious ways of thinking about them.

1

SCHOOLS AND CULTURAL DIFFERENCE

Almost from the beginning of the nation, schools have been thought of as both part of the solution and part of the problem of creating unity in diversity in the United States. Early on, Thomas Jefferson had a vision of mandatory public schools that could promote common beliefs, attitudes, and abilities that were, in his view, needed to make the American experiment in democracy succeed. Without an informed electorate, Jefferson argued, democracy would degenerate into a rancorous and ultimately fatal struggle among narrow and parochial interests.

By the last half of the nineteenth century, Jefferson's vision had taken hold across the nation. Eventually all states provided schooling at public expense and required families to send their children to school. As the flow of European immigration became a flood by the end of that century, the common education of the public schools came to be understood, especially in the cities, as Americanization. What Jefferson had seen as a rather limited *addition* to the education provided by family, church, and community became for the children of urban immigrants a *substitution* of American culture, language, and mores for those of the home.

This educational solution to the problem of unity in diversity was experienced by many to be part of that very problem. From the start, significant populations—notably African slaves, Native Americans, and, later, Asian immigrants—were simply excluded from the idea of a common education. When finally included in public schooling, children from these groups were usually segregated from their white peers and provided with an education that, at best, ignored their cultural and social background and, at worst, actively sought to strip them of their families' culture and language. In the west, for instance, Native American children were often involuntarily removed from their tribal communities to be educated in English-only boarding schools.

Many European immigrants resisted the enforced Americanization of the public schools. Some immigrant communities established schools that provided instruction in the native language. And many religious minorities sponsored their own alternatives to public schools. These efforts to maintain cultural and linguistic identity were often greeted with hostility by English-speaking and protestant majorities. During and after World War I, several states sought to prohibit instruction in foreign languages because such instruction allegedly fostered anti-American sentiment. In 1922, Oregon adopted a law, supported by the Ku Klux Klan and aimed particularly at Roman Catholics, that required all children to attend public schools. When in the mid-1920s the U.S. Supreme Court eventually upheld parents' rights to provide these private alternatives, the incompatibility of militant educational Americanization with the founders' ideal of unity in diversity was formally recognized in constitutional law.

Throughout the twentieth century, the meaning of that ideal has been further tested in the courts, in state legislatures and the Congress, and in the educational bureaucracy by members of those groups that had in the nineteenth century been excluded from publicly sponsored education. African-Americans have challenged segregation laws and other policies and practices that have limited their educational opportunities. Native Americans have fought for day schools and greater community control over their children's education. Spanish- and Chinese-speaking parents have sought educational programs that take into account their children's linguistic backgrounds. These ongoing controversies and others concerning school textbooks and libraries, home schooling, private religious schools, and the teaching of evolution reveal that the citizens of the United States are more uncertain than ever about what the ideal of unity in diversity should mean and about how our schools should help to achieve it.

FACTS, ETHICS, AND CULTURAL DIFFERENCE

Part of our confusion about the ideal of unity in diversity stems from our uncertainty over matters of fact. What are the children who are culturally or linguistically different from me and my children really like? What aspirations do they and their parents have? How do they behave? What school rules, curriculum, and teaching methods are most likely to help them realize their aspirations? What effect would those educational arrangements have on *my* children? Would my children do well under those conditions? Would they achieve the goals I have for them?

These and similar questions seek the *facts* about the members of different groups and how they interact with each other. And achieving the ideal of unity in diversity in any concrete school situation clearly depends upon these answers. The sort of unity that is possible in the education of a multicultural group of children depends to some extent upon what aspirations they happen to share. The diversity that is feasible in such a context similarly depends upon the extent to which the various cultural and linguistic differences are compatible. Thus, the facts about cultural and linguistic groups to which school children and their parents belong help to determine what options a society has for creating unity in diversity within particular school situations. There are, however, two things we should observe about these facts.

First, these facts are often extraordinarily difficult to come by. Much of what passes for facts about children of various ethnic or language groups is simply the result of historical prejudice or superficial generalization rather than serious study. And, as we will see in the specific cases to be presented later, even when we do look carefully and thoughtfully at children, it is often hard to agree upon a description of their characteristics, aspirations, and problems. One thing that makes this agreement about facts hard to achieve is that there is much diversity within cultures. The differences among Polish Americans or African-Americans or Japanese Americans are considerable. Any characterization of Japanese Americans, say, that neglects this diversity is more likely to be a stereotype than an accurate description. Cultures also change. Thus recent immigrants from Puerto Rico and Mexico differ because their common Hispanic heritage evolved under disparate social, economic, and geographic conditions before they arrived. Similarly, the culture of the descendants of the Japanese who settled in Hawaii is significantly different from that of those who settled in California because, despite their common origins, their ancestors had considerably different experiences after immigration. The facts about the members of the various cultural groups that make up the United States are, therefore, unusually complicated.

Second, these facts do not uniquely determine a solution to the problem of unity in diversity. A knowledge of the differences in religious practices, attitudes toward authority, or understanding of the natural world within a community may tell us whether unity in religious, political, or scientific belief will be hard or easy to achieve. But this knowledge does not necessarily reveal whether those beliefs are a legitimate part of the diversity we should tolerate or the unity we should foster. That our public schools might with relative ease erase the minor religious differences that exist within a particular community does not necessarily imply that they should do so.

In this case, we are likely to ask a different set of questions. Do I as a parent have a right to transmit my religious beliefs to my children without interference from the rest of the community? Do my children have a right to hold religious beliefs different from those of other children? Who should determine the precise beliefs that public schools will promote and why? What should we do if people with dramatically different beliefs move into the community?

These are *ethical,* not factual, questions. They ask what people *should* do from among the actions that the facts make possible—what responsibilities people have toward one another, what freedom they should exercise, how they should make decisions that affect themselves and others, what role tradition should have in people's lives. They demonstrate that the ideal of unity in diversity has a moral and not just a pragmatic meaning. That ideal concerns not only how culturally, religiously, and ethnically different people *can* live together but also how they *should* live together.

It is tempting to suppose that disagreements among the members of a multicultural society are entirely the result of a mutual misunderstanding of the facts. And we may hope that getting straight about the facts will resolve these issues. Unfortunately, such disagreements often prove to be more complex and difficult because they include ethical differences. Even worse, these ethical differences can themselves affect the interpretation and selection of relevant facts. In short, in many situations of multicultural difference, a consideration of ethics will be unavoidable.

It is with this ethical dimension of education in multicultural and multilingual communities that this book will be primarily concerned. The ethical issues raised in educational contexts are among the most difficult and controversial that Americans confront. As we seek to understand and resolve these issues, it is important to focus our attention on realistic problems. For this reason, this book will be centered upon descriptions of representative school situations in which these issues arise. Let us now consider one such situation in an effort to understand why these issues seem to be so complicated.

As we have already noted, American cultural and linguistic groups are themselves enormously diverse. As a result, the cases presented in this book do not pretend to represent the beliefs and characteristics of all members of the groups they include. For example, many Americans of African and European origin will not share any of the viewpoints described in the following case. Nevertheless, we believe that such cases faithfully capture some of the issues that arise when people with various backgrounds encounter one another in educational contexts.

JEFFERSON HIGH SCHOOL

Jefferson High School is, by almost any measure, one of the real successes of Iron City's fifteen-year-old desegregation plan. City officials point to Jefferson's natural advantages and the leadership of an extraordinary principal to explain the school's success.

Jefferson is located between Hiram Hill, an almost exclusively white upper-middle- and middle-class neighborhood, and Kaneville, a neighborhood of small apartment complexes and row houses that has for generations served working-class families as a step away from the overcrowded conditions of Iron City's central district. In serving Hiram Hill and Kaneville, Jefferson had long maintained a reputation for serious study and academic excellence, a reputation that inspired gratitude and loyalty among its alumni and their parents. In the years prior to desegregation, Kaneville had become the residence of an increasing number of African-American families. Nevertheless, the Iron City school board's periodic redrawing of Jefferson's attendance area resulted in a student body that was never more than about 10% black. Indeed, these school board actions were a significant part of the evidence that led to the federal court's desegregation order.

That order required the integration of both the school's student body and its faculty. The former was accomplished easily by an adjustment of attendance area boundaries that initially resulted in a student body that was 40% black and 60% white. In the first few years, demographic changes in Kaneville and, to a lesser extent, Hiram Hill and the decision by some parents to send their children to private schools increased the proportion of black students to around 60%, where it seems to have stabilized.

The integration of the faculty was one of the first responsibilities of Rosemary Taylor, an African-American vice principal of a central city high school who was appointed principal at Jefferson in the second year of desegregation. The appointment of a known and trusted leader encouraged many of Iron City's most experienced and talented black teachers to seek transfer to Jefferson. Equally attractive to teachers, both black and white, was Mrs. Taylor's approach to the educational program for Jefferson's newly integrated student body.

Mrs. Taylor was convinced of the crucial role of high intellectual and behavioral expectations in the promotion of academic success among students. As a result, she wished to continue Jefferson's traditions of a rigorous academic curriculum for all students. At the same time, Mrs. Taylor believed that two changes were necessary for this approach to succeed in a racially integrated setting. The standard academic curriculum, she believed, almost entirely neglected the involvement of African-Americans in the development of American society and civilization. Thus, neither white nor black children understood their society as a joint venture to which their ancestors had—for better and worse—contributed and for which they themselves had a shared future responsibility. This understanding, she thought, would produce the mutual respect and confidence necessary, first, for amicable relations between European- and African-American children reared in segregated neighborhoods and, second, for the maintenance of a serious attitude toward academic and vocational achievement. Furthermore, this understanding required a thorough revision of the entire curriculum to include as a matter of course the contributions of and relations between the races; the addition of a unit on George Washington Carver here or a semester of African-American studies there would be insufficient. For this purpose, she charged committees of teachers to conceive, design, and implement a revised curriculum in all subjects, a task that introduced a continuing vitality and thoughtfulness into the intellectual life of the school.

In addition, Mrs. Taylor recognized that order and academic motivation were not all that Jefferson's integrated student body needed for success in a scholastically demanding program. Many of the new students had attended segregated elementary and junior high schools that were poorly staffed and funded. Therefore, these students would need remediation, assistance, and guidance to prosper at Jefferson. Mrs. Taylor asked the school PTA and guidance counselors to establish a program of academic support to meet these needs. Their planning resulted in a system of early identification and counseling of students with difficulties, an academic big brothers and sisters program, a tutoring program before and after school, the opening of the school library for supervised study in the evenings and on Saturdays, and visits to the homes of students with special problems. Not only school staff members but also community and student volunteers were systematically involved in these efforts.

Although there were some difficulties in initiating these curricular and support programs, Mrs. Taylor's enthusiasm and commitment and her ability to obtain needed additional resources from city school authorities led to their gradual implementation over the first five years of her administration. And these initiatives seemed to produce results. Jefferson had the lowest dropout rate of any Iron City High School; 80% of entering students earned their diplomas. Sixty percent of these graduates went on to some type of postsecondary education. Standardized test scores were significantly above city averages and a little higher than national norms. Equally important, Jefferson had maintained strong community support during the period of transition to a desegregated school. Students developed a genuine pride in Jefferson, and parents and other community members showed their confidence in the school through continuing involvement in the academic support programs.

Despite the overall success of Jefferson, parents and teachers have recently begun to express concern over whether all students are benefiting equitably from the school's program. There are some real disparities in the achievement of black and white students at Jefferson. The dropout rate for blacks is about 25%, whereas that for whites is only 10%. The median white student at Jefferson scores about ten percentile points higher on standardized tests than the median black student. The greatest differences occur in postsecondary school attendance: 45% of Jefferson's black graduates continue their education; 80% of the white graduates do so. And more blacks go on to trade schools and junior colleges than do whites, who generally attend four-year colleges.

Some parents and teachers regard these differences as inevitable though unfortunate. Black students at Jefferson, they point out, do better than in any other Iron City high school. Moreover, student aspirations and performance depend not only on what the school does but also on parents' educational background, community influences, and the family's economic resources. Jefferson has done a great deal to compensate for these factors, but some of them are beyond the reach of the school. It would be too risky to tamper with a basically satisfactory school program when the chances of equalizing black and white students' achievement any farther seem so slender.

Others in the school community, including Mrs. Taylor, are less satisfied with the status quo and wish to consider changes that might reduce these apparent inequities. The principal has therefore asked Alex Andrews, a young and respected white social studies teacher, to chair a teacher task force to address this issue. She reported this action to the PTA, who decided to ask their curriculum committee, chaired by James Radner, a prominent black attorney, also to consider the problem. After over a year of work, the teacher and PTA groups have reached significantly different conclusions.

The teacher task force concluded that, although Jefferson's curriculum has been changed to recognize the value of African-American contributions to, and the reality of their experience in, American society, the way that curriculum is taught disadvantages most African-American children. As in other American schools, Jefferson's classrooms emphasize individual study and learning, quiet, constrained movement, and the artificial scheduling of activities. Success at Jefferson depends upon students' ability to see aspects or elements of the world as disconnected from the whole—as discrete and independent subjects such as history, psychology, and physics. Those subjects, moreover, place a premium on objective and impersonal judgment.

The teachers' reading and research have suggested that African-American students' families and communities and the African cultures from which they descended promote a style of understanding and acting in the world at odds with these procedures, assumptions, and expectations. What many scholars and observers have called black cultural style encourages verbal and physical expression, collective action and understanding, and an event-centered rather than a mechanical attitude toward time (Boykin, 1986). This heritage emphasizes holistic and spiritual conceptions of the world and respects emotional and subjective responses to experience. These differences between home and school put African-American students at a learning disadvantage in comparison with European-Americans, whose home culture is usually more consistent with Jefferson's approach to education. This disadvantage accounts in large part, they argue, for differences in African- and European-American school performance and for the alienation from school that leads to dropping out and the choice not to pursue education beyond high school.

To correct these inequities, the teachers propose significant changes in the way that Jefferson's classes are taught. First, they argue, the curriculum should be reorganized into units that would allow common themes to be studied from many points of view. Math, science, social-studies, and English teachers should plan and teach these units together. In this way, the subject matter that students learn will be more coherent and, thus, more consistent with the holistic view implicit in most African-American students' approach to learning. Second, classroom procedures must be changed. The students must be encouraged to be actively involved in their learning. Rather than learning by passive listening and reading, students must be challenged to observe, discuss, manipulate, and experiment with the subject matter they are studying. Tasks that emphasize these activities will, they argue, exploit African-American students' cultural preferences for expression, movement, and engagement. Moreover, school learning should be cooperative rather than individualistic and competitive. Tasks should be assigned to small groups of students who can stimulate, assist, and encourage each other to reach common goals and understandings. Finally, these new classroom procedures will necessitate a different approach to teachers' evaluation of student performance. Such evaluation must emphasize group success and students' contributions to it.

The PTA committee has suggested a dramatically different diagnosis of the disparity in black and white students' achievement at Jefferson. Academic and social success, they argue, is based upon students' acquiring the language and information assumed by a society's literate culture—the words, concepts, metaphors, ideas, and references necessary to understand the written and spoken discourse of university, government, business, and community leaders. Without this cultural literacy, as E. D. Hirsch (1987) has called it, students are locked out of full participation in the society's most powerful institutions and most significant decisions. Most of Jefferson's white students and a few black students become naturally conversant in this literate culture because they grow up in middle- and upper-middle-class families that participate in the culture. The vast majority of Jefferson's black students, however, do not have these home advantages. For them, the school is the only available means of access to what Hirsch calls literate culture.

According to the parent group, this difference in access accounts for the differences in school performance of Jefferson's black and white students. Standardized tests inevitably utilize the language and ideas of the dominant literate culture, and black students are, therefore, at a clear disadvantage on those tests. Academic high school courses implicitly assume a familiarity with this literate culture. Without that familiarity, many black students feel alienated from school and are likely to drop out. Even though they may have facilitated the integration of the school by producing an atmosphere of mutual understanding and respect, the curricular changes initiated by Mrs. Taylor, the parent group suggests, may have unintentionally disadvantaged black students further. By emphasizing events, people, and ideas not included in the dominant literate culture, Jefferson's curriculum deprives black students of information they need to succeed on standardized tests and, later, at college. Because its organization is based on concepts and ways of thinking from this literate culture, the new curriculum still produces cognitive confusion and alienation among disadvantaged blacks.

To address this problem, the PTA committee has proposed a program that provides Jefferson students with a more coherent and systematic initiation into the dominant literate culture. In the ninth and tenth grades, the academic subjects will introduce students to the basic language and information of this literate culture—the language of grammar, folklore, geography, history, literature, mathematics, science, and government in everyday use in the lives of those who influence American society. Although the organization of this material and the teaching methods to be used must be developed by Jefferson's teachers, their goal should be the mastery of this background information by all of Jefferson's freshmen and sophomores. In the eleventh and twelfth grades, then, students should have the understanding and confidence to succeed in a rigorous common program of standard college preparatory subjects: biology and chemistry, American and English literature, composition and speech, advanced algebra and analytic geometry, American history and political science. Beyond these common courses, students may elect subjects that reflect their own special interests or aspirations. But this basic program, the parent group insists, is necessary not only to prepare students for higher education but also to enable them to participate fully in American society whether or not they go on to college.

These two alternatives seem incompatible. The faculty task force has argued that the PTA proposal would only worsen the alienation of students at risk of failure and dropping out. The PTA committee has claimed that the faculty proposal would further widen the gap between what students learn at school and what they need to succeed in American society. There is, at the moment, no clear consensus among parents, teachers, and students in favor of either of these proposals. Many are satisfied with Jefferson's current program; others, though not fully satisfied, are worried that radical and untried departures from the status quo might undermine the hard-won peace and progress that Jefferson has achieved over the past decade.

Mrs. Taylor herself is uncertain in her judgment of the proposals. Both, she believes, have been carefully thought out. There seems, however, to be little empirical evidence about how either would work out in a school like Jefferson. Their adoption therefore would entail a real degree of risk. How should Jefferson and Mrs. Taylor proceed at this point? Why?

THE COMPLEXITY AND DIFFICULTY OF MULTICULTURAL CONFLICT

Everyone involved in the controversy at Jefferson High seems to agree on a wide variety of issues: What the school has accomplished under Mrs.

Taylor's leadership *has* been a comparative success; students at Jefferson, both African- and European-American, are better off than those in other Iron City high schools. Still, there are very real and troublesome differences in the outcomes for black and white students. It *would* be better if Jefferson could narrow these differences—if the school could improve black students' academic achievement and reduce their alienation from school. Furthermore, these differences in school outcomes are at least partially the result of differences in students' family and community backgrounds. To narrow these outcome differences, Jefferson must, therefore, recognize and respond to these background differences. In very general terms, then, the members of the Jefferson school community appear to agree upon the basic facts about the school, the goals for its improvement, and even the overall strategy by which that improvement can be achieved. However, some wish to keep the current program, others argue for sweeping changes to accommodate students' cultural styles, and still others seek equally dramatic changes to develop students' cultural literacy. Why, given so much basic agreement about the situation, are there such seemingly irreconcilable disagreements about Jefferson's educational program? To answer this question, we must look more deeply at the beliefs of the various members of the school community.

Although all three groups believe that the differences in black and white children's school performance are caused by differences in their experience, each emphasizes particular aspects of that experience. The current program is based on the idea that black children, in their daily lives, have been treated with suspicion, prejudice, and neglect by others. As a result, these children have come to doubt their own abilities, to reject the values of the society, or both. To compensate for this experience, the school needs to create a climate of mutual respect, understanding, and acceptance among students and to give them a chance to overcome any learning deficits that their previous experience may have created.

The teacher task force is concerned with quite a different aspect of African-American students' experience. African- and European-American communities, they contend, promote different perspectives on understanding, learning about, and acting in the world. Insofar as standard school subjects and methods reflect the European perspective, African-American students usually face a dual task in order to succeed in school; they must master not only particular skills and subject matter but also unfamiliar styles of inquiry, expression, and behavior. Schools can make this task more manageable by using learning activities that take advantage of skills and understandings that African-American students have already learned in their homes and communities.

The PTA committee stresses yet another difference in black and white students' experience—the concepts, ideas, and information that they learn from their parents. Because black children have less day-to-day access than whites to the larger society's language of power and success, black children's schools must concentrate explicitly on providing that access. Only then will all students have an equal chance to succeed.

The principal, teachers, and parents might very well agree that the students' experiences differ in these three ways and perhaps in others as well. But they apparently disagree about what aspects of that experience are most *important* for children. This is partly a disagreement about facts, about what *causes* children to stay in school and perform well. Some believe that students' self-respect and motivation are the crucial elements in school success, some claim that the compatibility of students' home and school experience matters most, and some believe that access to the language of power is of primary importance. But this is not only a factual dispute; these various causal theories also reveal differing beliefs about what contributes most toward the dignity and well-being of humans. This is, in other words, a dispute about ethical ideals.

The ideal at the heart of Jefferson's current program seems to be *respect*. According to this view, human beings thrive when those around them recognize the worth of their origins, abilities, and potential. The teacher task force, by contrast, emphasizes the ideal of *coherence*. For them, a life is most worth living when one is permitted to act in ways that are consistent with one's deepest beliefs, habits, and expectations. The PTA committee sees the ideal of *achievement* as central. Here, actually succeeding according to the standards of one's society, and having the tools and raw materials to do so, is what constitutes a meaningful and satisfying life.

One party to this dispute does not necessarily deny that the other parties' values exist; rather each party sees the others' values as secondary to and derivative of its own highest ideal. The teacher task force, for instance, would say that to show *real* respect for students, the school should enable them to make the most of their backgrounds and experience; for them, respect is secondary to and dependent upon the school's having an educational program that is consistent with the perspectives and practices of students' home and community lives. The PTA group, on the other hand, maintains that school success allows students to become truly worthy of respect in the society at large; they see respect as a predictable result of a school's promoting the central value of achievement. Similarly, in the current program and in that proposed by the PTA, coherence has a different meaning and importance than it has for the teacher task force. The current program is coherent in the sense that it aims to respect and develop each child's individual potential even if that potential has been given inadequate opportunities for development in the child's previous schooling or social experience. The PTA seeks coherence between the school program and the demands of the larger society, demands that may be greatly different from those of children's families or communities. Finally, all three programs claim that they will improve student achievement, but supporters of the current program and the teacher task force argue that achievement will follow naturally if students respect themselves and others, or if their school activities are consistent with their home lives.

What we have at Jefferson High School is therefore a complicated and tangled disagreement over both what the world is and what it should be. Let us note some additional features of this disagreement. First, the disputants have different views of the nature and importance of culture. The teacher task force's coherence-oriented program portrays culture as a feature of various subgroups within a society that depends upon the ethnic, religious, and geographic heritage of those groups and on how those groups have translated that heritage into contemporary styles of understanding and interaction. The PTA's achievement-oriented program, by contrast, identifies culture with the socially dominant mode of communication and action. Culture figures less prominently in Jefferson's current respect-oriented program; at most, culture is an aspect of the individual differences among students that must be understood and accepted.

Second, these three programs are connected with different traditions of thought and action. The coherence-oriented program places the ethnic group at the center of human experience. This emphasis is clearly related to the African cultures to which the teacher task force has traced the behavior and learning styles of African-American children. Those cultures' pursuit of a holistic view of nature and human activity seems to have inspired the conception and design of the coherence-oriented program. The ideas implicit in the respect- and achievement-oriented programs are, many would say, more typically American, but they appeal to quite different elements in American ideology. The respect-oriented program places the individual at center stage; the individual's own constitution, aspirations, and identity give meaning to his or her experience. The achievement-oriented program, by contrast, seems to imply that society at large provides the framework within which a person's experience has meaning. In short, these three programs can be connected to tribal, individualistic, and nationalistic traditions of thought.

APPLYING STANDARD ETHICAL PERSPECTIVES

Given the extent and severity of these disagreements and differences in thinking, one might say that the parties to the dispute at Jefferson High have different world views, at least with regard to the school's educational program. And it is these systematic disparities of belief and perception in disputes about, or arising from, cultural or linguistic differences that make these disputes so very hard to settle.

Over the past three thousand years, philosophers and other thinkers in the West have identified two basic approaches for resolving ethical disputes.

One standard approach says that we should resolve disputes by comparing the *outcomes* of the actions recommended by the disputants. If one action has better consequences than another, that is the right thing to do. Another approach says that we should compare the alternative *actions themselves* rather than their outcomes. If one action is inherently better than another, then that is what we should do. Let us see whether either of these standard approaches to ethical disputes can help resolve the dramatic differences we have seen at Jefferson High.

The first general approach, called consequentialism, holds that alternative actions or policies should be judged according to their outcomes. To apply this approach, we need to specify what outcomes are to count as morally good. The most influential version of this approach says that human well-being or happiness is the outcome that matters. However, as we have seen, the parties at Jefferson have radically different views about human well-being. People are well off, according to one group, when others recognize their fundamental worth as individuals, or, according to a second, when their lives are consistent with their background beliefs and practices, or, according to a third, when they are able to compete to the best of their abilities for society's rewards. When, as in this case, people disagree about what the morally best outcomes are, the consequentialist approach to ethics seems incapable of resolving disputes.

The other general approach, called nonconsequentialist or deontological ethics, holds that different actions or policies should be judged according to whether they are inherently right rather than according to their consequences. Here we need to determine what makes an action inherently right. The most influential version of this approach, proposed by the eighteenth-century German philosopher Immanuel Kant, maintains that an action is right when it respects the fundamental dignity of other human beings as persons with their own purposes and lives to lead rather than as objects to be used solely for others' purposes. Unfortunately, the disputants at Jefferson also have radically different views about human dignity and therefore about the right and wrong ways to treat others. This is most easily seen in the different interpretations that each group gives to the idea of respect. The current program maintains that respect for others as individuals is the basis for right action; we wrong others when we treat them as fundamentally inferior to ourselves. The coherence-oriented program emphasizes respect for others as members of ethnic, religious, or social groups; we wrong others when we alienate them from their backgrounds. The achievement-oriented program stresses respect for others as potential contributors to society; we wrong others when we neglect that potential. Thus, the nonconsequentialist approach does not help to resolve the disagreements at Jefferson; if anything, it only emphasizes how deep those disagreements are.

CULTURAL RELATIVISM AS A WAY OF AVOIDING DISPUTES

When confronted with deep and complicated disagreements like the one at Jefferson, we can try either to *settle* the dispute—to find ethical principles or procedures for reaching a rational resolution of it—or to *avoid* it—to find an approach that stops the debate without resolving it. Because the prospects for a resolution in this case appear so limited, avoidance, if possible, seems especially attractive. Cultural relativism, the doctrine that each culture defines ethical values of its own members but of no one else, has seemed to many a promising way of avoiding disputes between or about cultures. For if what the members of one culture mean by "good" or "respect" is different from what members of a different culture mean by those terms, it apparently makes no sense for them to argue about ethical matters at all.

Cultural relativism was developed by anthropologists at the beginning of the twentieth century as part of an effort to create a more objective way of learning about cultures than had been used previously. In studying various cultures, these anthropologists noted two things. First, while many cultural groups practiced customs and accepted mores that were dramatically different from one another, the resulting societies proved to be relatively stable and capable of meeting the needs of their members. Second, efforts to impose outsiders' beliefs and practices upon other cultural groups often had disastrously disruptive effects.

As a result, these anthropologists proposed, on the one hand, that ethical principles and concepts have meaning and application only *within* the cultural traditions in which they originate. If my culture defines "good" as "increasing human happiness" and yours defines it as "obeying the word of God," that moral concept has two different meanings that are equally valid because they are both culturally determined. On the other hand, these anthropologists suggested, what a person should do or believe is determined by his or her own culture. If my culture tells me that it is right to satisfy my own desires, that is what I should do even though your culture thinks it a sin. In both these ways, ethical values are relative to one's culture.

It has seemed to some, including the anthropologists that developed it, that cultural relativism provides a way of avoiding conflicts between cultures. For once people notice that their moral ideas do not apply to those outside their culture, mustn't they accept others' rights to live their lives according to their own cultural standards? And if they accept these rights, won't the members of different cultures be able to live harmoniously with one another? Doesn't cultural relativism, then, put a stop to the potential conflicts that modern multicultural societies face? To answer these questions, let us consider the implications of cultural relativism for the debate at Jefferson High School.

Cultural relativism is claimed to avoid conflicts *between* cultures. Thus, for cultural relativism to apply to a situation, the potential disputants must be able to recognize and agree upon the boundaries between cultural groups. This may be intuitively easy to do when the groups are historically and geographically distinct, as when, for example, the native residents of Massachusetts first encountered the English Puritans. But the members of a multicultural society share a place of residence and very often a long and intertwined history. Is the dispute at Jefferson High between cultures or within a culture? As it happens, the answer to this question is part of what is in dispute. The proponents of the coherence-oriented program identify Jefferson's African- and European-American children as members of distinct cultures, whereas the proponents of the achievement-oriented program see them as members of the national culture. Because the very definition of culture is part of what parents and teachers disagree about at Jefferson, it is hard to see how to apply cultural relativism to this situation.

The indistinctness of cultural boundaries in multicultural societies also creates another set of difficulties—the problem of overlapping group membership. Cultural relativism tells us that an individual's ethical values are determined by the cultural group to which he or she belongs. But to what group do Mrs. Taylor, the African-American principal; Mr. Andrews, the European-American chair of the teacher task force; and Mr. Radner, the black lawyer who chairs the PTA curriculum committee, belong, and to what ethical ideals do they, therefore, owe their allegiance? Let us examine just one of these cases.

Mr. Andrews has concluded that European- and African-Americans have different cultural backgrounds and belong, therefore, to distinct cultural groups. Although he grew up in a European-American family, he now finds himself a member of a predominantly African-American faculty of a school with a predominantly African-American student body. He has, moreover, studied and come to understand what he identifies as African-American culture and believes that his own teaching should embrace the perspectives and modes of action implicit in that culture. In this situation, should African- or European-American culture define Mr. Andrews' moral obligations? In fact, he identifies with both cultures. Should he then simply choose whatever moral values seem best to him in any situation? Or should he follow African-American cultural values when interacting with African-Americans and European-American values with European-Americans? Or was it morally wrong of him to have learned about and accepted African-American culture in the first place? For Mr. Andrews and many others in multicultural societies, these are important *moral* questions that cultural relativism does not even recognize, let alone answer.

So far, we have seen that cultural relativism is not especially useful in multicultural societies for two different reasons. The boundaries between cultural groups are themselves controversial, and many people in these societies are members of more than one cultural group. But there is one further consequence of cultural relativism that is even more disappointing: it may put an end to the debate over cultural conflicts but not to the conflicts themselves.

Cultural relativism instructs us that different cultures attach different meanings to moral language. What Mr. Radner means by a good life—success in the larger society—is inconsistent with what Mr. Andrews means—an internally coherent pattern of beliefs and action. Thus, any debate about the good life between these two is senseless; insofar as their cultural and linguistic differences make it impossible for them to determine what the good life really is, argument is pointless. Cultural relativism also tells us that Mr. Radner's beliefs are right for him because they are part of his culture. He believes that it would be wrong for him or anyone else to treat children in a way that imperils their chances for social success, and that Mr. Andrews' program would do precisely that. According to cultural relativism, then, Mr. Radner is morally required by his own beliefs to prevent Mr. Andrews from teaching in the way that Mr. Andrews thinks best. Thus, cultural relativism does not put a stop to this cultural conflict but only to the debate over it.

Contrary to appearances, cultural relativism does not necessarily imply that the members of one cultural group should respect or even tolerate the beliefs and ways of life of the members of another. If the members of one culture believe they have a duty to force their values on others or to interfere in others' lives, cultural relativism implies that that is what they should do.

In multicultural societies, where the contact between cultural groups is frequent and unavoidable, cultural relativism is quite possibly more a prescription for civil war than for intercultural harmony. In light of this implication of cultural relativism, it seems preferable to keep the debate over cultural differences alive in the hope that some satisfactory way of resolving them can be found.

THE SEARCH FOR RESOLUTIONS

Let us take stock of what we have learned so far about education in our contemporary multicultural and multilingual society. Cultural and linguistic diversity have been constants in the history of the United States since its founding. Finding a way to create unity within that diversity has been understood as crucial to the survival and vitality of American society. However, past attempts to fashion a society that realizes the ideal of unity in diversity have failed in two important respects.

First, those efforts—in which public schooling has played a prominent role—were often brutally repressive. Few Americans today find our history of ethnic, religious, and racial discrimination, segregation, and heavy-handed socialization to be ethically acceptable. Second, these efforts have not succeeded at putting an end to the conflict that arises from cultural and linguistic differences. If anything, contemporary multicultural conflicts seem even more complicated and difficult than those of the past. As we have seen in the case of Jefferson High School, centuries of American experience with cultural differences have produced situations that seem more confusing than ever. On the one hand, that experience has not produced general agreements about human well-being and dignity that permit the use of standard consequentialist and nonconsequentialist approaches to ethical problems in resolving multicultural and multilingual conflicts. On the other hand, the long-term and daily contact between members of different cultures in this society does not allow us to avoid these conflicts by withdrawing, as cultural relativism suggests, into our various cultural, linguistic, and ethnic groups. Such an attempted withdrawal would apparently only perpetuate the confusion and conflict without offering the possibility of reaching rational and mutually satisfactory resolutions.

Fortunately, our society is not wholly without resources for attempting to deal with these complex issues. In very general terms, the question that these situations of multicultural and multilinguistic difference pose is, How should a society proceed when its members disagree about what should be done? This is a classic question of political morality. It is a political question because it concerns the way in which societies make decisions and govern themselves. It involves morality because it asks what societies *should* do, not simply what they are likely to do. Several influential but significantly different ways of answering this question have been developed in the United States and elsewhere over the past three centuries. In the remainder of this book, we will consider the potential of three prominent approaches to political morality—namely, the liberal perspective, the democratic perspective, and the communitarian perspective—to conceptualize and resolve culturally and linguistically based controversies in education.

Each of these approaches places a familiar but different value at the center of social and political decision making: personal liberty, democratic participation, and community. These different basic values lead each perspective to approach ethical conflicts in different ways.

Liberalism tries to enable each person to become a self-governing, independent individual. In the Jefferson High School case, the liberal would ask which of the proposed alternatives most respects the individual rights of each person involved and which is most likely to encourage each child to become his or her own person. In this light, the liberal would probably be concerned about both the teachers' and the PTA's plans. After all, those plans define what is good for children in terms of their participation in a group, either their ethnic group or the system of achievement of the larger society.

Democratic theory, by contrast, tries to create a society in which all citizens have a fair chance to participate in making social decisions. Thus, democracy aims for the self-governing society, not the independent individual. At Jefferson High School, the democrat would want to ensure that the school program adequately prepares all children to take an active role in the society's political system. As a result, the democrat would have reservations about the current program, with its exclusive emphasis on individual potential, and about the teachers' plan, with its focus on the students' roles in their particular ethnic communities.

Finally, the communitarian seeks a society in which all members have a meaningful place in the immediate communities in which they live. Thus, the communitarian aims for the self-governing community, a group whose members' lives are informed by relationships and traditions that provide everyone with an authentic identity and role. At Jefferson High School, the communitarian would be critical of the current program and the PTA plan precisely because both tend to devalue the historical and social contexts in which Jefferson students must live, namely, their families and ethnic communities.

These brief sketches provide only the barest idea of the three perspectives. Each represents a sophisticated political tradition that has developed over many centuries. Accordingly, we will devote each of the next three chapters to a detailed explication and assessment of the perspectives. Of course, the point of looking at these traditions is to determine whether they can help us resolve cultural and linguistic issues that arise in schools. We will focus, then, on how each approach can be used to analyze and resolve realistic examples of these issues.

Most important, we will want to know not just how these approaches deal with cultural and linguistic differences in school settings but also whether the resolutions that they imply are satisfactory. These theories of political morality have been developed to deal with the full range of disagreements that may arise in a society, and not particularly with those that have cultural and linguistic origins. We will want to consider, therefore, how well they succeed in resolving this special category of disagreements. The discussion in this chapter has helped to reveal several different concerns that we should bring to bear on the assessment of an approach to resolving cultural and linguistic conflict in schools.

Conflict of any kind implies that there are differences between the parties—differences in beliefs, preferences, expectations, perceptions, habits, ways of living, and so on. But not all differences between people can reasonably be regarded as having cultural or linguistic origins. If I prefer to drive a Ford and you prefer a Chevrolet, this difference is not likely to have a cultural basis. Any approach to resolving cultural conflict must, therefore, be able to distinguish cultural from other sorts of characteristics and differences in some sensible way. For this purpose, an approach to these conflicts must include a workable conception of culture, one that will enable us to tell what differences and characteristics have cultural significance.

The situation at Jefferson High points out just how challenging the task of finding a useful conception of culture is likely to be, especially if it is to help us deal with issues that arise in a multicultural society. For we have seen that straightforward criteria of cultural identity—such as common group membership, historical origins, or geographic residence—are not very helpful in diverse and complex situations like that at Jefferson. There, group histories and identifications have become so intertwined and overlapping that any superficial conception of culture is likely to yield uncertain or conflicting results. Does, for example, Mr. Radner identify with European-American culture because he is a lawyer and lives in a predominantly white neighborhood, or with African-American culture because he grew up in a black family? Does the distinction between European- and African-American cultures make any sense in these circumstances? In this case and many others in multicultural societies, the need for a sophisticated conception of culture is clear.

We want a perspective on political morality to tell us what a culture is, in part to help us resolve these vexing questions. But we also want a conception of culture to be accurate, to correctly classify those cultures that most people recognize as such. Our Jefferson High School case, however, has also taught us that the definition of culture is itself one of the things about which people in a multicultural society may disagree. So in determining whether a perspective's conception of culture is accurate, we cannot employ a single detailed definition of culture to which we expect everyone to agree. Instead, we must be satisfied with a rough, intuitive understanding of culture against which the perspectives' conceptions will be judged.

We will develop these intuitions more fully in later chapters as we attempt to assess the adequacy of the perspectives' views of culture, but here are some of our starting points. First, a culture embraces beliefs, characteristics, and activities that are of great importance to people, including to some extent their fundamental values and outlooks, their accustomed and preferred ways of living, and even their personal identities. Second, cultures are shared and as a result have a group of some kind as their reference point. Finally, cultures have a historical dimension; cultural ideas and patterns of life are developed over significant periods of time.

Of course, the point of identifying characteristics that have a cultural origin lies with the assumption that those characteristics have or ought to have a special moral status in the resolution of social conflicts. This assumption reflects the idea that a person's cultural commitments are particularly profound, reaching deeply into his or her very identity. They provide at least part of the fundamental framework in terms of which people define both themselves and their world. People's cultural commitments, then, encompass their basic conceptions of their own personhood and well-being. As we have noted, personhood and well-being are perhaps the central concerns of ethics. For this reason, an approach to resolving cultural differences must not only identify cultural characteristics and commitments but also assign them a special ethical significance in the making of social and political decisions.

As we have seen, parties to the dispute at Jefferson High assume that what they take to be the culture of the school's students ought to have special importance in their education. The teacher task force, for instance, organizes its program around the African perspectives and practices they find to be implicit in African-American children's home culture. Unfortunately, in disagreements about or between cultures, two or more sets of such fundamental commitments are at odds with one another. In such a situation, then, it is impossible for a society to honor all of the cultural commitments of everyone involved in the dispute. An approach to resolving such disputes must clearly determine how those who hold the conflicting commitments will be permitted to act upon them or be constrained from doing so. The three proposals at Jefferson cannot all be implemented simultaneously, because each claims that a particular educational program is best for all of the school's students. A resolution to this situation, thus, must limit the implementation of the proposals in some way—perhaps by prescribing that one of the three should be chosen over the others or that each should be implemented for some, but not all, of the students.

Finally, we seek to *resolve* and not merely to end these cultural and linguistic disputes. An ethically adequate approach to these conflicts must also provide a good reason for constraining people's opportunities to meet their cultural commitments. At the very least, this reason should be understandable to those whose actions have been constrained; at best, it should be acceptable to them.

To sum up, an approach to resolving cultural and linguistic differences in education must meet four criteria:

1. It must include a conception of culture that permits us to distinguish between cultural and other sorts of differences, especially in multicultural and multilinguistic societies.
2. It must assign a special ethical significance to people's cultural commitments.
3. It must determine how people's cultural commitments are to be constrained when they come into conflict with one another.
4. It must provide a morally adequate and, if possible, mutually acceptable reason for such constraints.

Let us consider next how each of the three major political theories meets these criteria.

REFERENCES AND FURTHER READING

Banks, J. A. (1984). *Teaching strategies for ethnic studies* (3d ed.). Boston: Allyn and Bacon.
>   Includes short historical sketches of a variety of ethnic groups in the U.S. and recommendations for teaching ethnic studies to school students.

Boykin, A. W. (1986). The triple quandary and the schooling of Afro-American children. In U. Neisser (Ed.), *The school achievement of minority children: New perspectives* (pp. 57–92). Hillsdale, NJ: Erlbaum.
>   A revealing discussion of the social and cultural pressures that black children experience; includes a description of African influences on African-American cultural style.

Cremin, L. A. (1980). *American education: The national experience, 1783–1876.* New York: Harper & Row.

Cremin, L. A. (1988). *American education: The metropolitan experience, 1876–1980.* New York: Harper & Row.
>   These two volumes of Cremin's ambitious and wide-ranging history of American educational institutions include carefully documented discussions of the schooling of immigrants and minorities throughout the nation's history.

Hirsch, E. D., Jr. (1987). *Cultural literacy: What every American needs to know.* Boston: Houghton Mifflin.
>   The original statement of the theory of cultural literacy; includes arguments about the benefits of cultural literacy for minority children.

Sumner, W. G. (1907). *Folkways: A study of the sociological importance of usages, manners, mores, and morals.* Boston: Ginn.
>   An early and influential statement of cultural relativism by an important American anthropologist.

CHAPTER 2

The Liberal Perspective

As we saw in the first chapter, the presence of people from different cultural or linguistic backgrounds within a society can produce serious disagreements about what should happen in our nation's schools and classrooms. We also concluded that finding a conscious way to resolve these disagreements reasonably would, if possible, be better than simply ignoring them. In this and the next two chapters, we will examine three different approaches to resolving these disputes. Each of these approaches provides a different answer to the basic question of political morality: Why should people accept and obey the decisions of a political system, especially if some of them disagree with those decisions?

Now, not all differences and disagreements have a cultural basis. Obviously, people who are members of the same culture can have differences of opinion. And people who belong to the same culture can disagree even when their cultures do not speak to the issue at hand. A viable theory of political morality must, therefore, be able to resolve social disagreements of all kinds, whether or not those disagreements reflect differences of culture and language. In fact, all three perspectives that we will consider in this book were developed to deal with these more mundane, noncultural disputes. This fact creates one of the hardest problems we will be wrestling with throughout this book, whether a theory of political morality developed for ordinary disagreements can do an adequate job on the complex and difficult differences that arise between cultural and linguistic communities.

We will approach this issue in a similar fashion for each perspective. First, we will briefly examine an everyday disagreement that provides the intuitive basis for the perspective. Then, we will show how our intuitions about how to resolve that minor disagreement can be developed into a full-blown set of moral principles for an entire society. These principles, in turn, imply that the good society should establish particular institutions to enforce the principles, to resolve social disputes in a morally legitimate way, and to educate the members of the society.

Once we have explained the basic principles and institutions of a perspective, we will examine a complex case of multicultural conflict about schools. This case, like all those included in this book, is hypothetical, although it is based upon issues that actually arise in contemporary schools. Next, we will use the perspective to analyze and, if possible, resolve the problems presented by the case. And, finally, we will assess how well the perspective has met the four criteria of adequacy we proposed in the first chapter.

Let us turn now to the first perspective on political morality, namely, liberalism. To understand the basic idea of the liberal perspective, let us consider a familiar disagreement:

> Two children are squabbling at the art table over which of them should be allowed to use the orange clay. Marie wants the clay for the Halloween pumpkin she plans to create. Nate is recreating last night's dinner and needs the clay to make carrots. After calming tempers, the teacher simply divides the clay and gives each child half.

Why does this resolution seem reasonable? Each child has a good use for the clay, and neither seems to have any greater claim on it than the other; as a result, each seems to deserve a share of the clay. The teacher's resolution is right in that it gives each child what she or he deserves. It seems natural in cases like these to resolve differences by trying to create a fair outcome, one that respects the interests of everyone involved.

The liberal perspective simply extends this ordinary appeal to fair outcomes to the political process. When disputes arise in the larger society, the liberal perspective says that we should resolve them by dividing the disputed resources fairly, that is, according to what each person deserves. If we do so, then people ought to accept and obey the decisions made by such a political system because the results of those decisions are just. A legitimate liberal society is, we might say, one which attempts to provide substantive justice for all its members.

WHAT LIBERAL THEORY IS

In the most general terms, treating people justly means giving equal consideration to each person's interests. In the story of Marie and Nate, the teacher determines that both children have a legitimate interest in the disputed clay; since justice requires that she give equal weight to both of these interests, she must divide the clay equally between them. But in this situation, would it be right for the teacher to conclude that, because in her opinion Halloween is a frivolous holiday, Marie does not have any real interest in the clay and should not therefore receive a share? A theory of justice clearly requires an answer to the question of who should decide what is and what is not a legitimate interest that deserves to be taken into consideration. What distinguishes liberalism from many other theories of political morality is the answer that it gives to this question.

The Central Commitment: Neutrality to Individual Goods

Liberalism's answer to the question of who decides what is in a person's interests is straightforward—each person has the right to determine what is good for him- or herself. In other words, no one other than myself has the final say over what activities or pursuits are best for me. Although the case of children is complicated, as we will see shortly, this basic commitment of liberalism suggests that the teacher has no business substituting her judgment for Marie's in determining what is in Marie's interest. In making just decisions, then, a liberal society is *to remain neutral to each person's own vision of the good life* (Dworkin, 1978).

It is important to note from the very first that this commitment to neutrality *does not* mean that liberal justice requires that each person should get exactly what he or she wants. After all, what one person's vision of the good life requires may also be of interest to many others. And sometimes what would advance one's vision of the good—having another person be one's slave, for instance—obviously interferes with others' efforts to live the good life as they see it. All that liberal justice requires is that each person's self-defined interests be given equal weight in making decisions that affect those interests. Even if the teacher has no right to decide that Marie has no interest in the clay, she does not therefore have to give Marie all of the clay in order to treat her fairly. Instead, she must attempt to balance Marie's interests with those of others whose vision of the good gives them an interest in the disputed resource.

The Role of Government: Equal Facilitation of Individual Goods

Thus far, liberalism's answer to the question of why people should accept and obey the decisions of a political system is that a liberal system's decisions will reflect an equal consideration of the interests of citizens as those citizens themselves define their interests. But doesn't such a rule permit the government to deny equally the interests of all citizens? In the Marie and Nate situation, couldn't the teacher give equal consideration to the interests of both children by refusing to let either of them use the orange clay?

Although it may not be obvious, the answer to this question is a resounding No. In denying any citizen the fulfillment of his or her aspirations, a government must rely upon one of two quite different reasons—either that someone else has a legitimate claim on the resource that is needed *or* that the vision of the good of the citizen in question is not worthy of fulfillment. As we have seen, this second reason is ruled out by liberalism's commitment to neutrality; liberal governments have no business determining which of their citizens' visions of the good are worthwhile or not. Thus, the only condition under which a liberal government can deny its citizens the resources necessary to fulfill their visions of the good is when that distribution of resources would adversely and unequally affect the interests of other citizens. When the interests of no one else are at stake or when others' interests have been equally considered, then a liberal government is bound by the commitment to neutrality to grant me access to the resources I need to fulfill my aspirations. In other words, the teacher can act neutrally toward Marie and Nate *only* if she gives each a fair share of what they require to satisfy their own plans and purposes; equal denial of those interests violates the neutral stance that liberal authorities must take toward their citizens.

This discussion implies that liberal governments have one overriding goal—*to facilitate equally each citizen's efforts to realize his or her own vision of the good life*. To give any citizen a more than equal chance to fulfill his or her vision of the good is clearly inconsistent with neutrality. But so, too, is a decision to withhold available resources from a government's citizens, even if those resources are withheld equally from all. To meet this goal, then, liberal governments must seek to establish the legal, social, and economic arrangements in which all citizens are equally advantaged in the pursuit of their personal visions of the good life. Let us look more closely at some of the features of those arrangements.

BASIC INTERESTS AND INSTITUTIONS IN LIBERAL SOCIETIES

The task of liberal societies is to create the conditions under which their citizens have a full and equal chance to fulfill their visions of the good. The example of Marie and Nate that we have used thus far may have inadvertently left the impression that liberalism focuses mainly on the material conditions and resources in a society. However, many other things are also important to people's pursuit of their visions of the good. And, in fact, liberalism traditionally places the greatest emphasis on two other social conditions that facilitate individuals' efforts to live the good life as they see it—liberties and opportunities.

Full and Equal Liberty

Many, perhaps most, people hold beliefs about how to live that they think are unquestionably right and that, moreover, would be good for other people to hold as well. Religious beliefs in particular tend to have this character. Such beliefs, after all, have for those who hold them the ultimate authority—that of an all-knowing and all-powerful God. Often, the good life for people with these beliefs includes a commitment to spreading their beliefs to others. Persuasion is one obvious way to promote a vision of the good life, but other, more forceful, methods are available as well—brainwashing, indoctrination, deprivation of access to competing beliefs, and so on.

In general, however, a liberal government cannot permit the use of these coercive means of promulgating beliefs. Neutrality obviously forbids such a government from using its *own* power to promote one vision of the good in preference to others. For to do so, the government would have to decide which vision of the good is best for its citizens, something that neutrality clearly rules out. But governments not only exercise power themselves, but also make judgments about whether their citizens' attempts to exercise power over one another are legitimate or not. By allowing some citizens to promote their beliefs by coercive means, a government would in effect be showing a preference for certain visions of the good—namely, those of the socially powerful.

Because liberal governments must be neutral to visions of the good, they must also be committed to what John Stuart Mill (1859/1978) called the free marketplace of ideas. In this marketplace, all citizens are free to choose their own ideas, to express those ideas, and to make up their own minds about the value of others' ideas. The use of censorship and indoctrination are, in general, prohibited. *Freedom of conscience* and *freedom of expression* are, thus, basic rights of all citizens in a liberal society. Similar arguments support other sorts of freedom as well, in particular, *freedom of association*—the right of like-minded citizens to band together to pursue common purposes—and *freedom of the person*—the right of citizens not to be detained or otherwise restricted at the mere whim of government authorities.

In the United States, these basic liberties are explicitly recognized in the Bill of Rights, the first ten amendments of the Constitution. These liberties are protected by an array of governmental institutions, including a federal court system that is permitted to rule on the constitutionality of all laws enacted by all levels of government within the nation, an executive branch that is empowered to carry out those judgments, and a legislative branch that can enact laws enabling citizens to enforce their rights against one another.

Equality of Opportunity

In addition to the freedom to decide upon one's own vision of the good, individuals need access to the means for carrying out the visions that they choose. Among the most important means of pursuing one's good are, on the one hand, the knowledge and skills necessary to engage in the activities that one finds rewarding and, on the other hand, the chance to use one's knowledge and skill in those activities. If I, for instance, wish to become a musician, I need first of all to learn how to play the violin and, second, the chance to play with an orchestra.

As this example suggests, the freedom to act individually is usually insufficient for gaining access to these opportunities to learn and to engage in rewarding activities. Although I might learn to play the violin entirely on my own, access to skilled teachers is usually necessary. Similarly, to be a musician, a person usually needs the chance to play with other skilled individuals. In other words, education and employment are *social* opportunities in that they require access to, and the cooperation of, other people. In addition, these opportunities are more often than not in short supply; that is, there are more potential students of the violin than skilled teachers and more aspiring violinists than available chairs in orchestras.

A society that is attempting to enable its citizens to realize their visions of the good must find a fair way to distribute these scarce opportunities. This distribution must be fair in two senses; it must be fair to those who *want* the opportunities and to those who can *provide* them.

To be fair to those who seek these opportunities, factors that people can do nothing about and that are irrelevant to their ability to take advantage of the opportunities should not be considered in deciding what people should learn and with whom they should be able to work. Among these factors are a person's race, sex, ethnic background, nationality, family status, and religion. At the same time, certain other factors seem relevant to a fair distribution of opportunities. In education, these factors are concerned with each person's *potential* to learn—his or her native ability and motivation, for instance. In employment, these factors are concerned with each person's *productivity* on the job—such things as his or her level of skill and willingness to work hard.

Distributing opportunities according to potential and productivity also allows a society to be fair to those who make the opportunities available. This is clear in employment: An incompetent, careless, or lazy co-worker can make my own work less rewarding; he or she can, in effect, interfere with my effort to realize my vision of the good life. Selecting violinists based upon their musical productivity helps to promote other orchestra members' visions of the good and is, therefore, fair to them. Similarly, focusing scarce educational resources on the most musically promising students is likely to produce the greatest supply of accomplished violinists. This result will also enhance other musicians' efforts to pursue satisfying musical careers.

Finally, a liberal society must be committed to equality of opportunity in education and employment across the full range of skills and activities possible within that society. Neutrality requires that a liberal government promote whatever forms of life to which its citizens happen to aspire. In distributing opportunities for learning and work, therefore, a liberal government cannot restrict access simply because certain officials happen to believe that a particular way of life is inferior to others. The only legitimate reason for restricting such opportunities is that such a restriction is needed to protect others' rights to pursue their own lives as they see fit.

In summary, then, liberal societies are required to provide their citizens with equal opportunities to participate in the activities that fulfill their visions of the good. In doing so, such societies must distribute educational opportunities according to individuals' potential and employment opportunities according to individuals' productivity.

In general, the major institutions for delivering these opportunities are a public educational system and free labor markets. In a liberal society, public schools and colleges are to provide all people with the educational resources and activities necessary to develop their potential, and free labor markets are to allow individuals to compete for available jobs on the basis of their qualifications. However, the actual operation of these institutions may depart from liberal ideals significantly enough to require corrective governmental action to enforce the civil rights of the members of various minorities and to compensate these individuals for disadvantages that stem from past discrimination. Several relatively recent developments in U.S. education can be understood as efforts to regulate schooling and labor markets to meet the requirements of equal opportunity. Among these actions are the Supreme Court's desegregation decisions; Titles VI (education) and VII (employment) of the Civil Rights Act of 1964; Title IX of the 1972 Amendments to the Elementary and Secondary Education Act (sex discrimination); the Supreme Court's 1974 *Lau v. Nichols* decision (bilingual education); Title I, now Chapter I, of the Elementary and Secondary Education Act of 1965 (compensatory education for poor children); affirmative action requirements in employment; and the Education for All Handicapped Children Act of 1975.

Resolving Conflicts in Liberal Societies

Our discussion of Marie's and Nate's dispute at the art table has already revealed the basic principle that liberal societies must follow when their citizens' visions of the good bring them into conflict—*the parties to the dispute are to be neither relatively advantaged nor disadvantaged in their pursuit of the good life as they see it.* However, the importance of basic liberties and opportunities to each person's pursuit of the good life complicates the implementation of this principle of equal advantage.

Let us suppose that my aspiration to become a musician would be advanced by your becoming my involuntary servant for several hours a day. Your polishing my violin, turning the pages of my music, keeping the instrument in tune, and so on would give me more time to develop my musical skills through devoted practice. Let us add two additional features to this situation—first, that because of past disadvantages I have suffered, I will not without your help have an opportunity to develop my talents that is equal to that available to others in the society; and, second, that the demands I make on your time and effort would not impair your opportunities to develop your own potential, that the time I seek you would otherwise spend sleeping or relaxing. Should a liberal society require you to assist me against your will?

In this situation, we are asking whether it is permissible to trade one person's liberty for another's equal opportunity. In general, liberal political morality does not permit such tradeoffs (Rawls, 1971, pp. 541–548). Because the freedom to choose and act upon one's own vision of the good is viewed as central to a liberal government's basic task of facilitating its citizens' pursuit of their goods, liberty is, as a rule, granted highest priority in resolving disputes. If, in a conflict between citizens, one person's basic liberties are at stake and another's are not, then the conflict should, in general, be resolved in favor of the first person. To use Ronald Dworkin's (1976) graphic terminology, rights and liberties function as trumps in a liberal society; that is, a claim based upon one's basic rights or freedoms is of absolutely higher priority than a claim based upon other kinds of interests—in particular, a person's interests in equal opportunity or material welfare.

Similar arguments suggest that equal opportunity has priority over material welfare. Opportunities provide one with the basic means to enter the system in which the material rewards in a society are distributed—skills and the chance to be judged according to one's qualifications. Those who have been allowed to enter the distribution system are thereby absolutely advantaged in their effort to realize their visions of the good over those who have not been admitted. Neutrality and the principle of equal advantage, therefore, imply that one person's interests in being admitted to the competition for material goods are more important than another's interests in keeping the material goods he or she has gained by participating in that system.

In applying the principle of equal advantage, then, a liberal society must pay attention to the kinds of interests involved in the dispute. Because of their relative importance in each person's attempt to live the good life as he or she sees it, basic liberties and equal opportunities will take precedence over other sorts of interests that may be in conflict.

EDUCATING CHILDREN IN LIBERAL SOCIETIES

Many readers, I suspect, found the discussion of the conflict between Marie and Nate to be somewhat peculiar, perhaps even entirely inappropriate. Suppose Marie had done nothing but make pumpkins at the clay table for the past three weeks. Shouldn't the teacher, then, have simply encouraged her to do something else and to let Nate have the orange clay? Suppose the teacher had instructed the children to make things that represent their favorite holidays. Shouldn't Marie's project have taken priority over Nate's? In general, don't adults have the right or even the duty to control and make judgments about children's activities that would be inappropriate if they were dealing with other adults?

The basic moral concepts of the liberal perspective—neutrality, liberty, equal opportunity, equal advantage—apply most directly to adults. These concepts assume either that the people to whom they are applied already have a vision of the good life or that they are capable of making reasonable judgments about such a vision. In attempting to give two people equal opportunities to fulfill their visions of the good, one has to be able to identify what those visions actually are. In granting someone the freedom to determine his or her own beliefs, one has to assume that that person has the intellectual skills and background to make meaningful use of that freedom. But neither of these assumptions is true of children, especially of the very young. Children simply do not possess a considered and systematic view of their own good, nor do they have the understanding and experience to evaluate the multitude of possibilities for living that society makes available to them.

Even though it is not possible to apply the basic concepts of liberal political morality to children, however, they are not just an ordinary part of the environment, a natural resource to be used by adults to advance their own projects and aspirations. For children, unlike trees and mountains, have the potential to develop a sense of their own good. And this potential implies that adults owe special obligations to children that are different from those that they owe to other adults. In the most general terms, adults owe children a liberal education (Ackerman, 1980). Let us examine the features of such an education.

Initial Socialization

Even though children do not come into the world with an established view of the good, each child has the potential to follow an enormous variety of paths in life. Any particular child might become an antique dealer or a race car driver, a Roman Catholic or a Buddhist, a Republican or a Democrat. Seriously embarking on one of these paths often closes off a great many other possibilities. If Marie spends her youth preparing to be an electrical engineer, she will at some point foreclose any chance she may have of becoming a ballet dancer. Hence, the crucial educational question for liberalism is how these momentous decisions about the course of children's lives can be made in a way that is consistent with neutrality.

For ten to fifteen years, children are not able to make these decisions on their own. And at least some of these decisions *must* apparently be made during childhood. Children must learn one or two languages and be able to function within a limited community in order to enjoy robust and satisfying lives as adults. But the need for adults to make these decisions for children poses a real threat to neutrality, for such decisions inevitably reflect the adult decision maker's own beliefs about what ways of living are most worthwhile. The problem for liberal societies, then, is how to permit adults to make these decisions without, on the one hand, showing a nonneutral preference for some visions of the good or, on the other, undermining the rights to self-determination that children are supposed to enjoy once they become adults.

The liberal solution to this problem traditionally has two distinct parts (Mill, 1859/1978, pp. 103–106; Ackerman, 1980, pp. 139–154). The first is to decentralize control over child rearing by making parents responsible for the early socialization of their own children. In this way, the possibility that a single faction of adults who hold a particular vision of the good will monopolize control over child rearing is avoided. Because children will be socialized into various visions of the good in roughly the same proportion as those visions are represented in the adult population, a liberal government has from the perspective of the society's adults maintained its neutrality.

From the children's perspective, however, this is anything but a neutral solution to the problem of child rearing. A child can have no choice about his or her parents, and their vision of the good is imposed upon the child in ways that would be illegitimate among adults—the child is effectively indoctrinated into the parents' view, and alternative views are heavily censored. At most, this socialization leads children to live a life that is best from their parents' perspective. Because the primary goal of a liberal society is to enable its citizens to live the life that is *from their own perspective* best for them, parental socialization cannot be the only education that a society provides to children.

Schooling

The goal of this additional education is to enable children to become their own persons, to develop personal visions of the good that they have chosen for themselves. A child's personal vision of the good may turn out to be the same as that imposed by the family in the process of initial socialization, but it need not. As a result of this possible tension between the educational goals of families and of the larger society, liberal theory usually assigns the task of enabling children to become their own persons to a distinct institution, the school.

This task of the school has several related aspects. First, the school should enable each child to understand himself or herself. This self-understanding includes a knowledge of the child's own talents and the extent to which the exercise of those talents is rewarding to the child. Marie needs, in other words, the chance to experience and explore her various intellectual, artistic, social, athletic, and other potentials.

Second, the school should provide to children an acquaintance with a reasonable range of the alternative visions of the good present within their society. For most people, these existing views of the good—occupational, religious, cultural, communal, and so on—establish the alternative possibilities for living one's life in a particular society, and the social context within which one's life will be led. Marie needs here an understanding of the opportunities within her society for realizing and exercising the talents that she finds to be rewarding.

Third, the school should promote an understanding of the system of political morality that governs citizens' actions and choices within the child's society. In a liberal society, this political morality establishes the framework within which one is permitted to pursue one's life—what minimum obligations one has to others and what rights one can expect others to respect. Marie needs to know what freedoms, opportunities, and responsibilities within society as a whole she will have as an adult.

Finally, the school should develop each child's capacity for critical judgment. This capacity enables one to foresee the realistic consequences of one's own decisions and actions. Marie needs to know how to reason logically and to understand the natural and social worlds in which she lives well enough to comprehend the meaning and potential of the alternatives that her society presents to her.

If a school succeeds at these tasks, it places the child's initial socialization in the context of the larger society—the possibilities for and limitations upon living outside one's immediate family. It also gives each child the understandings and skills necessary to make personally meaningful choices among those social possibilities—a knowledge of one's own potential and the ability to assess which of the possibilities presented by one's society can best realize those aspects of one's potential that are most rewarding. Against this background, each child can develop and affirm a way of life that is truly his or her own.

Allowing each child to become his or her own person through liberal education is a prerequisite for providing equal educational opportunities for all. Before Marie's learning can enhance the life she aspires to, she must have her own vision of that life. Thus, liberal societies assign two distinct but related tasks to schools. Schools must enable children to have their own visions of the good and also provide them with a chance to acquire the knowledge and skills necessary to pursue those aspirations. Once children have developed a vision of the good, schools must, in other words, also provide to children the equal educational opportunities that we have already discussed. Of course, much of what children learn in order to choose their life plans will also help them carry out those plans. Critical judgment, for example, is necessary not only for deciding among the possibilities available in one's society but also for pursuing one's choice effectively. However, if Marie chooses to become an electrical engineer, she will need more than general good judgment; she will need to know the physics of semiconductors, the logic of computational systems, and so on. For this reason, educational justice in a liberal society includes a commitment to both common and differential learning.

WE HAVE NOW ASSEMBLED a general picture of how liberal societies operate. Liberalism answers the basic question of political legitimacy—Why should citizens obey the decisions of government when they disagree with those decisions?—by making sure that each person's self-defined interests have been taken into account in society's effort to resolve disputes among its citizens. We have seen that, based upon the fundamental commitment to neutrality, such societies prize basic liberties and equal opportunities for all adults. To prepare children for their adult lives, liberal societies must provide an education that, on the one hand, enables each child to become his or her own person and, on the other, allows each a chance to acquire the specific skills and knowledge required by his or her own vision of the good. Let us now consider how this liberal perspective applies to one concrete educational dispute that may arise in a multicultural society.

We wish again to remind readers that these cases are not intended to represent the beliefs and characteristics of all members of the groups they include. Obviously, many rural communities would disagree with the school board in this case. Similarly, many evangelical Christians will have beliefs different from those attributed here to the pastor who takes issue with that school board.

HARDY SCHOOL DISTRICT

Hardy, a western farming community of about one thousand, has seen better days. Forty years ago, at twice its current size, Hardy served as the economic and social center for the family farms that were gearing themselves to meet the increasing agricultural demands of postwar America. Now, the remaining farmers truck their harvest past Hardy's abandoned grain elevators and stockyard forty miles along the interstate to the city of Alston, Hardy's economically diversified, increasingly populous, and far more successful neighbor. The farms that have survived are larger than ever, including land bought up or leased from their less successful neighbors, and fully mechanized. Those who had to quit farming or who lost work on those farms or in local businesses sought jobs in Alston or elsewhere. Some have kept their homes in Hardy out of an attachment to friends or family, but many others have drifted away, tired of the morning commute or drawn into the communities of their urban co-workers. And many farm women have taken jobs in the city to make ends meet while their husbands struggle to continue the work that they know and love best. Lately, a few city-dwellers have bought or built houses in Hardy, seeking a quieter life. But these newcomers work and, like the majority of their neighbors, do most of their business in the city.

Hardy's schools, an elementary school housing grades K–7 and a high school, both built in the 1950s on a single campus, have long been a point of pride to the community's residents. Parents in Hardy have traditionally agreed about their schools' basic purpose, to enable their children to become literate, self-disciplined, and patriotic adults. And they have consistently supported the schools through participation in school board elections and meetings, attendance at athletic events, home enforcement of teachers' recommendations for children, and, to the best of their ability, property tax assessments. In turn, the schools have responded to their community's expectations, focusing academic work on a thorough mastery of the basic skills, promoting orderly and polite behavior among the students, emphasizing school spirit and patriotic values. And Hardy's children have generally succeeded in meeting these expectations; they consistently score above national norms on standardized tests of reading and arithmetic, are respectful toward their teachers, and have had their share of success in their rural athletic conference.

Over the past few years, however, community concern over the schools has been gradually emerging. To some extent, this concern has been stimulated by the national debate over public education; Hardy's citizens are no less worried about the country's international economic competitiveness than are others all across the nation. Those who work in the city also hear about some of the special programs and opportunities that their co-workers' larger and more affluent urban and suburban schools are able to make available. But the real source of the growing concern is closer to home; Hardy's dwindling economy has meant that most local children do not and cannot make their adult lives in their home town. Most who seek employment after completing high school move to Alston. And about half of Hardy High School's graduates go on to college or vocational school. In these activities, even the young people who have done well in Hardy's schools seem to find themselves at a disadvantage. The best entry-level jobs require considerable sophistication as well as adequate basic skills. Similarly, getting into and succeeding in college or vocational school demand a kind and level of achievement that few of

Hardy's graduates attain. While they score reasonably well on general tests such as the SAT, Hardy's students perform much more poorly on subject-specific achievement tests in literature, chemistry, higher mathematics, and history. Those who seek vocational training find themselves competing with other students who received hands-on and on-the-job training in high school.

This concern has led Hardy's school board to seek new ways in which their small, rural school can provide educational opportunities that are comparable with those available elsewhere. One thing became clear from the beginning: With only about three hundred children, fourteen teachers, and one administrator, Hardy could not duplicate the specialized curricula offered by urban and suburban schools. The schools' response to this concern would have to be accomplished within current staffing patterns, state curriculum and graduation requirements, and the available budget for materials and supplies. Given these constraints, the school board determined that policy changes at the administrative level probably would not address the issue in any important way. Somewhat reluctantly, the board did decide to facilitate parental requests to send their children to schools in other districts, but, to the relief of the board, only a few parents took advantage of that opportunity. It became obvious last fall that a successful approach to the community's concern over the breadth and relevance of the school programs would require changes in the basic curriculum and that such changes would require the help and involvement of teachers.

Don Argus, the combined district superintendent and elementary/secondary principal, suggested that the board invite Jill Schultz, the fourth-grade teacher, and Bill Anderson, one of the high school's two English teachers, to work with him to propose ways of modifying the curriculum to meet these concerns. After meeting together many times, discussing their ideas with other teachers, and talking informally with some of the most interested parents, Mr. Argus, Mrs. Schultz, and Mr. Anderson presented their proposal to the board at the last school board meeting.

The proposal calls for two basic changes in the schools' educational program, one beginning in the fourth grade and the other in the ninth. The elementary reading program has been strictly tied to a textbook series in which specific reading skills are developed at each grade level and in which students' work focuses on the reading material in the text. Most of the material consists of innocuous stories, some descriptive pieces, and occasional poems. Mrs. Schultz, who has taught in Hardy for six years, has found her students to be not very interested in or informed by what they read in the basic text. In fact, she and the fifth-, sixth-, and seventh-grade teachers have tried informally to supplement the text when they happen to find something appropriate. For these teachers, the replacement of this mundane textbook with a variety of timely and informative reading materials seems to provide an obvious opportunity to make the elementary curriculum more broadly educative than it now is. The readings will come, by and large, from contemporary magazines and newspapers and will be selected to represent a broad range of subjects: science, current events, geography, careers, the arts, and politics, as well as literature. The upper elementary teachers will work together to establish a file of articles and stories that will enable them to implement the new reading curriculum over a four-year period beginning with the fourth grade. They will use this material to teach the same reading skills as before, drawing when appropriate on the old textbook for lessons and exercises.

At the high school, the English and social studies teachers propose to replace their separate classes in these subjects with a four-year-long, double-period course in world humanities, beginning in the ninth grade. Here, too, the teachers seek to broaden their focus to include technology, art, music, and social science as well as the traditional political history, literature, and language. Ninth and tenth grades will emphasize these subjects in the United States, while eleventh and twelfth grades will study international relations and world cultures. Team teaching will allow for greater coordination within the curriculum, and the double period will permit longer and more serious classroom discussions, as well as individual and group projects in which aspects of these subjects can be studied in greater depth. Eighth-grade English will continue to be a year of transition to high school studies in which students review and consolidate their basic skills. This program will also be phased in a year at a time to enable teachers to plan the new curriculum systematically.

At the initial presentation of this proposal in April, the school board, chaired by Betty Larsen, a respected member of one of Hardy's founding families, was impressed by the thoughtfulness of the plan. It appeared to meet many of the community's concerns. It also seemed to be feasible, given the teachers' willingness to undertake the hard work of curriculum revision that the plan entailed. Because the proposal represented a significant change, however, Mrs. Larsen asked Mr. Argus to circulate a summary of it to parents and other community members so that the board could hold a formal hearing at their May meeting. No one at that meeting had anticipated the adamant opposition of Reverend William Creasey, the pastor of a new but thriving evangelical Christian church in suburban Alston who had moved to Hardy only a few months before.

Reverend Creasey's Independent Gospel Church is committed to the literal truth of the Christian scriptures as a guide to everyday living. In its five-year history, the church has been most attractive to a growing number of relatively young, largely middle-class families from a variety of religious backgrounds who are seeking a stable and morally traditional community for themselves and their children. The recently finished church building teems with activity all weekend and every night of the week; prayer meetings, Bible study groups, and a full program of youth activities provide the structure and involvement that the Reverend Creasey's congregants demand.

Over the past three years, the reverend and several church members have expressed increasing dissatisfaction with their suburban public schools. Some of the school instruction, especially in health and science, directly contradicts what their children are taught at home and in church. But, more important, their children's classmates do not understand, and sometimes make fun of, the church community's social and behavioral requirements—the church's young people, for example, must pray before lunch and cannot attend school dances, participate in certain playground games, or celebrate certain secular holidays; at home, they do not watch popular television programs or play video games. Many parents in the church feel that the public schools make their children feel isolated and, in some cases, tacitly encourage rebelliousness against family authority. The church has seriously considered establishing its own Christian academy, but the expense of such an undertaking and some parents' concern over the educational viability of what would initially be a very small school led church leaders to postpone those plans indefinitely. Indeed, this decision is what prompted Reverend Creasey to move his family to Hardy. Two church members who live in Hardy have found the very traditional educational program and small-town atmosphere to be much more appropriate for their children than that of the larger, more diverse, and cosmopolitan schools of suburban Alston.

As he made clear at the Hardy school board's public hearing, the proposed changes are the very antithesis of what Reverend Creasey seeks for his children—a solid basic education that supports or, at the very least, does not compete with, the rigorous moral instruction provided at home. The Creaseys carefully control their children's access to secular journalism. Often, magazines and newspapers are a distraction from the sacred texts, prayers, and reflections that form the foundation of Christian living. At worst, and especially for children, they offer deceptive temptations to stray from the paths of right thinking and action. The utility of what the teachers call mundane and uninteresting reading textbooks is that they provide the opportunity for children to practice reading skills *without* conveying ideas or values that might contradict or provide alternatives to their family's beliefs. Teenagers do, of course, need to know something about the beliefs and activities of others whom they will encounter as adults. Traditional English and history courses do a reasonable job of providing such information. But the proposed humanities course goes too far in attempting to encourage students to *appreciate,* to see the value of, those alternatives. In short, according to Reverend Creasey, both proposed changes violate the religious freedom of the family, its prerogative to live according to its members' own convictions without interference from governmental authorities.

The members of the Hardy school board consider themselves religious people, although none is a member of Reverend Creasey's church. But, to a person, they simply do not feel any contradiction between the proposed curriculum and the religious and family values to which they are as strongly committed as Reverend Creasey. How, they ask themselves, could reading a newspaper be un-Christian? How could it threaten parents' authority over their children? How could an appreciation of other times, places, and cultures be morally suspect? At the same time, the board members are intensely aware of their duties as public officials to honor all citizens' right to follow their own religious convictions. Isn't Reverend Creasey's obvious sincerity adequate evidence that the new curriculum would interfere with those rights? Should they reject the proposal, then, even though they believe it will help to meet their and the larger community's concerns over the educational adequacy of Hardy's schools?

THE LIBERAL CONCEPTION OF CULTURE

Intuitively, the dispute between Reverend Creasey and his followers, on the one hand, and the larger Hardy community as represented by the school board, on the other, has all the earmarks of a cultural conflict; it reflects deep-seated and sincere convictions about matters of central importance in the lives of the disputants. As we consider this dispute from the liberal perspective, then, we need to understand how liberal societies think about culture. As we will see, such societies recognize two different ideas of culture.

In the first place, a person's culture is the system of beliefs, preferences, aspirations, and affiliations represented by his or her own vision of the good life. Reverend Creasey and his flock have a definite and shared culture in this sense. They believe that the best life is lived according to the explicit principles, rules, and models set forth in the Christian scriptures. Moreover, Christ's return to earth in order to rescue all true believers before the terrible tribulations described in Revelations is an immediate and impending reality. Therefore, to depart, even temporarily, from the Biblical way is to put oneself at risk of having to endure those tribulations, with the likely result of eternal damnation. There is no place in this view for experiments in living or learning by trial and error. The task of the church community is vigilant, mutual discipline in the ways of the Lord—to constantly reiterate the rules for Christian living, to observe those rules in fellowship with one another, to defend members against temptations to break the rules, and to bring others, especially their own children, into the community (Ammerman, 1987).

The visions of the good life of Hardy's other citizens are considerably more diverse. They have not only varying religious convictions but also different views about the role of religion in their lives in relation to their occupations, recreational activities, and social relationships. For some, as with Reverend Creasey, religion is the organizing principle for the good life. For others, religion is but one element of their vision and, in some cases, is subsidiary to the demands of work or friendship or politics. But despite this range of differences, most citizens of Hardy emphasize certain aspirations for their children—including a desire to enable them to succeed at college and in the workplace—that are of secondary importance to Reverend Creasey. On one level, then, the conflict in Hardy is between the cultures represented by different individual visions of the good life.

There is, however, another dimension of culture in liberal societies. Such societies are collectively committed to certain political and social values: neutrality, liberty, equality of opportunity, and liberal education. This liberal political culture defines the rights and responsibilities of citizens no matter what their individual cultural commitments happen to be. The dispute in Hardy can be seen as a conflict between those who accept this overarching set of political values and those who do not. The proposal before the school board is intended to broaden the educational experience of Hardy's children beyond what their families can provide. It also is an attempt to enable children to take full advantage of the range of educational and employment opportunities available in the larger society. For these reasons, the proposal can be seen as an effort to meet a liberal society's responsibility to provide children an education that allows them to become their own persons and to acquire the skills and knowledge that their emerging visions of the good life require. In opposing this proposal, at least for the reasons that he cites, Reverend Creasey shows that he does not accept some of the political values of a liberal society. Although he claims freedom of conscience for himself and the members of his church, he is not willing to have his children educated in a way that permits them to decide freely whether to adhere to their families' religious beliefs or to adopt some other vision of the good. He believes instead that the role of the school is to reinforce the values and perspectives that children learn in the home. Although we do not have enough information to describe Reverend Creasey's preferred political culture in full detail, we can conclude that, in respect to the education of children at least, it is at variance with liberalism. Thus, the dispute in Hardy is also a conflict between alternative political cultures.

THE DISPUTE IN LIBERAL PERSPECTIVE

Reverend Creasey and the members of the Hardy school board want different things for their children, then, in part because they have different ideas about the good life and in part because the disagree about the political values that should govern their society. How, from the liberal perspective, should these differences be resolved?

As we have seen, liberal societies are to resolve disputes according to the principle of equal advantage: the parties to the dispute are to be neither relatively advantaged nor disadvantaged in the pursuit of the good life as they see it. This principle clearly applies to the first level of cultural conflict present in this situation. Reverend Creasey will not be able to live up to his own ideals of the good life if his children are exposed to the new curriculum; on the other hand, that curriculum *is* consistent with Hardy's other citizens' aspirations for their children. In this light, the proposed curriculum would place Reverend Creasey at a disadvantage in his effort to live the good life as he sees it, at least in comparison with his neighbors.

However, a third set of interests that we have not yet considered is at stake in this situation—those of the children who are to be educated. Because children do not come into the world with particular visions of the good, liberal societies define their interests as the development of the capacity to be their own persons—in other words, the abilities necessary for choosing, understanding, and carrying out their own ideals for living. Reverend Creasey sees things differently; for him, the interests of children are defined solely by their parents. In particular, he believes that his own children have an exclusive interest in becoming good evangelical Christians. Here, as we have noted, Reverend Creasey disagrees not just with his neighbors but also with the basic principles of liberal political morality.

This second level of dispute is crucial for applying the principle of equal advantage, because it determines whether there are two or three sets of interests to be considered in this situation. For if we side with Reverend Creasey in this matter, the children's interests are already included in those of their parents. What, then, should a liberal society do when some of its citizens' conceptions of the good lead them to deny fundamental liberal political principles?

We have already considered a similar situation in our discussion of the use of coercive methods for promoting beliefs. A liberal society must be neutral to *all* of its citizens' conceptions of the good. Hence, it cannot permit the rich and powerful to engineer others' beliefs. Similarly, such a society cannot permit adults, who have a natural if temporary advantage over children, to use their power to coerce belief. Just as the vulnerability of powerless adults is no grounds for ignoring their interests, the simple fact that children cannot tell us whether their long-term interests will be different from those of their parents does not imply that they have no independent interests that deserve to be taken into account—interests in developing their self-understanding, broadening their experience, refining their judgment, and comprehending their political rights and responsibilities. In other words, when some citizens' private beliefs conflict with liberal principles, a liberal society cannot permit the exercise of those beliefs to impair others' legitimate interests. Thus, such a society must recognize three sets of interests in applying the principle of equal advantage to the situation in Hardy: those of Reverend Creasey, his neighbors, and the town's children.

In determining how these interests are to be balanced under this principle, we must remember that from the liberal perspective certain interests have priority over others; liberty is more important than equal opportunity, which, in turn, is more important than individual claims to material wealth. Just as a person who is not allowed to compete equally in the labor market is absolutely disadvantaged in comparison with those who are, so a child who is denied the chance to understand her talents and proclivities or to develop independent judgment is disadvantaged in her effort to make use of the freedoms and opportunities provided to all adults in a liberal society. If I am unable to make sensible and personally meaningful decisions about my life, the freedom to make such decisions has little value to me.

This line of reasoning suggests that children's interest in a liberal education is more important than *any* interests of adults to pursue their own visions of the good, including their interests in religious freedom. As a result, the principle of equal advantage must assign priority to the educational interests of Hardy's children. For to sacrifice those interests in order to enhance Reverend Creasey's or any other adult's religious liberty would leave those children absolutely disadvantaged in comparison with adults. Thus, to be equally advantaged, children must be given a liberal education. The basic liberal principle for adjudicating disputes implies, therefore, that the Hardy school board should implement the new curriculum proposal.

The consequence of this decision is, unfortunately, that Reverend Creasey will probably find it harder to live up to his ideal of the good life than most of his neighbors will. For his children will learn things at school that will challenge what they are taught at home and in church. This decision to provide a liberal education is *not* based on the assumption that Reverend Creasey's conception of the good is inferior to his neighbors'. Instead, it is based on the conclusion that children's interests in a liberal education are more fundamental than the reverend's or his neighbors' interests in pursuing their established visions of the good. A liberal society cannot promise all its citizens equal success in fulfilling their aspirations, especially if those aspirations require others to sacrifice their basic right to self-determination.

At the same time, however, the fact that Reverend Creasey's view of the good is in some respects incompatible with liberal principles does not imply that a liberal society need be openly hostile to him and his ideas by, for example, omitting all mention of Christian fundamentalism from the curriculum or even condemning such ideas as irrational or inhumane. Sometimes, neutrality to religion is interpreted to mean that the religious dimension of human life should be ignored by the public schools. This policy is inconsistent with liberal principles in two ways. First, it disadvantages people like Reverend Creasey in their pursuit of the good life more than is necessary in order to provide a liberal education to children. And, second, it gives those children a less than fully liberal education because it neglects some possibilities for living that many find to be fulfilling.

Therefore, while the Hardy school board should attempt to broaden and diversify the curriculum as the teachers propose, it should also make certain that the content of that curriculum does not ignore or demean either religion in general or Christian fundamentalism in particular. It may also wish to consider in this light whether other school policies—such as restrictions on students' private religious practices during school hours or the use of school facilities for extracurricular religious activities—should be modified in order to fulfill its commitment to neutrality.

THE ADEQUACY OF LIBERAL THEORY IN MULTICULTURAL CONTEXTS

Now that we have analyzed a case of multicultural conflict from the liberal perspective, let us consider how satisfactory that perspective has proven. At the end of the first chapter, we proposed four tests for assessing the adequacy of an approach to resolving multicultural differences:

1. Does the approach represent culture adequately?
2. Does it assign a high ethical priority to cultural values?
3. Does it produce clear and definite resolutions for cultural conflicts?
4. Are those resolutions acceptable to the parties involved?

Let us examine each of these questions in turn.

The Conception of Culture

Liberalism identifies culture with individual views about the good life. This understanding of culture captures many of our intuitions about it—that culture is related to the very meaning of a person's life, what one considers to be the purposes of living; that someone's culture is intimately connected with his or her identity, how one understands the world and one's place in it; that culture organizes a person's goals and activities in life. Liberalism can, in other words, distinguish between someone's more profound and permanent interests and his or her superficial preferences or passing fancies.

At the same time, however, a personal view of the good life does not have some of the central features of culture, namely its historical and social dimensions. Cultures represent patterns of belief, practice, and commitment that have developed over considerable periods of time—usually generations if not centuries. Similarly, cultures are shared by the members of a community. Liberalism does not distinguish between visions of the good that have a culture's historical and social foundation and those that are wholly idiosyncratic or that represent a major break with tradition. Thus, liberalism recognizes some but not all of the important characteristics of culture.

The Ethical Priority of Culture

Individual views of the good have special importance in liberal ethics; they define the very purpose of society since, as we have seen, the function of liberal government is to create the circumstances in which its citizens can pursue their conceptions of the good. Since cultures constitute, from the liberal perspective, a vision of the good life, they are assigned the highest ethical priority. However, cultures share this priority with other, more individual visions. The simple fact that a person's conception of the good is widely shared and based upon historical traditions does not give it any special ethical status in comparison with other conceptions of more recent vintage or revolutionary character. In liberal societies, cultural values are given the same protection—through freedom of conscience and association, for example—as all other individually accepted values.

The Power to Resolve Disputes

The basic commitment of a liberal society—to maintain neutrality toward all citizens' conceptions of the good life—is deceptively simple. Neutrality implies that liberal societies should follow the principle of equal advantage when their citizens disagree. This principle holds that in resolving a disagreement, the interests of the parties should be equally served. As we have noted, however, some interests are, from the liberal perspective, more fundamental than others because, unless they are preserved, the other interests have little value in the pursuit of one's vision of the good. As a result, liberalism places its citizens' interests in a specific priority order:

1. Liberal education
2. Liberty
3. Educational opportunity
4. Economic opportunity
5. Material welfare

This ranking produces complicated rules for applying the principle of equal advantage to particular instances of conflict among citizens: When the interests of the parties are of different types (liberty for some and material welfare for others, for example), the higher interest is to be favored; when the interests of the parties are of the same type (educational opportunity for all, for instance), those interests are to be equally balanced.

To be sure, all this complexity in liberalism's approach to disagreements demands a great deal of careful thought when making decisions about specific cases. Nevertheless, this approach has two real advantages. First, the list of various kinds of human interests that are morally important allows liberal theory to apply to a wide range of conflicts. Liberalism is not, for instance, limited only to quarrels over material resources. Second, the priority ranking of interests allows liberal theory to produce definite decisions about how those interests are to be treated. That ranking determines what should be done when different sorts of interests are at stake, without requiring an intuitive and probably inconclusive balancing of radically different kinds of human goods. After all, how much money is the freedom to worship as one pleases really worth? By assigning a high priority to basic liberties, liberalism obviates the need to answer such questions. As we have seen in the Hardy case, the principle of equal advantage is able to produce clear decisions even when some parties to the dispute reject basic liberal assumptions.

The Acceptability of Resolutions

One thing that can make a decision hard to accept is that it is capricious, not based upon any reasons except the decision maker's whim or preference. A decision made according to the principle of equal advantage cannot be arbitrary in this sense since that principle requires that decisions be based upon the actual interests of the parties involved. In the Hardy case, Reverend Creasey's freedom of conscience, on one side, conflicts with other parents' freedom of conscience and children's right to become their own persons, on the other side. The decision to implement the new curriculum is justified because of the priority of liberal education over liberty. Thus, liberal societies can always provide a reason for their decisions beyond the mere desires of the decision makers. Moreover, because liberal education provides an understanding of liberal political principles to all citizens, these are reasons that the parties to the dispute can comprehend.

Decisions of liberal societies often prove unacceptable to the parties on two other grounds, however. First, the reasons for the decision are often of secondary importance to the parties. What Reverend Creasey cares most about, for example, is saving his children from eternal damnation. And yet this overriding interest of his is not directly included in the rationale offered for the school board's decision. Their reasons are not his most important reasons.

In fact, neutrality requires this to be so. Because a liberal society cannot prefer one conception of the good over another, it must find more general and universal ways of thinking about its citizens' interests—liberty, opportunity, and so on. To Reverend Creasey's question, "But don't you *care* about the fate of my children's souls?" a liberal society must answer, "Yes, but only to the extent that we are committed to protect your right and that of other citizens to believe whatever seems best to you about such matters." Such a response is likely to strike Reverend Creasey as a peculiar way of caring about the issue that defines his very existence.

From the reverend's perspective, his society's attitude toward the community and traditions in which he participates will seem equally peculiar. His convictions about how to raise his children are *not* simply a matter of individual choice but a reflection of a shared way of life rooted in a long and venerable religious heritage. Yet all that matters to his society is that the reverend happens to define his good in a particular way. The highly individualized perspective of liberalism fails to capture the social and historical dimensions of Reverend Creasey's and, indeed, other citizens' beliefs. Here, again, the rationale for a liberal society's decisions will fail to reflect what many citizens find most important in their lives, their genuinely cultural commitments.

Second, the liberal approach to decision making provides no mechanism for changing a decision once it has been taken. In matters of principle, decisions are to be made according to a judicial model in which social authorities hear the evidence, apply the principles to that evidence, and render an impartial judgment. As long as the evidence is complete and the principles have been correctly applied, that judgment is final. In liberal societies, the ordinary politics of constituency building, lobbying, and compromise have a role only in matters where principles are indeterminate or inapplicable. In Hardy, where the principle of equal advantage has a clear application and a definite result, the denial of Reverend Creasey's request and the rejection of the values upon which it is based are permanent and irrevocable. Thus, the Reverend has not simply suffered a temporary defeat that might, through hard work and shrewd politicking, be reversed at a later date. The very clarity and finality of decisions based upon liberalism's substantive principles of justice make it all the harder, therefore, for some citizens to live with them.

A REVIEW OF LIBERALISM'S ADEQUACY

The liberal perspective's clearest strength in multicultural contexts lies with its ability to specify clearly and definitely what should be done even when disagreements run deep and emotions run high. Liberalism seeks to treat the members of different cultures fairly by representing their interests in very general and common terms. Its principles organize those interests into a hierarchy of value by placing at the top those interests that seem to be prerequisites for benefiting from the others. This process of abstracting from the concrete values and commitments of particular cultures comes at a fairly high cost, however. By viewing human interests as individual, liberalism tends to ignore the social and historical character of culture and to count conceptions of the good that are novel and idiosyncratic as morally equivalent to cultural commitments. This is especially troubling in the case of children, who are viewed as having no genuine culture until they have developed the capacities needed to choose a conception of their own good. Even worse, the liberal perspective on cultural differences produces resolutions to conflicts that many members of society may find hard to accept: First, the justification offered for those resolutions omits or abstracts from people's most important values; second, liberal societies offer those who are dissatisfied with a particular decision no way of working to change it.

REFERENCES AND FURTHER READING

Ackerman, B. A. (1980). *Social justice in the liberal state.* New Haven: Yale University Press.
>An important contemporary statement of the principles of liberal political thought, including a chapter on liberal education.

Ammerman, N. T. (1987). *Bible believers: Fundamentalists in the modern world.* New Brunswick, NJ: Rutgers University Press.
>A sympathetic sociological and anthropological portrait of a Christian fundamentalist church community.

Dworkin, R. (1977). *Taking rights seriously.* Cambridge, MA: Harvard University Press.
>An influential analysis of the way in which rights function in liberal societies; see especially the title chapter.

Dworkin, R. (1978). Liberalism. In S. Hampshire (Ed.), *Public and private morality* (pp. 113–143). New York: Cambridge University Press.
>A clear statement of the underlying assumptions of liberal political theory.

Mill, J. S. (1978). *On liberty* (E. Rapaport, Ed.). Hackett. (Original work published 1859).
>The classic defense of individual freedoms from a utilitarian perspective.

Rawls, J. (1971). *A theory of justice.* Cambridge, MA: Harvard University Press.
>A systematic and influential argument for liberal political principles; a very difficult book that is significantly responsible for a renewed interest in liberalism in the United States and elsewhere in the world.

CHAPTER 3

The Democratic Perspective

In societies that encompass a variety of cultures and languages, there are likely to be serious disagreements about how people should lead their lives, disagreements that can become particularly severe when the shaping of the next generation's expectations, abilities, and values are at issue. The three perspectives we analyze in this book attempt to resolve these disagreements in ways that the parties can accept even when they do not get their own way. As we have seen, liberalism resolves these disputes by ensuring that society's decisions will produce fair outcomes in which the self-defined interests of the parties have been equally taken into account.

Democratic theory develops from a different but equally familiar perspective on everyday disagreements. To understand the intuitive starting point of the democratic perspective, let us consider another dispute between Marie and Nate:

> Nate and Marie are at it again. A box of new books has just arrived to supplement their classroom library. As a reward for finishing their reading workbook assignments, their teacher allows the children to choose a book from the library and to read it quietly on their own while the other students finish their work. As usual, Nate and Marie are among the first to complete their seat work. Unfortunately, the same book has caught the attention of both Nate and Marie; each insists on being the first to read it. Unlike the orange clay, being first cannot be equally divided between them, especially since the teacher wants the children to read independently. In this situation, the teacher simply flips a coin to determine who will have the book first. Marie correctly calls the toss and gets the book.

Once again, the teacher's approach to this dispute seems eminently reasonable. In this case, it is impossible to resolve the dispute by creating a fair outcome. After all, only one child can be first even though they have an equally good claim on that privilege. Instead, the teacher uses a *fair procedure* for deciding the issue, a procedure that recognizes the validity of each child's claim but that will, nevertheless, give the book to one child rather than the other. The child who loses can accept the result because he or she has had a fair chance to win.

The democratic perspective extends this ordinary idea of fair procedures to the political process. A democratic society must establish processes for making social decisions that recognize the stake that various parties may have in those decisions. From this perspective, those parties ought to accept their society's decisions because each has had a fair chance to influence the decision-making process. While liberalism aims at substantive justice, then, democracy, we might say, attempts to provide procedural justice for all of the members of society.

WHAT DEMOCRATIC THEORY IS

Justice, as we noted in the last chapter, requires that people be fairly and equally treated when social decisions are made. Liberal theory proposes that the *outcomes* of those decisions should be regulated to reflect an equal recognition of the parties' interests. Democratic theory, by contrast, proposes that fair and equal treatment of the parties should be preserved by regulating the *process* used to make social decisions. The outcomes that result from such a fair process will, from this perspective, be just even if they do not represent a balance of interests, that is, even if some people's interests are more fully served than those of others. After all, Marie does get to read the disputed book first. There can, in other words, be clear winners and losers as a result of a fair process.

What, then, is a fair process? In general, coin-flipping is a peculiar way to make important decisions, even though it seems intuitively fair in the dispute between Marie and Nate. We would not think it appropriate to decide whether to put someone in jail or to build a new school by flipping coins or rolling dice. Nor would it seem fair for the teacher to base her decision on a coin flip if Marie and Nate had agreed upon who should go first. The coin flip seems right in this situation only as a tie-breaker, a way of producing a decision when opinion is equally divided. Thus, the coin toss is part of a larger process in which the parties have had an opportunity to express their opinions and to have those opinions taken into account in the final decision. A fair process, then, is one in which the parties' opinions about what should be done are related to the decisions that are made.

In this situation, however, would it be right for the teacher to decide that, because Nate is a special favorite of hers, only his opinion is worthy of consideration and that, therefore, he alone should determine who reads the book first? A theory of procedural justice must answer this question of whose opinion is to matter in the social decision-making process. And, historically, a wide range of answers to this question has been given at various times and places; the opinions of people of aristocratic descent or of a particular race, of people who own sufficient property or are members of the male sex have been deemed worthy of attention in the making of social decisions. The hallmark of the modern democratic perspective is the answer that it gives to this question.

The Central Commitment: Universal Participation

The literal meaning of "democracy"—government by the people—implies that everyone's opinion is to count in making social decisions. But there are many different ways of counting people's opinions. For example, when women were excluded from American politics, it was often assumed that their views were adequately represented by their fathers', husbands', or brothers' opinions. Modern democratic theory generally rejects such assumptions, holding that each person should have *the right to participate actively in the decision-making process that shapes his or her society.* From the democratic perspective, then, it would have been wrong for the teacher to base her decision only on Nate's opinion about who should read the book first, although, as we will see shortly, children pose a special challenge for democratic theory.

Before considering in more detail how a democratic society operates, it will be helpful to note two significant differences between the liberal and democratic perspectives. First, although both liberalism and democracy value the individual members of society, they interpret that value in different ways. Liberalism emphasizes *individual interests,* whereas democracy focuses on *individual opinions.* Now, I can have opinions on an almost unlimited range of subjects—from whether a state on the other side of the country should allow a nuclear power plant to be built, to what my neighbors should watch on television, to how I should lead my own life. For the liberal, opinions of this last sort—one's own vision of the good life—are of special moral and social significance; they constitute each person's self-defined interests, which a liberal government has a duty to facilitate. Of course, my vision of the good life can imply that I have an interest in what other people do because others' actions can affect my chances to lead my life as I see fit. But these legitimate interests in others' actions need not be identical to my opinions about their actions. I can, for example, have an opinion about what my neighbors should watch on television even though what they watch has no material effect on my own life. In a liberal society, my opinion about my neighbors' television viewing habits in this case is of no particular importance in society's decisions. By contrast, democratic societies do not in general pick and choose among their members' opinions. With some exceptions, which we will discuss in a moment, *all* of an individual's opinions have a legitimate role in the decision-making procedures of a democracy.

As a result of this difference in which opinions are relevant to social decisions, there is a second important difference between liberal and democratic societies. A liberal society must, under certain conditions, decide to allow a person to act in certain ways even if no one else in the society thinks he or she should do so. Neutrality requires a liberal society to permit me to pursue my vision of the good life as long as it does not interfere with others' pursuit of their visions. Again, with some notable exceptions, this is not true of a democratic society. Others' opinions about my behavior, whether or not those opinions reflect their holders' self-defined interests, are generally relevant to the decisions that a democratic society makes. To use Amy Gutmann's (1987) apt phrase, democratic societies engage in conscious social reproduction. They are involved in the collective and deliberate shaping and reshaping of the society as a whole based upon their members' informed opinions about what that society should be like. As a result, very few decisions are beyond the authority of the collective opinions of the members of a democratic society.

With these distinctions in mind, let us turn to the question of exactly what decision-making procedures and social institutions are necessary to maximize citizens' participation in the decisions that shape their society.

The Role of Government: Maintaining Majority Rule

A democratic society answers the basic question of political morality by telling its citizens that they should accept and obey society's political decisions because they have all had a full and fair chance to participate in the making of those decisions. For this participation to be meaningful, the society's decisions must depend in some way upon what the citizens want the decisions to be, upon the citizens' political opinions. Democratic societies therefore need a rule for translating their members' various opinions into collective decisions.

One such rule might be to require a consensus on every decision, in other words, to require *everyone* to agree to each decision. In the case of Marie and Nate, for instance, this rule implies that neither should be allowed to read the book until they both agree about who should go first. The consensus rule would, in effect, give everyone a veto over the society's decisions.

Of course, such a rule seems eminently impractical; if everyone had to agree to every decision, almost nothing would ever be decided. But practicality and expedience are not the criteria we ought to apply here. If our primary concern was that social decisions be made quickly and easily, we might just as well appoint a dictator and let his or her opinion decide every social issue. What we seek is not an expedient decision rule but a *fair* one. And from this ethical perspective, the rule of consensus might seem to be justified. After all, consensus appears to guarantee that every social decision has actually been accepted by all members of a society. Apparently, then, no one could challenge the legitimacy of a society's decisions because everyone has actually agreed to them.

But this justification is only superficially plausible. Consensus is not only impractical but also unfair. In fact, upon careful inspection, consensus turns out to be morally equivalent to dictatorship. To see why, let us reconsider the dispute between Marie and Nate.

Suppose that Marie does not actually care about reading the book first; instead, what really matters to her is that Nate *not* be allowed to read it. The consensus rule permits Marie to get her way no matter what Nate or anyone else happens to think. It allows her opinion alone to determine what will happen; she has, on this matter at least, become a dictator. The consensus rule is unfair, therefore, because it allows those who wish nothing to happen the absolute and final authority to get their own way.

Individual dictatorship and consensus are unfair for the same reason. Each allows the opinions of some people to count more than those of others in determining what society should do. The basic commitment of democracy that *all* should participate in social decisions is clearly incompatible with a decision rule that allows any one person's opinion to carry the day. This line of reasoning can be extended to show that allowing any two individuals to either veto or determine a decision is also both unfair and inconsistent with universal participation. Following this argument to its logical conclusion, the only decision rule that both accords equal weight to individuals' opinions and permits universal participation is one that decides issues as a bare majority of society's members wishes. The basic function of a democratic government, then, is *to ascertain and carry out the will of the majority.*

BASIC CONDITIONS AND INSTITUTIONS IN DEMOCRATIC SOCIETIES

As we have seen, democracy involves the deliberate shaping and reshaping of a society based upon what a majority of its citizens wants that society to be. The task of a democratic government is to create a fair procedure whereby that collective self-determination can take place. In the end, that procedure will generate specific results, such as the decision about whether Nate or Marie will be allowed to read the book first. But for those decisions to be morally legitimate, they must be made under fair conditions.

Political Rights

One thing that might cast doubt on the fairness of a decision-making procedure is, as we have already noted, that it does not take everyone's opinions equally into consideration. This might happen in one of two ways. First, certain kinds of opinions might be repressed in the decision-making process, no matter who happens to hold them. A society might, for example, forbid the expression of the belief that the means of economic production should be collectively owned. Second, certain people, no matter what their opinions are, might be excluded from the decision-making process. Here, a society might prohibit all people who practice a particular religion from voting in elections. To guard against the dangers of repression and exclusion (Gutmann, 1987), democratic governments establish and guarantee to their citizens certain political rights.

Chief among these rights is the *freedom of opinion,* the right to hold and express without social penalty whatever beliefs one wishes about the overall form of one's future society and the specific decisions that one's society confronts. Second, democratic societies protect their citizens' *freedom of political association,* the right to form coalitions of like-minded individuals in order to advance their shared opinions in the political process. Finally, democracies enforce the *freedom to vote one's conscience.* This complicated right implies that democracies must establish a formal mechanism, the vote, whereby a government periodically surveys the opinions of its citizens, takes all citizens' opinions equally into account according to the principle of one person/one vote, and guarantees that no one will be punished for voting as he or she thinks best (Dahl, 1956).

Taken together, these rights ensure that a society's decision-making process fairly reflects the actual opinions of its citizens. They allow individuals to hold any opinion they think best, to promote their opinions in cooperation with others, and to communicate their beliefs to government officials without fear of reprisal. These rights guarantee that no opinion will be repressed and that no person will be excluded from the process of collectively determining the society's future. They do place certain limits on the decisions that a democratic society may make about its own political processes. It cannot decide, for instance, to outlaw certain political parties (unless those parties are likely to use democratic processes to destroy democracy). The institutions that enforce these limitations are often similar to those used by liberal societies to protect their citizens' basic liberties—constitutional provisions implemented by a court system that has the power to nullify democratic decisions that violate those provisions. These provisions in the United States include such things as freedom of the press, freedom of peaceable assembly, the right to petition the government for redress of grievances, nondiscriminatory voter registration rules, and fair apportionment of elective offices.

However, the political rights of a democracy are, despite some superficial similarities, different in substance and purpose from the personal liberties of a liberal society. Liberalism's freedoms of conscience and expression, for example, are intended to allow each person to live his or her own life as he or she sees fit. Democracy's freedom of opinion, by contrast, allows each person to express his or her belief about how people should live, but does not guarantee that he or she will be allowed to live in that way because the majority may decide otherwise. Liberal freedoms place direct limitations on the substance of a society's decisions, but democratic freedoms place such limits only upon the procedures whereby decisions are made.

Information and Deliberation

There is yet another way in which a political process can be unfair. If citizens do not understand the meaning or consequences of their opinions about their society, democracies may make decisions that those citizens ultimately find impossible to live with. Suppose, for instance, that the teacher had not told Marie and Nate that the first person to read a new book has to make an oral report to the entire class. Under these circumstances, when Marie wins the toss and finds out about the book report, she is likely to conclude that she has been unfairly treated. Here, the coin-flipping procedure that we have described would not be fair precisely because neither child knows in advance the full ramifications of his or her wanting to be the first to read the book. A fair procedure requires, therefore, that the participants be reasonably informed about the decisions they are making.

Democratic theory does not require that the decisions of a fair process be "good" decisions according to some external criterion—that they, for instance, promote the greatest happiness for the greatest number or that they lead to the salvation of the most souls. Rather, democracy simply requires that the participants in a fair process have a reasonable understanding of what they are getting themselves into when they make particular decisions. A fair process, in other words, is one that includes informed decisions. Such a process involves *thoughtful deliberation based upon relevant information*.

Traditionally, three institutions have been charged with the task of meeting these requirements of information and deliberation. In addition to its role in serving freedom of opinion, a free press has been expected to inform citizens about the issues that they will decide. Since Thomas Jefferson's plea for an educated electorate, public schools have been recognized as a way of promoting among the general populace the knowledge and skills necessary for informed decision making. And, finally, deliberation requires a public forum in which decisions may be debated and made. Public assemblies—sometimes in the form of town meetings but usually in the form of elected, representative legislatures and councils—are democracy's ultimate deliberative bodies.

Resolving Conflicts in Democratic Societies

The teacher's disposition of Nate and Marie's disagreement over the book suggests the basic principle for resolving conflicts within democratic societies—*any decision made according to a fully fair decision-making process is morally binding upon all the parties to the dispute*. This principle of pure procedural justice implies that the results of a fair process are just, whatever those results turn out to be. Democratic theory defines a fair process as one in which all members of a society have a right to participate and in which all decisions are rendered according to the opinions of a majority of its members. Thus, in democratic societies the principle of pure procedural justice implies that those who oppose the majority's decision have a moral obligation to comply with that decision. Such political minorities form what has been called a loyal opposition; they are to be loyal to the majority's decisions despite their opposition. This opposition is not necessarily futile, however. Today's decisions may be reconsidered tomorrow, and revised if a sufficient number of citizens have changed their opinions in the meantime. If the decision-making process remains fair according to democratic principles, these revised decisions are just.

We have also seen that democratic theory places two conditions upon fair political processes in addition to the general requirements of universal participation and majority rule. Such processes must, first, respect the political rights of citizens to freedom of opinion, to freedom of association, and to voting their own consciences. And, second, these processes must involve deliberation based upon relevant information. These conditions upon fair procedures in democracies can complicate the resolution of conflicts. For some decisions of democratic societies can affect directly or indirectly the extent to which these conditions are realized within those societies. Obviously, a decision to disenfranchise a particular group of citizens would fall into this category. But so, too, might a decision to exclude particular subjects or ideas from the public school curriculum have an effect on freedom of opinion or citizens' ability to deliberate reasonably on various public issues.

Decisions of this kind, which affect the fundamental fairness of a society's decision-making processes themselves, must have a special status in democracies. For according to the principle of pure procedural justice, a society's decisions are not morally binding unless they are arrived at by means of a fair process. There may be situations in a democracy, therefore, in which a conflict should be resolved in favor of a political minority, situations in which adhering to the majority's opinion would render the decision-making process unfair according to democratic principles. In other words, maintaining democratic procedures takes moral priority over other matters. For without such procedures, no social decision is morally legitimate.

EDUCATING CHILDREN IN DEMOCRATIC SOCIETIES

As was the case in the previous chapter, the discussion of Marie's and Nate's dispute in this chapter may strike many readers as odd. Although it is not unimportant to find fair ways of settling disputes between children, many other considerations besides fairness seem relevant to this situation. Perhaps Marie had never before shown a particular interest in books. Mightn't the teacher, then, be justified in favoring Marie as a way of stimulating this emerging interest? Or suppose that Nate has not yet met the teacher's expectations for independent reading in that particular week. Here, wouldn't it be right to let him go first? In children's education, procedural fairness seems to be a secondary consideration.

Indeed, the entire set of moral concepts central to democracy—participation, majority rule, political rights, information, and deliberation—do not seem to apply very readily or directly to children. These concepts make certain assumptions about the motivations and abilities of those to whom they are applied. They assume that participants bring some vision of the society as a whole to the process of social decision making, that they are able to engage in that process in a peaceful and deliberative manner, and that they are able to govern their actions according to the results of that process. Young children do not have these capabilities and characteristics and therefore are not citizens of the democratic society fully deserving of the rights and responsibilities we have discussed.

Children do, of course, have the potential to become citizens, that is, to develop the capacities that would allow them to participate in the democratic process. And democratic societies have two different reasons for developing that potential. On the one hand, children are an important means for a society to realize its collective vision of the future. A democracy's decision to have clean air, for example, implies that it will build and maintain scrubbers to neutralize industrial emissions, require catalytic converters on automobiles, and so on. That decision also implies that the society must produce engineers capable of designing such devices, technicians able to install and maintain them, and consumers willing to tolerate the costs and inconveniences associated with such measures. Children are therefore one of the resources that a democracy has available for carrying out its collective decisions about its own future, and education is a means of developing that resource. Because a democratic government has a moral responsibility to carry out the decisions of the majority, it has a duty to educate children in ways that will realize the majority's vision of the future.

However, children have the potential not only to carry out the results of the democratic process but also to engage actively in the process itself. Democracy's fundamental commitment to universal participation implies that everyone must be given the formal opportunity to take part in society's decision-making processes, but does a democracy also need to develop individuals' abilities to participate effectively in those processes, to use their political rights skillfully and intelligently? A pragmatic response to this question might suggest that it would be difficult to educate children to carry out the decisions of a democracy without developing at least to some extent the abilities necessary to make those decisions (Dewey, 1916/1966). But some majoritarian decisions might actually require the neglect of some children's potential to participate effectively in democratic processes. A majority's desire to achieve a certain standard of living might require a cadre of workers willing to do difficult and inherently unrewarding labor for very low wages, labor that would be refused by people with the ability and motivation to take advantage of their political rights. Or a majority might wish to neglect the political education of a particular group of children against whom the majority is prejudiced. Under these conditions, would it be permissible for a democratic society to refuse to develop some children's potential to participate effectively in the democratic process?

We have already discussed why such neglect is inconsistent with democratic principles. The moral legitimacy of democratic decisions rests upon the assumption that those decisions are made according to a fair process, one in which all citizens have had a full and equal chance to participate. By failing to develop some citizens' potential to participate in that process, a society undermines the future fairness of the process and thereby the moral legitimacy of the resulting decisions. To be and remain a democracy, a society must therefore provide to all children a political education that develops their capacities to take advantage of the political rights and responsibilities they will enjoy as adults. Second-class citizenship has no place in a democracy (Gutmann, 1987).

As a result, education in democratic societies serves two different and sometimes conflicting functions. The *political* function aims at the reproduction of democratic decision-making procedures and is governed by the basic moral principles and concepts of democratic theory. The *societal* function aims at the construction of future states of society according to the will of the majority and is governed by the actual results of the democratic political process. If these two functions come into conflict, political education takes precedence over societal education so that the society's decisions retain their moral authority.

Political Education

The purpose of this aspect of democratic education is to develop in young people the skills, knowledge, and dispositions that will enable them as adults to participate fully in the processes of democratic decision making. To this end, a democracy's educational institutions, particularly public schools, must make it possible for children to have their own visions of the society's future and their own opinions about the political decisions that their society confronts. For most people, developing this vision of the society depends in part on a knowledge of the range of such visions available within the society. Thus, Nate needs an understanding of his society's important political issues, the various positions on those issues that are possible, and the rationales for those positions.

The schools should develop in children the intellectual skills and knowledge necessary for them to make independent and critical judgments about the social visions available within their society. Nate needs, first, sufficient information about how the world works and what the people in his society are like and, second, sufficient command of the processes and standards of rationality to reach his own considered judgments about the most desirable future state of his society.

Having developed such a vision of the good for their society, children must be capable of entering effectively into the processes of democratic decision making. Here, Nate needs to acquire the powers of expression, persuasion, and negotiation, as well as a knowledge of political institutions that will enable him to make the most of his freedoms of opinion and association. He needs to develop the disposition to seek relevant information and to deliberate thoughtfully as he exercises his freedom to vote his conscience. And, finally, Nate needs to develop a democratic sense of justice that will enable him to accept the rule of loyal opposition when he is in the minority, and to avoid the abuse of power that undermines the fairness of the political process when he is in the majority.

Societal Education

Beyond providing the education necessary to maintain the fundamental fairness of political procedures, democratic societies are also obliged to enable their citizens to participate in the social arrangements that result from those procedures—the specific economic, cultural, and interpersonal institutions and activities authorized by the majority's vision of the good for the society. Because the ability to participate in these institutions depends significantly on citizens having the chance to acquire the particular skills and knowledge needed for such participation, democratic societies are committed to equal educational opportunity. But democracy's version of equal opportunity differs from liberalism's version in two crucial respects. First, the kinds of educational opportunities that democratic societies offer to their citizens are determined by majority rule, whereas those in a liberal society are governed by individuals' personal visions of the good life. The social roles for which a democracy provides a chance to prepare are, thus, a matter of collective decision rather than individual aspiration and negotiation. The portion of its citizens' potential that a democracy must seek to develop is politically rather than individually determined. Of course, this societal education in a democracy will by necessity be adapted to the talents and proclivities of those who are being educated. But this adaptation is a pragmatic consideration rather than a moral commitment to the sanctity of individuals' self-definitions.

In a related vein, the basis for democracy's commitment to *equal* opportunity is different from liberalism's. In liberal societies, equal opportunity reflects the commitment to neutrality, the conviction that it is unfair to prefer one individual's personal view of the good life over another person's view. In democracies, the goal of societal education is to bring about the social conditions preferred by the majority. Like any society, a democracy seeks to achieve its goals efficiently. As economists have long argued, equal educational and occupational opportunity promote social efficiency. After all, the larger the pool of candidates for society's roles and positions, the more likely that society is to find or develop the abilities it requires. Moreover, because democracies cannot create a category of second class citizens by neglecting some people's basic political education, there is no group of children whom it would be efficient to exclude from the system of societal education. Thus, democracy values equal opportunity for its efficiency in carrying out the majority's decisions and not for its connection to any individual right of self-determination.

In part, societal education in a democracy is specifically vocational, a way of preparing individuals to fill particular roles within the society. But as John Dewey (1916/1966) pointed out, democracies encounter unanticipated problems in their efforts to realize the will of the majority, and they also constantly redefine themselves as the beliefs of the majority evolve. Hence, societal education in a democracy need not be narrowly or exclusively vocational but should emphasize general problem-solving abilities and a degree of adaptability to changing social conditions and expectations as well.

WE NOW HAVE a general idea of how democratic societies operate. Democracies respond to the basic question of political legitimacy—Why should citizens obey a government's decisions when they disagree with them?—by creating a political process in which all have a fair chance to affect the decisions that are made. This process must respect adults' rights to freedom of opinion, of association, and of voting their conscience, and must involve thoughtful deliberation based upon relevant information. To enable children to participate in their society when they become adults, democracies provide a political education that allows children to develop their own opinions about the society's future and to engage in its decision-making processes. Democracies also provide a societal education that permits children to qualify for roles in the institutions determined by majority rule.

Let us now consider how this democratic perspective applies to another concrete educational dispute that may occur in a multicultural and multilingual society. As in previous cases, the beliefs and characteristics described here are not intended to characterize Anglo and Mexican American, much less all Latino, populations in general. Latinos are an especially diverse group in this country, ranging from the descendants of early Spanish colonists to more recent immigrants from throughout the Caribbean, Mexico, Central America, and South America.

LA ESPERANZA MIDDLE SCHOOL

Like many communities of the American Southwest, San Pablo's ties to Mexico are long-standing and vital. Despite a complex history of Native American, Spanish, and Mexican influence, waves of Anglo immigrants after 1850, in the 1930s, and more recently in the 1960s have meant that political power has long resided in the Anglo community. In the past thirty years, the historic flow of Mexican immigrants became a flood, resulting in the development of barrios geographically, culturally, and linguistically demarcated from the Anglo residential areas.

Until the mid-1970s, public education was conducted exclusively in the English language, with the result that few Mexican American children completed high school and fewer still excelled academically. At that time, pressure from the Mexican American community, supported by federal authorities and courts, led to the institution of a transitional bilingual program in San Pablo's elementary schools. Upon entry into the school, students' language skills are assessed; students whose proficiency in English is limited are placed in bilingual classrooms. In the first two grades, bilingual classes provide early reading instruction in Spanish, and teach mathematics, social studies, art, and so on in Spanish, but they also include intensive instruction in oral and written

English. In grades three and four, children learn to read English and are instructed in their other subjects in a mixture of Spanish and English. By the fifth grade, reading in Spanish has been phased out, and most of the instruction in other subjects is conducted in English. In fact, with some exceptions, Mexican American and Anglo fifth graders are integrated into the same classrooms and taught by the same teachers, most of whom are monolingual English speakers. Although there are special arrangements for teaching English as a Second Language to recent immigrants, middle and high school instruction is in English with elective Spanish language and literature classes available from eighth grade on.

Under this program, the school attainment of Mexican American students has improved but still lags that of Anglo students. About 70% of San Pablo's Mexican American females graduate from high school, compared with a graduation rate of about 80% for all Anglo children. However, only about 60% of Mexican American males finish high school. About a third of the Mexican American high school graduates go on to college or postsecondary vocational school, compared with over half of the Anglo graduates. The majority of the city's young Mexican Americans seek local employment, and many secure relatively low-paying jobs.

The difference in school attainment by Mexican American females and males is reflected in, and according to some, caused by, a social phenomenon that has become a source of sometimes bitter controversy within and between the Anglo and Mexican American communities. Over the past fifteen years or so, gang membership and activity among teenage boys and young men in the barrios have grown dramatically. Most members of the Anglo community view this development as an unmitigated evil. For Anglos, the congregation of groups of young Mexican American males on the streets, their seemingly raucous and defiant behavior, and the occasional violence within and between gangs is an open threat to public order and safety.

Members of the Mexican American community tend to have a different, if equally concerned, view of these events. Traditionally, Mexican American boys are expected to develop a degree of independence from their families at an earlier age than Mexican American females or Anglo children of either gender (Brussel, 1971, p. 171). In early adolescence, Mexican American males spend less time with their families and more time with other teenage males, developing the male friendships and attitudes that will eventually prepare them for their adult roles and responsibilities as heads of families and in the male-dominated public life of the community.

Unfortunately, the educational, economic, and social conditions in San Pablo lead some young Mexican American males in directions that are at odds with the community's traditional cultural expectations. Their alienation from school and the general shortage of gainful employment, combined with a growing reluctance among some young men to accept and be satisfied with the low-paying jobs that are available to them, mean that for some young Mexican American men early independence does not produce the anticipated integration into adult-male family and community responsibilities. In some cases, this independence from family authority, and solidarity with their age mates, develops instead into self-destructive patterns of defiance, alcoholism, and violence that bear only a superficial resemblance to the masculine ideal of *machismo*. Although most young Mexican American males do not ultimately fall into these patterns, far too many do. Many Mexican American families regard this situation with grave concern because it represents a significant threat to their community life—an estrangement of their sons and a loss of responsible husbands for their daughters.

La Esperanza Middle School was established fifteen years ago on the border of the barrio and an Anglo neighborhood. Its purpose is to address the academic and social needs of preadolescents with a special emphasis on the needs of barrio children, as perceived by the members of the San Pablo school board. La Esperanza, spanning grades six through eight, enrolls most of San Pablo's Mexican American children in that age group who do not attend Catholic secondary school; over half the student population is Mexican American. The school's academic purpose is, through classes conducted entirely in English, to consolidate children's language skills and to establish the basic background in academic subjects necessary for success in the high school. The middle school format was selected in order to begin this process while the influence of most children's families is still strong and before the complications of puberty set in.

As noted, this strategy has succeeded for most Mexican American and Anglo students. Nevertheless, a worrisome split in La Esperanza's student body has developed, involving a significant minority of students who are alienated from school. Largely, though by no means exclusively, Mexican American and male, this alienated group is marked by high rates of truancy and disruptive behavior in school. Most of these students are assigned to the school's lowest academic track and tend to band together in classrooms, the school cafeteria, and elsewhere on the school grounds, which sometimes leads to open and occasionally violent conflict with other students. According to school authorities, these alienated students frequently drop out of school when they reach sixteen, and some become involved in gangs outside of school. School efforts to cope with these students have included counseling, contact with parents, tutoring, and a variety of disciplinary measures. These efforts have not been especially effective in reducing the size of the alienated group, although some teachers and students believe that such measures have helped to keep its members from becoming a source of excessive disorder.

For many members of San Pablo's Mexican American community, progress toward the social equality that the political and legal victories of the 1960s and 1970s had promised now seems increasingly and frustratingly out of reach. Recognition of Mexican Americans' legal and civil rights, and the establishment of bilingual education in schools, did put an end to some of the most egregious forms of discrimination and neglect and has opened new doors of opportunity for some. But the hope for full social and economic parity with the Anglo community has gone unfulfilled. Indeed, some believe that this modest and incomplete progress has come at a very high price—the disintegration of a distinctive and coherent Mexican American culture.

In response to this frustration and concern, a small group of middle school teachers has, with the encouragement of some parents and community members, proposed a Spanish-language school-within-a-school for La Esperanza. Raoul Hernandez, a veteran social studies teacher at the middle school, has assumed leadership in developing the proposal. The plan would create a separate educational program at La Esperanza that parents and students could elect and that would be located in a wing of the middle school. Comprising six teachers and 150 to 200 students in the three grades, this program would include instruction entirely in Spanish in four subjects—Spanish-language and social studies classes that would emphasize Mexican American literature and heritage, as well as classes in mathematics and science. In addition, students in the program would study English for one period each day and would have one period in which they would take required or optional classes (such as physical education, home economics, and art) with students from outside the program.

In presenting this proposal to the San Pablo school board, Mr. Hernandez argued that the city's schools have proven ineffective for many Mexican American children in two ways. First, the transitional bilingual program in the elementary school, he suggested, leaves many Mexican American students without a real command of either Spanish or English, especially insofar as those languages are required for serious academic work. By the fifth grade, Mexican American students have stopped using Spanish in the academic context, but many have learned only enough English to get by in school, but not to excel. Second, just as students are beginning to seek their adult identities, the middle school classes' almost exclusive emphasis on the English language and Anglo culture leaves many young Mexican Americans without a meaningful cultural context in which to do so. This can be especially confusing for some young Mexican American males whose efforts to develop toward masculine independence are neither understood nor supported in the school environment. Indeed, much of the alienation among these students is, according to Mr. Hernandez, an unintended consequence of the current middle school program.

Mr. Hernandez argued, further, that the proposed Spanish-language program can meet both of these difficulties—at least for some students. By increasing language instruction to two periods a day, the proposed program will emphasize skills particularly needed by some Mexican American students. And by including both Spanish and English, this instruction will promote the balanced development of the students' linguistic potential. Moreover, the academic course work of the proposed program will be more accessible for students whose skills in Spanish are better developed than their English-language skills. No longer would such students be consigned to the lowest track, in which their access to academic subject matter is restricted. Enhanced attention to Mexican American history and culture in these classes will provide a more supportive context for many students. Finally, the teachers in the proposed program will be able to meet the developmental and social needs of the students by providing strong male role models for the boys, maintaining culturally appropriate forms of discipline, and communicating effectively with the students' families. In sum, Mr. Hernandez claimed that the Spanish-language program can both promote greater academic achievement for the students who opt for it, and help to overcome the alienation that produces disruptive behavior in the school and may lead eventually to the gang activities that concern both the Mexican American and Anglo communities.

This proposal has produced considerable controversy among school board members and in the San Pablo community at large. Discussions in the Mexican American community have generated a broad spectrum of reactions. Mexican American parents are divided about whether it would be a good idea to enroll their children in the Spanish-language alternative. Many parents feel that such a program would ultimately disadvantage their children; they fear that it would interfere with their children's acquiring facility in English, and thereby with their ability to take advantage of educational and economic opportunities in the larger society. Others, however, see the program as a chance for their children to perform academically in a language in which they feel comfortable and in a social environment that is consistent with their family and community values. In fact, some believe that the new program would enable their children to maintain those values more easily than is possible in the regular school program. Still others see the proposal as a way of helping their children overcome or avoid alienation from school. Members of the Mexican American community generally agree, despite their differences over what they want for their own children, that the new program is worth trying for those who want it and, perhaps, as a deterrent to gang membership for at least some teenagers. After all, the current efforts of school authorities, social agencies, and police have done little to remedy the situation and, in the view of some, may actually be making it worse. All in all, then, La Esperanza's Mexican American parents, and community in general, strongly support the proposal as an option for some parents and students.

The Anglo community is far more skeptical about the value of the proposal. Very few Anglo parents are interested in enrolling their own children in the program. Some believe that the program might contribute to combating the gangs. Others support the proposal out of respect for the cultural values of Mexican American parents. But many in the Anglo community see the program as a form of social segregation and cultural isolation that may have a variety of harmful effects. Some view the continued separation of Anglos and Mexican Americans as inherently wrong, like the segregation of blacks and whites in other U.S. cities; they worry that the proposed program might unintentionally prolong old hostilities between the communities. Some believe that the program would insulate participating children from the political, social, and economic values of mainstream America, preventing them from acquiring the skills (especially in the English language) and attitudes necessary for full involvement in the larger society. Others are concerned that the program would preserve and promote what they consider to be a sexist bias in Mexican American culture, that it would perpetuate the unjust male dominance already present in the public life of the Mexican American community and discourage Mexican American females from taking advantage of the wider range of life choices available to them in the regular curriculum. And a few people are concerned that the program might even promote more gang activity because it would reinforce the students' strong identification with Mexican American culture. In the end, although a significant number of Anglos support the program, especially in the neighborhood served by La Esperanza, a large majority of them in the city as a whole are opposed to it.

Opinion about the program among members of the school board is divided along community lines. The two Mexican American board members favor the program, as does one Anglo member from the La Esperanza neighborhood. The four remaining Anglo members are opposed to the plan. Two of these opponents, however, are concerned about the legal consequences of their opposition; they suspect that national Latino activist groups may attempt to convince local Mexican Americans to take the board to court if the proposal is defeated, and that the entire school district's policies and practices toward Mexican American children might then become subject to constitutional challenge.

Based on their personal appraisals of the proposal, a majority of school board members (and of the entire San Pablo community) oppose the Spanish-language program for La Esperanza Middle School. Nevertheless, those most directly affected by the proposal, Mexican American and Anglo parents from the school's attendance area, are in favor of the proposal. And the threat of constitutional litigation further complicates the situation. How, then, should this case be resolved?

THE DEMOCRATIC CONCEPTION OF CULTURE

The dispute in San Pablo is, at least in part, a cultural conflict. Some Anglo and Mexican American parents have different views about the rearing of their children and about the patterns of adult life that upbringing is intended to foster. These differences are the result of long-standing traditions of ethnically and linguistically distinct communities, and they represent fundamental and personally compelling convictions of the members of those communities. The dispute over the new program at La Esperanza arises in part from these differences in perspective on the means and purposes of child rearing, differences that lead to a degree of mutual misunderstanding and, perhaps, suspicion between the communities. Let us consider, then, how the cultural elements of this dispute appear from the perspective of democratic theory.

As we have noted, democratic theory distinguishes two different types of political beliefs—beliefs about a society's basic political processes and opinions about particular political issues. The basic political process in a democratic society must meet certain standards of fundamental fairness—participation, majority rule, and so on. Such standards can and should be enforced even if members of the society have beliefs that conflict with them. These standards constitute the basic political culture of democratic societies.

Some of the arguments on both sides of the dispute in San Pablo appeal to these democratic principles. Some people who support the proposal charge that the regular school program is antithetical to the language and traditions of the Mexican American community; as it stands, the middle school thus represses the values and beliefs of that community and is, as a result, undemocratic. Others claim that the new program would prevent participating students from receiving the basic political education that is the birthright of all members of a democratic society. And some argue that the proposed program would promote what they believe to be sexist values in Mexican American culture and would, therefore, violate the democratic principle of nonexclusion. All these arguments allege that the Spanish-language program is either required by or prohibited by the morally authoritative political culture of a democratic society. The dispute in San Pablo can, from this perspective, be seen as a disagreement between those who share democratic political culture and those who do not.

Most political issues in a democracy, however, do not have an effect upon the basic fairness of the society's political procedures. Rather, differences of opinion on most issues reflect alternative visions of the best collective future for the society, all of which are consistent with basic democratic values. Many of the arguments in San Pablo can be understood in this light. Some people prefer more linguistic and social variety; some prefer less. The city's adults differ in the amounts and types of camaraderie among male adolescents they find appropriate and worthy of perpetuation. And they have varying opinions about the amount of social integration they deem desirable. From this perspective, the conflict in San Pablo is between groups of people who have differing visions of their city's and country's future. Those who hold similar visions of the future might be thought to represent a particular cultural viewpoint within the larger society. Because there is a clash of social visions in San Pablo, there is also, in a special sense, a clash of cultures.

THE DISPUTE IN DEMOCRATIC PERSPECTIVE

Education from the democratic perspective has two primary functions. First, it develops the knowledge, skill, attitudes, and values that are necessary for maintaining a democratically fair decision-making process. Second, it is a way of bringing about the collective vision of the future that results from that process. Because the political function of education takes moral priority over the societal function, we must analyze the dispute over the proposed Spanish-language program at La Esperanza from the political perspective first.

The Political Education Perspective

Several arguments in this case maintain that the new program is either required by or prohibited by the democratic commitment to enable children to participate appropriately in society's decision-making processes. Some people charge that the program is required by democracy's principle of non-repression, that without the program some children will be denied their Mexican American heritage and that, therefore, Mexican American values and ideas will be unfairly repressed.

Nonrepression is, of course, a basic democratic value, but exactly how does it apply to this case? Opinions are repressed when a society does not permit their expression in the process of social decision making. Those in San Pablo who make the nonrepression argument want more than simple expression of opinions, however; they wish to preserve a way of life, to allow at least some children to observe and perpetuate the traditions of Mexican American culture. Democracy, though, does not guarantee that everyone will be able to live the life that he or she prefers, only that people will have a fair chance to influence the decisions about the ways of life that will be permitted within that society. As we have noted, there can be clear winners and losers in a democracy as long as the process for choosing the winners is fair.

From the democratic perspective, then, the important question in San Pablo is whether it is *necessary* to have a Spanish-language school program in order for the members of the Mexican American community to have their opinions taken seriously in the political process. The answer to *this* question is not at all clear. If Mexican American beliefs and ideas can be successfully communicated in English, it does not seem necessary to provide a Spanish-language program. But even if they cannot, how would the proposed program be of any help? Having a minority of children who grow up fluent in Spanish does not guarantee that Mexican American ideas will get a fair hearing if those ideas cannot be expressed and explained adequately to those who speak only English. If ideas are language-specific, the democratic principle of nonrepression seems to require that *all* children learn all the languages spoken in a particular society. The nonrepression argument, therefore, proves either too little or too much. If Mexican American culture can be successfully translated into English, the proposed program is *unnecessary* to prevent the repression of those ideas. If that culture cannot be adequately communicated in English, the proposed program is *inadequate* to prevent repression. In either case, the principle of nonrepression does not imply that a democracy must adopt the elective Spanish-language program proposed for La Esperanza in order to safeguard the fairness of the political process.

A similar fate befalls the argument of the program's opponents who claim that democracy requires all citizens to share a common language and that the program should not be allowed because it would prevent some children from becoming sufficiently fluent in English, the predominant language of American politics. This argument is based upon what may turn out to be a false assumption, that the proposed program will permit some children to complete school without a sufficient degree of English literacy to participate in American politics. After all, program participants will complete the elementary school bilingual program before they enter middle school, will study English for an hour a day in the middle school, and go on to the regular high school program. And, of course, they are growing up in a society in which English is the primary language of the media and commerce. But for the sake of argument, let us suppose that at least some participants would develop too little proficiency in English to enter directly into a political process conducted in English.

What can a democracy do when some citizens cannot communicate directly with one another? If translation between the two languages is possible, a democracy could simply provide for it in the political process—ensure that political documents are available in both languages, provide translators at political events and legislative sessions, and so on. Of course, such arrangements might be inconvenient or expensive, but when translation is possible, democratic principles do not require all citizens to acquire a common language.

Suppose, however, that translation is not possible, that some Anglo beliefs, values, or attitudes cannot be adequately expressed in Spanish and vice versa. Does this possibility justify the requirement of a single, common language in a democracy? Fair political processes in a democracy do demand satisfactory communication among citizens—for participation, information, and deliberation all require that mutual understanding of citizens' opinions be achieved. If some opinions held by Anglos cannot be expressed in Spanish, there is good reason for Spanish speakers to learn English. But the same argument applies to English speakers as well. If Anglos, despite the best efforts of translators, cannot make sense of Mexican American opinions, then they should learn Spanish. Once again, if translation is not possible, universal bilingualism is the logical consequence of democratic principles.

In this way, a consideration of the communication requirements of democracy also proves too little or too much. If translation is possible, it is not *necessary* to require everyone to learn English. If translation is not possible, requiring everyone to learn English is not *sufficient* for democracy; everyone must learn Spanish as well.

Finally, let us consider the claim that the proposed Spanish-language program is prohibited by democratic principles because it promotes sexist values. Sexism clearly violates the democratic principle of nonexclusion. Providing different opportunities for boys and girls to learn what is necessary for participating in society's decision-making processes, or promoting attitudes that discourage girls from taking advantage of opportunities to develop and use their abilities to participate in democratic politics, has the clearly discriminatory effect of excluding some future citizens from involvement in social decision making. Thus, avoiding and, when necessary, opposing sexism must be a fundamental commitment of democratic societies.

However, such a commitment does not imply that alternative Spanish-language programs like that proposed for La Esperanza Middle School must be forbidden. Rather, it implies that any school program, whether conducted in Spanish or English, and whether it emphasizes the history and literature of England, the United States, or Mexico, must be nonsexist. If the original plan for the new program betrays a bias against women, then like any program, it must be modified to exclude that bias. Perhaps, such modifications would make the program less attractive to some parents or other citizens, but the democratic principle of nonexclusion does not absolutely prohibit the use of any particular language or cultural orientation in schools.

To be sure, the popular cultures of the United States, Mexico, and many other nations are sexist in different ways. Similarly, different languages subtly promote and reflect varying discriminatory beliefs and traditions. What may be needed to combat sexism effectively in one culture may be considerably different from what is appropriate for another culture. A separate Spanish-language program could, if carefully designed, provide an opportunity to deal with the specific forms of gender bias that Mexican American children may confront in their daily lives. In this way, the new program could prove even more effective in overcoming sexism for some children than a nonsexist English-language program. In any case, having two nonsexist alternatives in school seems no less justified according to democratic principles than having only one.

In sum, the arguments based upon democratic political education in this case seem to be inconclusive. Establishing the new program is either an unnecessary or an insufficient response to the democratic concern over the repression of Mexican American values and beliefs. Similarly, banning the new program is either an unnecessary or an insufficient response to the problem of maintaining an effective medium of communication in a democracy. And, finally, democratic opposition to sexism implies at most a modification, rather than a prohibition, of the proposed program.

The Societal Education Perspective

In general, democratic majorities are free to enforce whatever social arrangements they prefer as long as the process they use to make such decisions is fair and those arrangements will not create unfair political processes in the future. We have found that the new program at La Esperanza is neither required nor prohibited by democratic concerns over the fairness of future political processes. In other words, separate Spanish-language and Mexican American culture alternatives in schools are not a necessary part of children's democratic political education, nor are they inherently antithetical to that education. It appears, therefore, that the citizens of San Pablo are free to adopt or reject the proposal based upon their current opinions about the most desirable future for their society. The proposal concerns what we have called children's societal education, about which political majorities are to have the final decision.

All that is necessary to make a democracy's decisions about societal education legitimate is that those decisions are made by means of a fair process. The procedures used by the San Pablo school board seem to meet that requirement. There has been a free and open public debate about the proposal. Citizens on both sides of the issue have had a chance to explain their opinions and to present information in support of those opinions. Members of the school board have had the opportunity to argue over, and to deliberate thoughtfully about, the decision.

One aspect of the situation in San Pablo, however, reveals an unfortunate ambiguity in democratic theory's definition of fair procedures, an ambiguity that creates serious uncertainties in applying democratic principles to this case. A majority of those most immediately affected by the decision about the new program, the citizens of San Pablo served by La Esperanza, are in favor of the program. Yet a majority of citizens of San Pablo as a whole oppose it. The laws of the federal government, representing the political opinions of the citizens of the entire nation, also apply to this situation although their precise interpretation is not yet clear. Which majority should govern the La Esperanza decision—that of the school community, the city, or the nation?

From the democratic perspective, the answer to this question must depend exclusively on whether the decision-making process would be more fair if it were assigned to one of these levels of government. In a democracy, a procedure is fair when it enhances citizens' participation in the decisions that shape their society's future. But here is where the ambiguity appears.

On the one hand, it seems intuitively fair to give those who are more immediately affected by a decision a greater say in making that decision. Allowing La Esperanza's parents to decide about the new program would enhance their participation in the control of their own and their families' lives. On the other hand, it also seems fair to give everyone affected by a decision a chance to participate in it. The lives of the children educated at La Esperanza will not be confined to the neighborhood of the school or even to the city of San Pablo. Moreover, people who will never come into direct contact with those children have opinions about the education they should receive and the society in which they should live, opinions that from a democratic perspective give them a legitimate political interest in such matters. From this point of view, a much larger group of citizens should be involved in the decision about the program.

Democratic theory is ambivalent about school, local, or national control of education. When majority opinions at these various levels differ, as they do in this case, the implications of democratic theory are troublingly uncertain. In short, although democracy's commitment to the principles of participation and majority rule is unequivocal, the political realities of local and regional differences of opinion and ambiguities in our intuitions about fair political procedures make the most appropriate meaning of those principles unclear.

In light of this ambiguity in interpreting the principles of democracy, it may seem best for (national?) majorities to determine what decisions should be assigned to the various levels of government. Thus, the final decision about the proposed program should be made by the school board because previous decisions at the national and state levels have assigned authority over school programs to school districts. If so, the new program should not be adopted, because a majority of the San Pablo board opposes it. But this solution to the practical problem of jurisdiction does not resolve the issue of moral legitimacy that these difficulties raise.

Democracy provides moral legitimacy for social decisions by ensuring that those decisions are fairly made. When intuitions about fair processes conflict in a way that apparently cannot be resolved by democratic principles, the moral legitimacy of social decisions is undermined no matter how authority to make such decisions is distributed. For those on the losing side of such decisions can, with some degree of plausibility, maintain that their loss resulted not from a lack of political power or persuasiveness but instead from the unfairness of assigning the decision to a particular level of government.

THE ADEQUACY OF DEMOCRATIC THEORY IN MULTICULTURAL CONTEXTS

Our analysis of the situation at La Esperanza from the democratic perspective has affirmed the San Pablo school board's rejection of the proposed Spanish-language program because the program is neither necessary for, nor antithetical to, children's basic political education; because the school district has been assigned political authority over decisions about children's political education; and because they have used democratic procedures in making the decision. Let us consider how well democratic theory, especially as it applies in this case, meets the four criteria for adequacy that we developed in the first chapter.

The Conception of Culture

Democracy identifies culture with citizens' shared opinions about the future of their society. This way of thinking about culture coincides with some features of our intuitive understanding of that idea. For example, it explains how a society may embrace many different cultures. From a democratic perspective, a culture is a political faction, a group of people who hold similar opinions about certain decisions that will shape their society's future. Because there may be many political factions in a democracy, there may then be many cultures. The democratic view of culture also meets one critical objection to the liberal view—that it is excessively individualistic. Political factions are groups; therefore, culture in a democracy is a collective rather than an individual phenomenon.

Unfortunately, the democratic conception of culture is open to objection on other grounds. The members of a political faction share particular political opinions, but they may do so for very diverse reasons. Some citizens of San Pablo support the proposed program because they share the language and way of life upon which the program is based. But many Anglos also support the program, some because it promises to reduce gang violence, some because they prefer a more diverse society, and some because they believe it would enhance the academic performance of Mexican American children. In other words, a political faction is a coalition of people who may have radically different histories, ways of life, and even aspirations for their own and their children's future. But a culture is more than a temporary and coincidental sharing of political opinions. It involves a shared history and way of life, characteristics that have no particular political significance in democracies. Cultures imply that their members have a deep personal stake in them. But people may be members of a political faction on a whim, that is, even though the positions of the faction do not affect their lives in a profound and meaningful way. Moreover, cultures have a permanence not necessary to political factions, which can arise quickly and disappear once a particular controversy fades. The democratic view of culture seems, therefore, insensitive to the depth of commitment, historical origin, and continuing nature of culture.

The Ethical Priority of Culture

Cultural commitments, like other political opinions, do have real moral significance in democracies. Citizens are guaranteed the freedoms to hold and express whatever political opinions seem best to them. Thus, everyone's cultural values and beliefs have certain fundamental protections in a democracy. Moreover, citizens' political opinions are the basis upon which a democracy is to make its collective decisions about the present and future states of the society. Cultural commitments thus figure into democratic societies' political deliberations.

Although democracies provide a definite role for culture in the political life of society, that role is limited in two ways. First, cultural beliefs are no more important than other sorts of political opinions. The simple fact that a person's opinion has its origin in a historical or communal context gives it no special status in democratic decision making. Second, democracies do not guarantee that citizens with particular cultural commitments will be allowed to conduct their lives in accord with those commitments. Freedom of opinion ensures one the right to hold one's cultural beliefs but not necessarily to live them. A democracy gives individuals a chance to persuade others to let them live the life they prefer, but it also permits majorities to decide otherwise. To put the matter in another way, the political value of a cultural commitment in a democracy depends upon the number of citizens who hold it or can be persuaded to respect it. Democracies protect the political beliefs of minorities but do not necessarily guarantee minorities' rights to practice their cultures even when such practices are compatible with fair political procedures. As we saw in San Pablo, democratic majorities are not required to provide school programs that reflect Mexican Americans' cultural commitments as long as their political participation is guaranteed in other ways.

The Power to Resolve Disputes

The dispute-resolving power of a theory of political morality depends upon two things—whether the theory covers all the various types of disputes that can arise within a society and whether it provides a definite resolution for the disputes that it does cover. Democratic theory clearly meets the first criterion. It divides disputes into two types, those that affect the society's decision-making procedures and those that do not. For the procedural disputes, democratic theory defines a prioritized set of criteria for maintaining the fairness of the decision-making process:

1. Democratic political education
2. Political rights of opinion, expression, and voting
3. Deliberation and information
4. Majority rule

Criteria at the top of this list are prerequisites for those below. Thus, for example, it is fair for majority opinion to determine social decisions only if that opinion is informed by a reasonable understanding of the implications of the decision for the members of the society. These prioritized principles of fairness provide an orderly, if complex, way of resolving disputes about a democracy's political processes, or about other matters that impinge in some way upon citizens' opportunities to participate fully and freely in those processes.

All other disputes in a democracy are to be decided by means of these fair procedures. There is in principle no dispute too private, too idiosyncratic, or too trivial to be submitted to public debate, deliberation, and decision. Of course, democracies typically maintain a wide variety of nonpolitical institutions for making everyday decisions or resolving minor disputes, institutions like the family and economic markets. But such societies have the authority to modify, regulate, or even eliminate those institutions in order to realize their citizens' collective vision of the future as determined by the democratic political process.

The second virtue that an approach to dispute resolution must have is the ability to reach clear and definite decisions about controversial issues. On this criterion, democratic theory fares less well. As we saw in the San Pablo case, democratic theory is ambiguous in assigning clear decision-making jurisdiction to various levels of government. There is, therefore, one type of dispute over fair decision-making procedures that democratic principles are unable to resolve. But this is a crucial defect in multicultural societies, where there are likely to be significant local and regional differences of political opinion. In these societies, different decisions will be reached depending upon the level of government to which a dispute is assigned. Thus, the ability of democratic societies to reach clear and unambiguous resolutions of at least some nonprocedural disputes is undermined by their inability to resolve jurisdictional disputes on the basis of principle.

The Acceptability of Resolutions

As a practical matter, democratic societies *do* assign particular decision-making responsibilities to various levels of government—sometimes by convention or tradition and sometimes by explicit majority vote. From the democratic perspective, any assignment of decision-making jurisdiction seems morally arbitrary, and as a result any decision made at the assigned level will seem unfair to some citizens when a more favorable decision would have been made by a smaller or larger unit of government. In other words, some nonprocedural decisions in a democracy will appear to be arbitrary to some citizens even though all the rules for fair decision making have been followed. Thus, the inability of democratic principles to settle jurisdictional disputes also weakens the moral authority of some decisions made in nonprocedural disputes.

This lack of moral authority, in turn, makes those decisions hard to accept. The more culturally diverse a society is, the more often the outcomes of social decisions will depend upon the unit of government to which they are assigned. When there are concentrations of minority cultural groups in particular geographic areas, social decisions assigned to small localities are more likely to reflect minority cultural beliefs than decisions assigned to larger units of government. But local assignment of decisions will seem unfair to members of the cultural majority or, possibly, to members of other cultural minorities. Similarly, state or national assignment of decisions will seem unfair to local cultural minorities. As a result, it is likely that large numbers of decisions in democratic but multicultural societies will seem unacceptable to many citizens because they have been determined by democratically arbitrary assignment to particular jurisdictions.

Thus, members of the La Esperanza Middle School community will be not only disappointed that they lost the debate over the new program, but also concerned that it is unfair for the city-wide school board to make this decision when no one outside the school is immediately affected, and when the proposed program would not impair children's political education. This unresolvable concern about the fairness of the decision-making process will make it hard for the members of the school community to accept the decision even though they may be committed to the principles of democracy.

Two other features of the democratic approach, however, tend to make its decisions acceptable to the losers of the democratic debate. First, the debate is conducted by the citizens themselves in their own terms. Unlike liberalism, democratic theory does not require a decision based upon an analysis of citizens' interests in such abstract terms as liberty or equality of opportunity. San Pablo's Mexican Americans are free to explain their culture and their aspirations for their children using the concepts and language that make the most sense to them. If *machismo* is central to their vision of the good person and the good society, they do not need to represent or misrepresent that ideal as an *individual* vision of the good. Similarly, the members of the school board are free to decide whether and to what extent Mexican American culture is compatible with other citizens' visions of the future and should therefore be maintained and promoted in the public schools. They need not inquire about such abstruse and theoretical matters as children's personal liberties or their abilities to become their own persons. Moreover, democratic procedures and the political education that supports them promote widespread mutual understanding of citizens' various perspectives, values, and aspirations. Thus the citizens of San Pablo and their school board have an opportunity through public debate and deliberation to achieve a realistic appreciation of what the decision about the new program means to various members of the Mexican American and Anglo communities.

At times, of course, the effect of a decision on the fairness of society's future political processes must be considered, and some decisions will be made on procedural grounds rather than for citizens' personal reasons. Nevertheless, democratic decisions are far more sensitive to citizens' ways of thinking and their actual desires than liberal decisions tend to be.

Second, most social decisions in a democracy are revisable. Liberal societies produce definite and permanent resolutions based upon fundamental principles of substantive justice, but because democracies are based on procedural justice, democratic decisions, except those required to keep political procedures fair, are subject to revision if a majority can be convinced to change its mind. Because most democratic decisions are not final, those who oppose particular decisions still have the opportunity to persuade others of the rightness of their cause. Although citizens in a liberal society can only complain about principled decisions that they do not agree with, citizens in a democracy can work to change those decisions.

Whereas democratic ambiguity about the assignment of jurisdiction over particular decisions can lead those who disagree to find those decisions unfair, these two additional features of democracy can help to mitigate this problem. That most decisions are made on the basis of citizens' personal reasons, and that the chance exists to have unfavorable decisions reversed, make it easier to live with those decisions.

A REVIEW OF DEMOCRACY'S ADEQUACY

The hallmark of democracy is the political process in which all citizens have the right to express their visions of the society, explain the value of those visions to one another, and decide collectively on the shape and direction of their society. This process has a number of virtues in multicultural and multilingual situations. It provides a vehicle for the public expression of cultural norms and beliefs and establishes a social context in which citizens can come to comprehend and value one another's points of view. And, as John Dewey (1916/1966) observed, it maintains a mechanism of continuous and mutual adjustment of society's institutions to its members' evolving interests and aspirations.

But there is a downside to democracy for the members of minority cultures. By treating cultural groups as but one of many political factions, democracy ignores the historical and communal dimensions of culture. By treating cultural commitments as mere political opinions, democracies can outlaw activities and practices central to the continuance of minority cultures even when those practices have little material effect on other citizens' ways of life. That there can be clear winners and losers in a democracy means that the tyranny of the majority, so eloquently described by Alexis de Tocqueville (1848/1969) over a century ago, can be a real threat to the survival of minority cultures in democratic societies. And the inability of democracies to resolve jurisdictional disputes based upon principles undermines the very moral authority that fair procedures are supposed to confer upon social decisions. When the resolution of particular disputes depends upon the morally arbitrary assignment of jurisdiction, as frequently will be the case in multicultural societies, many citizens will perceive those decisions as unacceptable because they are arbitrary.

REFERENCES AND FURTHER READING

Brussel, C. B. (1971). Social characteristics and problems of the Spanish-speaking atomistic society. In J. C. Stone and D. P. DeNevi (Eds.), *Teaching multicultural populations: Five heritages* (pp. 169–196). New York: Van Nostrand & Reinhold.

    A brief but useful analysis of the characteristics of Mexican American families, communities, and values. The book that includes this essay contains other informative chapters on various aspects of African-American, Puerto Rican, Native American, Asian-American, and Mexican American culture and experience.

Dahl, R. A. (1956). *A preface to democratic theory.* Chicago: University of Chicago Press.

    An influential explanation of the nature and value of interest-group democracy, in which politics is based on factions that form around particular issues rather than competing, large scale political ideologies.

Dewey, J. (1966). *Democracy and education.* Chicago: Free Press. (Original work published 1916).

    The classic progressive definition of democracy as an interdependent social and educational system aimed at the solution of common problems.

Gutmann, A. (1987). *Democratic education.* Princeton, NJ: Princeton University Press.

    An important contemporary conceptualization of a constrained form of democratic society in which education plays a central role. This book includes informative applications of democratic theory to a wide variety of educational issues at the elementary, secondary, and university levels.

Tocqueville, A. de. (1969). *Democracy in America* (G. Lawrence, Trans.; J. P. Mayer, Ed.). Garden City, NY: Doubleday. (Original work published 1848).

    An appreciative and critical nineteenth-century European perspective on American democratic attitudes and institutions that articulates issues of democratic theory that continue to be of concern today.

CHAPTER 4

The Communitarian Perspective

The liberal and democratic traditions described in the last two chapters represent the most familiar approaches that Americans bring to the question of political legitimacy. As we have seen, liberal theory maintains that people should obey their society's decisions when those decisions fairly reflect all its members' individual interests. Democratic theory, on the other hand, holds that citizens should accept social decisions that are made according to a fair procedure that takes into account all citizens' opinions about what should be done.

These approaches to political morality share certain commitments. Both, for example, emphasize and protect citizens' freedom to hold and express their own beliefs. But they also differ in significant ways. Liberalism is fundamentally committed to allowing each individual to pursue his or her own vision of the good life as long as others also have a fair chance to do so. Democracy, by contrast, permits informed and deliberative majorities to define future states of their society in ways that may prevent some citizens from pursuing their personal visions of the good. Liberalism and democracy each offer different advantages and disadvantages in attempting to resolve the conflicts that arise in multicultural societies. Liberalism's view of culture as entirely a matter of individual belief is less satisfactory than democracy's recognition of culture as a group phenomenon. On the other hand, democracy's ambiguity about the jurisdiction to which social decisions should be assigned makes its resolutions of cultural conflicts less definite than those produced by liberal principles. We will consider these and other comparisons in greater detail in the next chapter, but in this chapter we will develop a third important approach to political morality—the communitarian perspective.

Although communitarian thought is less commonplace than liberalism and democracy as a public ideology in the United States and other Western nations, it also develops from a familiar perspective on everyday disagreements. Once more, let us consider one such disagreement as a way of understanding the ethical basis of communitarianism:

Despite, or even because of, their conflicts in school, Marie and Nate have become good friends. Marie and her mother have invited Nate to play at their house on a crisp Saturday morning in November. Things go well until lunchtime, when Nate asks for juice with his sandwich as he usually has at home. Marie's mother requires her to drink milk at each meal even though Marie does not particularly care for it. Marie's mother accedes to his request, and Marie asks, "Why should I have to drink milk if Nate doesn't?" Her mother explains that families have different ideas about what is best for their children and that she has Marie drink lots of milk because she believes it will help Marie grow up to be healthy and strong. With some disappointment, Marie accepts her mother's explanation and drinks her milk.

Why does this seem like such a natural way of dealing with the conflict between Marie and her mother? Marie's mother does not justify the different treatment of Marie and Nate on the grounds that Marie's fundamental interests are different than Nate's; she does not, in other words, appeal to the idea of a fair outcome to meet her daughter's complaint. Nor does she claim that the different treatment is the result of a fair procedure in which Marie's, Nate's, her own, and perhaps others' opinions have been equally taken into account. Instead she appeals to the special relationship between her and Marie, on the one hand, and between Nate and his parents, on the other. The different treatment is justified because the two families have different ways of doing things, and because the special relationships between family members create special responsibilities and rules within the family that do not necessarily apply to outsiders.

Communitarian theory extends to the political arena this idea that particular relationships can create valid moral responsibilities that apply only to people within those relationships (Dworkin, 1986). From this perspective, the members of a political community do stand in a special relationship to one another created by their shared historical, social, cultural, and geographic context. As a result, the members of such a community have special obligations to one another that are defined by the practices, goals, roles, rules, and other traditions of their community. The members of this community ought, then, to accept political decisions of their community when those decisions are consistent with the obligations that grow out of these relationships and traditions. Both liberalism and democracy are based upon an ethic of *justice*; they seek courses of action that are fair to the members of society. Communitarianism, by contrast, is based upon an ethic of *association*; it seeks courses of action that are justified by the relationships that exist among the members of a political community.

WHAT COMMUNITARIAN THEORY IS

Most Americans intuitively accept the idea that intimate relationships—like those among family members, friends, and lovers—create special responsibilities for the participants in those relationships. I *do* have responsibilities to my children that I just do not have to strangers. When my son's feelings are hurt by the thoughtless and cruel behavior of a playmate, I must comfort him in ways that are certainly not required and might even be inappropriate in the case of a child I do not know. I can reasonably expect the kind of help from a friend that I would not ask for from the telephone operator, for example.

Most political relationships, however, are not personal and intimate in this way. Most people are not even acquainted with all of their neighbors, let alone everyone in their town, state, or country. And the circle of their friends and relations is even smaller than that of their acquaintances. What sort of *political* affiliations can create ethical responsibilities analogous to those that exist between family members and friends?

The most famous modern answer to this question has not found wide acceptance among Americans and now seems to be losing influence throughout the world as well. Karl Marx and Friedrich Engels (1848/1972) proposed that individuals' relationship to the means of economic production creates economic classes within which there exist special ties of solidarity. In the capitalist era, Marx and Engels claimed, those who own capital, the bourgeoisie, and those who do not, the proletariat, constitute the primary social classes. Within each class, individuals are united by shared circumstances, values, and aspirations, even across national boundaries. The two classes are, however, locked in a continuing conflict that will only end with a violent revolution from which a unified communist society will inevitably emerge.

Most nationalist ideologies also have a communitarian character. The British empire, for example, was founded on a belief in the superiority of British civilization and a commitment to promulgate British values and institutions throughout the world. Adolf Hitler also proposed a communitarian political ideology, in which the members of what he called the Aryan race were claimed to have a special relationship with one another and a moral status superior to that of nonmembers.

Against this historical background, many people are deeply suspicious of the communitarian perspective on political morality. Nevertheless, most individuals also experience bonds of association with others that go well beyond their immediate intimate relationships. Many people, for instance, feel a duty to help a member of their church who is in need, even if that person is not an acquaintance. Some American Jews feel strong ties to Israel, even though they have no friends or relatives there. Many first- and second-generation immigrants feel a special obligation to assist those who are newly arrived from their own country of origin. Americans abroad often feel a special kinship to other Americans they encounter, although they have never met before. Some belong to civic or fraternal organizations that extend fellowship and assistance to members who are visiting from other parts of the country. Others feel particular attachments to their town, the college from which they graduated, or the region of the country in which they grew up.

Contemporary social scientists, moreover, are finding that large numbers of Americans feel a need for bonds of association that are increasingly hard to establish in a highly mobile and individualistic society. Robert Bellah and his colleagues (1985) reported a significantly unsatisfied desire for mutual support, involvement, and commitment—for, in other words, community—among the more than two hundred Americans from all sections and social groups in the country whom they interviewed and observed over a five-year period. In fact, Bellah argues that the prevailing liberal and democratic ideologies are at least partly responsible for our society's diminishing capacity to satisfy or even acknowledge these desires for fulfilling human relationships. These perspectives' emphasis on individual freedom, competition, and self-reliance has, he concludes, produced institutions and expectations that ignore and often militate against the values of cooperation and mutual devotion to common enterprises.

The moral and political significance of these bonds of human association was recognized in the slogan of the French Revolution—"Liberty, Equality, and Fraternity." What the French called fraternity is now most often referred to as community, and many contemporary liberal and democratic thinkers have attempted to find a place for this value in their political theories. Some, like John Rawls (1971), have argued that bonds of community would spontaneously arise in a well-ordered liberal society. Others, like Robert Nisbet (1953), have proposed that we ought to think of democracy as a fair way to resolve differences, not between individuals, but between the communities that naturally occur within society—families, religious organizations, work groups, and so on.

One obvious problem with these efforts to incorporate the value of community into liberal and democratic thought lies with the assumption that there is no conflict between substantive or procedural justice, on the one hand, and the responsibilities that arise in human relationships, on the other (Dworkin, 1986). These conflicts seem very real, however; indeed, they have been a major theme in Western literature from Sophocles' *Antigone* to Shakespeare's *King Lear,* Dickens's *Hard Times,* and Harper Lee's *To Kill a Mockingbird.*

Thomas Gradgrind in *Hard Times,* for instance, establishes a school for his own and other children based upon efficiency, the utilitarian principle of justice. The children's lives, governed by a stern and systematic application of this principle, are well disciplined but joyless. One of Gradgrind's daughters discovers among working class friends acceptance into a network of human relationships in which she finds support, identity, and a kind of fulfillment not possible, according to Dickens, in a world regulated by the austere dictates of justice.

Dickens, like many other authors, reminds us that the requirements of justice may sometimes conflict with those of community. In liberal and democratic societies, justice takes moral priority over other values. When the demands of community conflict with individual self-determination in a liberal society or majority rule in a democratic society, community must take second place. Even worse, Dickens implies that fulfilling human associations may not even emerge in a society committed single-mindedly to justice. As Bellah (1985) has observed and philosopher Michael Sandel (1982) has argued, liberalism's and democracy's assumptions about human nature and their political institutions may make it difficult for people to enter into the types of relationships necessary for true community to develop and prosper. There is reason to question, therefore, whether liberalism and democracy can give full expression to the value of community.

Despite the inadequacies of past communitarian theories, the idea of community still exerts a powerful attraction, based in part on our common experience of the value of membership in, and identification with, particular social groups. Liberalism and democracy, moreover, may not be consistent with community. It is necessary to consider, therefore, how well the communitarian perspective on political morality on its own terms can address the conflicts and problems that arise in multicultural and multilingual societies. To do so, we must first consider the basic principles and institutions of a communitarian society.

The Central Commitment: Maintenance of Community Traditions

Ronald Dworkin (1986) has recently attempted to articulate a general theory of community that is a useful point of departure. Obviously, a community is a group of people but not just any random aggregation of individuals. Thus, a collection of strangers shipwrecked together on a desert island is not a community. There must be some established and ongoing patterns of interaction—relationships, interlocking roles, shared practices, mutual understandings, and so on—that bind a group into a community. But not just any set of arrangements among individuals will do. A Japanese manufacturer and an Egyptian farmer do not become members of a community when they sign a contract to trade raw cotton for finished textiles. The relationships among community members are pervasive; that is, they involve a wide range of interactions. Those relationships also have a historical dimension; they are not just contemporary developments. Finally, those relationships are socially prescribed for the members of a community, and thus the responsibilities that they involve are not fully matters of individual choice. In other words, the patterns of interaction among community members constitute a network of continuing and shared traditions that significantly define the identities, roles, and responsibilities of those individuals.

These characteristics of community can be illustrated on a small scale in the relationship between Marie and her mother. In the mother-daughter relation, the lives of these two individuals are thoroughly intertwined; their responsibilities are not exhausted by any limited and explicit set of rules, although rules are involved in their relationship. Clearly Marie did not choose to be a daughter and therefore has not directly consented to the responsibilities of that role. And the precise nature of their relationship is determined by the customs of their larger society and by the specific history of their shared lives.

The existence of such a network of traditions that unite a group of individuals defines what Dworkin (1986) calls a "bare" community. But our interest in community is not merely sociological but moral. After all, we are seeking an answer to the question of political legitimacy, of why the members of a community *should* accept and obey decisions even if they disagree with them.

However, not every set of traditions and customary relationships can morally compel obedience. The institution of slavery probably provides the most obvious illustration of this principle. Slaves and slave-masters alike are born into their roles, roles that in most slave-owning societies have been defined by a long history and deep-seated social conventions. The relationship between slave and slave-master is genuinely pervasive, prescribing nearly all interactions between the parties. In short, a slave-owning society meets the criteria of a bare community. And yet we believe that neither the slave-master nor the slave is morally required to carry out the responsibilities that derive from their relationship, or even to permit that relationship to continue. Clearly, then, a community must be more than "bare" in order to meet the test of political legitimacy.

A community must meet at least two additional criteria in order that it have a morally valid claim upon the allegiance of its members. First, the purpose of the community and, thus, of its specific customs, roles, and responsibilities must be to serve the well-being of its members. One purpose of a family, for instance, is to enable children to grow up healthy. Marie's mother's rule about milk drinking represents not simply an arbitrary exercise of her power over her daughter; instead, it is a reasonable attempt to carry out that beneficial purpose of the family. These general purposes have, moreover, higher priority than any particular rules that may be in effect. If Marie develops an allergy to milk, then her mother is obliged by the beneficial purposes of the family to change her specific rules.

Suppose, however, that Marie's mother reacts to the discovery of her daughter's milk allergy by saying that it is just too inconvenient to provide some other source of calcium. Most people would find such a reaction morally problematic. This response would reveal that in this particular family the well-being of the child takes a clear second place to the most trivial interests of a parent. But families and other communities are supposed to serve all their members' interests, even if such obligations sometimes involve sacrifices for some. In other words, a community must demonstrate roughly equal concern for the well-being of each of its members.

A society that maintains the institution of slavery does not pass either of these additional tests for a moral, as opposed to a bare, community. The purposes of such a society are not concerned with the well-being of the slaves. Rather, slaves' interests, to the extent that they count at all, are purely subordinate to the owners' interests. A slave-owner might attempt to maintain the health of a slave in the same way that he would maintain his farm equipment, that is, as a means of enhancing the profit he accrues from ownership. But the owner who neglects the slave's health does not violate a responsibility he has to the slave. Moreover, the owner is not expected to sacrifice his own well-being to that of the slave, to treat the slave's well-being as roughly equal to his own. In these circumstances, the existence of a bare community that embraces slaves and slave-owners does not generate a moral obligation for community members to carry out the traditions of that community.

Once a society *does* meet the requirements for both a bare and a moral community, however, communitarian theory holds that the responsibilities that attach to the society's traditions become obligatory for its members. Why would this be the case? Why does membership in a moral community imply that one has a duty to fulfill the roles and carry out the responsibilities that such membership entails, even if one does not immediately wish to do so?

On the one hand, the pervasive nature of the society's practices implies that each member of the society has a fundamental ownership in those traditions. Indeed, the traditions help to define the identity of each person in the community. Marie's role as a daughter is a central part of who she is, not just an imposition upon her. Carrying out the traditions, then, is not just a matter of obeying externally imposed duties; rather, it involves each person's acting as he or she really is. In this way, in carrying out a tradition the members of a community are being true to themselves; they are acting *authentically.*

On the other hand, by meeting the two criteria for a moral community, the traditions express a concern for the well-being of the community members. Thus, in carrying out such a tradition, a person is acting in the interests of others. At the same time, those traditions reflect as a whole a roughly equal commitment to the well-being of each community member. When community members carry out their prescribed roles, they participate in a pattern of activities that redounds to the benefit of all, including themselves. By accepting her family's mealtime rules, Marie is not sacrificing her own welfare. Thus, carrying out a tradition of a moral community has the result of promoting the welfare of oneself and other members of the community.

These two conclusions about action that accords with the traditions of one's moral community imply that such action is morally right on both consequentialist and nonconsequentialist grounds. First, the actions have good consequences for the members of the community. And, second, the actions can be regarded as inherently right because they are consistent with the character and identity of those who undertake them. As a result, communitarians argue, members of a moral community have an obligation to carry out the traditions of their community.

We now have the communitarian answer to the question of political legitimacy: Members of a moral community should obey decisions that they disagree with when those decisions accord with the established traditions of the community. And the central commitment of a communitarian society follows directly from this conclusion—*to maintain the community's traditions.*

Before considering the details of a communitarian society, it is important to note two consequences of our analysis thus far. Communitarian theory is, in the first place, different from cultural relativism. There are, to be sure, certain similarities between communitarianism and cultural relativism. Both maintain that what is morally right is defined by the cultural group of which one is a member. Communitarian theory requires that one's cultural group must meet the criteria of moral community before its traditions become obligatory. Cultural relativism, by contrast, does not impose any such qualifications. At most, the cultural relativist requires one's cultural group to be a bare community. The cultural relativist would hold, therefore, that the traditions of a slave-owning society impose moral obligations upon its members. As we have seen, the communitarian does not reach this conclusion, because a community does not impose legitimate moral obligations upon its members unless that community's purpose is to benefit all its members in roughly equal measure. The communitarian perspective applies external moral criteria to cultural communities and is, therefore, able to distinguish between morally legitimate and illegitimate communities and their practices. As a result, communitarian principles can settle some conflicts between cultures in a way impossible for cultural relativism. If such conflicts arise between morally legitimate and illegitimate communities, communitarian theory gives clear priority to the claims of the legitimate community.

At the same time, it is important to notice that moral communities do not necessarily meet the requirements of substantive or procedural justice. The criteria for a moral community are internally focused; that is, they require the traditions of the community to be in the interests of the members of the community, but say nothing about the effect of those traditions on nonmembers. At the very least, then, moral communities may treat the members of other communities unjustly. Moreover, even though a moral community must express an equal concern for the well-being of its members, that concern need not take the form of any particular theory of justice. It is possible, for example, for a society to treat its members equally without permitting anyone the freedom of expression or freedom of opinion that are central to liberal and democratic theories of justice. Thus, a morally legitimate community may treat its own members unjustly, at least from the liberal or democratic perspective (Dworkin, 1986, pp. 202–206).

The Role of Government: Enforcing and Interpreting the Traditions

There is a strong utopian tendency among communitarian thinkers in the West that has led many to challenge the necessity of government in a true and morally legitimate community. For instance, Karl Marx (1875/1972), in one of his rare speculations about the future, suggested that in a true communist society the state would wither and die because the need to enforce the rules of one economic class upon another will have disappeared. If people grow up in a system of traditions that express an equal concern for their well-being, these thinkers ask, why would there be any reason to use the coercive power of government to maintain the traditions of the community? Wouldn't people voluntarily play the roles, follow the rules, and observe the customs to which they have been socialized? The communitarian perspective that we have developed thus far suggests two reasons why government may be needed in a moral community.

First, individual resistance to traditions may arise from ignorance of the whole scheme of cooperation on which a moral community is based. A moral community maintains a pattern of interactions among community members that, as a whole, benefits each member in roughly equal measure. This does not mean, however, that every practice in the community individually benefits every person equally but only that the entire scheme of practices is mutually beneficial.

For example, Marie's family may have a rule that she must make the beds every morning. To be sure, Marie derives a certain benefit from this rule in that her own bed gets made. Yet others in her family receive this same benefit without having to expend any energy in bed making. Of course, this rule is part of a larger scheme of cooperation in which other family members cook the meals, earn income, mow the lawn, and so on. Yet Marie, like most children, may resist her bed-making duties because she does not or perhaps cannot understand the whole system of interdependence within her family. From a narrow perspective, it may look to Marie that she is giving more than she gets. But she benefits, in ways that may not be readily apparent to her, from the entire system of family responsibilities.

In this way, it may be necessary for a moral community to enforce particular roles and responsibilities upon individual members even though that community meets the requirement of roughly equal concern for each member's well-being. This will be especially true in larger communities, in which the duties of individual community members are more differentiated and specialized. In such communities, it may be difficult for individuals to appreciate the benefits they receive from the actions of community members they do not know or whose activities they do not understand. The larger and more complex a community becomes, the greater the need for governmental enforcement of individual responsibilities.

Second, nothing in the definition of a moral community implies that its traditions are perfect. Individual resistance to tradition may arise from a variety of imperfections in a community's practices that, from the community's own perspective, may require modification of those practices. For example, circumstances within the community may change so that the old practices are no longer adequate to meet the community's purposes. We have already noted that Marie's family will need to change their food rules if Marie develops an allergy to milk.

Similarly, sometimes a community's practices may be unclear or ambiguous. Marie's family has a rule that requires her to make the beds every morning before she leaves the house. Does that rule apply when she is visiting her grandparents' house or only in her own house? At times, then, a community's rules may need to be amplified or clarified.

A community's traditions may even conflict with one another. After all, those traditions develop in the course of an actual historical and social process in which the conflict may not have become apparent or important. Suppose that Marie's family has a rule that she may not disturb her family before ten o'clock on Saturday mornings but that she may play in the house or in the neighborhood with her friends. Without realizing it, Marie's family has created an inconsistent set of rules, one that requires her to make the beds before she leaves the house and another that permits her to play outside before her parents get up. Such conflict can also require modification of a community's practices.

Finally, a community's practices may simply not serve their purposes very adequately. One aim of the milk-drinking rule is to ensure that Marie maintains an adequately nutritious diet. But suppose she just doesn't like the taste of milk and, as a result, dawdles so long over her meals that her family cannot be certain that she is eating properly. In this situation, there may be other rules that might serve the family's purposes better, such as requiring Marie to eat cheese or broccoli every day.

Thus, a variety of imperfections in a community's practices—new circumstances, lack of clarity, conflict, and ineffectuality—can all produce resistance to those practices that requires modification of the traditions rather than simple enforcement. What is required in these situations is improvement of the practices, not to meet some external standard of adequacy but to meet the community's own internal commitments to its members. The maintenance of a community's traditions, therefore, goes beyond the mere preservation of the status quo.

Dworkin (1986) has argued that the process of changing a community's traditions to overcome these imperfections involves the reinterpretation of those traditions in light of their intended purposes. After all, if the point of such change is to further the purposes of the community, then any proposed modifications must be judged according to the principles underlying the old, inadequate practices. New food rules for Marie must, for example, be judged according to whether they will provide her with a nutritious diet.

In the next section, we will deal with this process of interpreting a society's traditions in more detail. At this point, however, let us simply note that this kind of interpretation is not something that is appropriately accomplished by individuals acting on their own. Such interpretation and subsequent modification of tradition aims to further the collective purposes of the community, not just the purposes of individual members. Here, then, is another role for government in a moral community. An appropriately constituted government can take the community-wide perspective necessary for the evolving interpretation of traditions.

In sum, government from a communitarian perspective has a dual role in maintaining the community's traditions in light of its members' resistances to the roles and responsibilities those traditions prescribe. On the one hand, government is *to enforce traditions* when those resistances result from community members' inability to comprehend the entire scheme of mutual benefit that constitutes a moral community. On the other hand, government is *to reinterpret the community's traditions* when those resistances result from imperfections in the community's practices.

BASIC GOODS AND INSTITUTIONS IN
COMMUNITARIAN SOCIETIES

The criteria for a moral community hold that a fundamental purpose of the community is to benefit its members in roughly equal measure. At the heart of such a community, then, lies an implicit or explicit theory of what is good for each individual. Unlike liberal societies, communitarian societies are committed to some particular theory of the good; they cannot maintain neutrality toward the personal visions of the good that their members may happen to accept (Sandel, 1982). The conceptual constraints on this theory of the good are that it be inclusive of all community members and that the value it ascribes to the particular goods for the various members be roughly equal. Within these constraints, moral communities may define the good differently for different people—for men and women, blacks and whites, children and adults, rulers and ruled, and so on. That is, as long as what a community defines as good for men is valued equally with what it defines as good for women, those goods may be utterly dissimilar—for example, political virtues for men and domestic virtues for women. Of course, a moral community need not make distinctions of this kind; it may also define the good for each member as the same as that of everyone else.

However a community defines the goods of its members, those goods must be realistically compatible with one another. It must be possible, in other words, for the community to promote the goods of all its members simultaneously. At least, these goods should not conflict with one another; at most, they should be interdependent. Ideally, then, it would be best if the conditions and activities necessary to generate the goods for some members would also promote the goods of others.

Despite these moral and practical constraints, there is room for enormous variation in the theories of the good held by particular morally legitimate communities. Although moral communities must all aim to benefit their members equally, they may operate in dramatically different ways. The particular institutions, practices, roles, and customs of a community must be adapted to the goods that it is committed to create and allocate. Unlike cultural relativism, communitarian theory does not sanction all actual social arrangements. Nevertheless, it is compatible with a wide range of actual and possible forms of society.

Because of the permissible variation in social organization of moral communities, it is difficult to specify in any detail the institutions that such societies share. At the very least, however, communitarian societies must carry out the two governmental functions that we have identified—enforcing and interpreting the societies' traditions. For the purpose of enforcement, most large and many small political communities rely upon the institution of the law—an explicit, usually written, statement of the traditions—including prescribed roles, duties, and activities, and their purposes. The law is understood to transcend, and to provide a framework for, the actions and aspirations of individual community members. In a profound sense, moral communities are thus governed by the rule of law, the idea that no individual stands above or outside of the shared commitments and prescriptions of community tradition. Everyone, no matter how great or small, is governed by the purposes and rules that constitute the law of the land. Rooted in longstanding tradition, the law is not to be abrogated for the convenience of any particular individual or any segment of society, even a political majority.

Often, the most central features of the law—those that define the community's theory of the good, its essential purposes, and perhaps its most basic practices—are codified in a basic document, a civil constitution or a religious text, which specifies an immutable core of the community's commitments. This constitution defines implicitly or explicitly, and usually at a very high level of generality, the fundamental rights and duties of community members. Although the precise content of these provisions depends upon the community's specific theory of the good, they do create enforceable expectations about the actions and responsibilities of community members.

Carrying out the general purposes specified in a community's constitution usually requires a code of more concrete rules, or statutes. Effective enforcement of community traditions implies that these rules be specified in considerable detail, so that the actions of individual community members can be judged to conform or not. The level of detail required for enforcement opens up the possibility that such rules may be imperfect means of achieving the community's purposes. Therefore, statutory rules are subject to modification, amplification, amendment, and repeal in a way that the constitution is not.

We have arrived at the second function of communitarian government—interpreting the community's traditions. Under a system of law, even enforcement requires a degree of interpretation. Whether a community member's actions do or do not conform to a rule necessitates an inquiry into the meaning of the rule. Often this inquiry is straightforward; the meaning of a statute requiring people to drive on the right side of the road is not difficult to discern. But enforcement also requires that the rules be applied to particular cases in which a community member is alleged to have violated a rule. Here, the community's commitment to enforce tradition requires the collection and analysis of evidence about the individual's actions: What did the accused offender actually do? Is that action a violation of the applicable rules? Is the evidence of the violation sufficient to find the accused guilty? After all, a commitment to enforce traditions implies that community members who actually obey the traditions should not be wrongly punished. Thus, even enforcement requires the making of deliberative judgments.

The need for deliberation is especially evident in confronting the various imperfections in a community's rules that we have considered: new circumstances, ambiguity or lack of clarity, conflict, and ineffectuality. Evaluating the appropriateness of a community's rules requires a reflective assessment in light of the fundamental aims of the community. So, too, does the enactment of new or modified rules. The purpose of a change must be to bring a community's practices more fully into line with its general and traditional commitments to the well-being of its members.

These requirements for careful and thoughtful judgment in the enforcement, evaluation, and modification of a community's rules imply the need for a deliberative body of some kind invested with appropriate authority. A council of elders is a familiar model of such a body in small communities. Larger communities may delegate these functions to a variety of institutions: courts, legislatures, bureaucratic offices, and so on. Although these institutions may bear a superficial similarity to those in liberal and democratic societies, their fundamental purposes are quite different. Liberal legislatures are guardians of individual interests; they are to establish the conditions and enforce the rights necessary for individual citizens to live their own lives as they see fit. Democratic legislatures are representative decision makers; they are to realize the vision of society desired by a majority of their citizens. Communitarian legislatures are interpreters of tradition; they are to enact laws that faithfully carry out the traditional purposes of their community. Communitarian legislators are not simply representatives of the opinions of community members; they are both dedicated to the community's traditions and possessed of the wisdom necessary to make the difficult interpretations and judgments that maintaining those traditions may require. Even if they are, according to the community's traditions, popularly elected, communitarian legislators, judges, and civil servants should act like members of a council of elders.

Resolving Conflicts in Communitarian Societies

As we have already noted, the traditional practices of a community may be imperfect in a variety of ways. Those traditions may be ambiguous, ineffectual, or inadequate for problems that arise in new circumstances; some of a community's practices may even conflict with others. These imperfections can produce disagreement between the members of the community. When there is no established practice for dealing with a novel situation, for instance, community members may have conflicting opinions about what rules should apply in this case. There are many ways of coping with Marie's new allergy to milk. What precise course of action should her family take? Liberals would choose the alternative that would best reflect Marie's and others' self-defined interests. Democrats would choose the alternative that reflects the opinion of the majority. Communitarians apply a different principle—*choose the alternative that most fully advances the traditional purposes of the community.*

Applying this principle requires a process of deliberative interpretation of the community's traditions. Since no concrete rule exists for this situation, one must look for principles that underlie the community's other practices and that might provide some guidance in this case. Marie's family must consider what purposes their existing food rules serve. Do those rules aim to maximize Marie's chances to grow up physically healthy? Do they aim to make meals easy to prepare or especially good tasting? Are they designed to conform to the family's religious beliefs? These and perhaps many other considerations provide the criteria for developing a rule that applies to the new circumstances.

A similar process of deliberation must be used to resolve the conflicts that arise from the other sorts of imperfections in a community's practices. In those cases as well, existing community rules are in some way in need of modification or elaboration. Thus, what should be done cannot adequately be determined by current practice. Here, too, the community needs to consider what changes, if any, are best suited to meeting the collective purposes and commitments they share.

The rule that results from this process of deliberation may or may not conform to the community members' actual opinions about what should be done. Indeed, the course of action that best preserves the community's traditions may not even have occurred to any community member prior to the process of deliberative interpretation. And while the most appropriate rule does reflect the community's definition of the interests of its members, it need not conform to the personal preferences and desires of those it directly affects.

EDUCATING CHILDREN IN COMMUNITARIAN SOCIETIES

Despite their many differences, liberalism and democracy share a common perspective on children. The primary moral concepts of these ideologies—such as neutrality for liberalism and participation for democracy—do not directly apply to children. As a result, children are not citizens of these societies. However, they do constitute a special class of noncitizens; although children do not have the rights and responsibilities of citizens, the society does have a distinctive obligation to them, an obligation to enable them to become citizens. Thus, education in these societies is seen, at least in part, as a preparation for citizenship.

Communitarian societies, by contrast, do not treat children as outsiders. Indeed, the commitment to the equal benefit of all community members forbids such treatment. To be sure, communities do establish roles, responsibilities, and rules for children that are usually markedly different from those that apply to adults. But these are roles *within* the community, in the same way that there may be different roles for men and women, for example. Children's roles are determined, moreover, by the community's theory of the good for its various members. They are the recipients of the particular benefits that the society defines as appropriate to their nature and status, not simply aspirants to benefits that society reserves for adults. Thus, children are viewed as full, if distinctive, participants in the community rather than potential applicants for citizenship.

The fundamental commitment of a communitarian society defines the purpose of education—to maintain the community's traditions. Those traditions apply to children and adults alike. In principle, therefore, communitarian societies do not make a fundamental distinction between the education of adults and children. As we have seen, maintaining a community's traditions requires, first, the enforcement of the roles and responsibilities that the community assigns to its members and, second, the interpretation of the community's traditions.

Education in the Community's Conventions

To enforce traditions, communitarian education must develop the attitudes, knowledge, and skills that enable community members to carry out the responsibilities of their current or future roles. The details of this education in convention depend entirely upon the particular roles that individual community members occupy. Because moral communities can take an enormous variety of forms, the specific content, timing, and method of communitarian education will be equally various. Nevertheless, education in convention will share three general features.

First, much communitarian education will take place within community roles. Because from the communitarian perspective all community members occupy particular roles, individuals learn the conventions of their community "on the job." A child, in other words, learns the role and responsibilities of childhood in his or her particular community while actually occupying that role. He or she learns that role by being exposed directly to others' expectations, exhortations, directions, and sanctions, rather than by learning *about* those expectations beforehand. Much of the role learning throughout communitarian societies, for adults as well as children, has this immediate quality. Even the transition to new roles can take the form of an apprenticeship in which the individual, under the guidance of a knowledgeable role occupant, learns a new role simply by doing what the role requires. Such on-the-job learning is especially suited to communitarian societies because they can prescribe the roles that their members are to take. Liberal and democratic societies, by contrast, must permit their citizens a degree of personal choice about their roles that, in turn, requires those citizens to know something about those roles before they undertake them. Of course, communities can, depending upon their traditions, permit their members to exercise some choice about their roles. Similarly, liberal and democratic societies can make some use of apprenticeships. But communities' reliance upon tradition, rather than individual or collective decision-making, as a determinant of social roles and relationships makes within-role learning a typical feature of communitarian education in convention.

Second, communities have a need to educate their members about how the community as a whole functions. As we have noted, governmental enforcement of traditions is necessary because some members of the community may not fully comprehend how they benefit from undertaking the responsibilities that community tradition assigns to them. To minimize the use of coercion, therefore, a community must promulgate some general understanding of the mutual interdependence of its members' roles—a knowledge of what roles exist, what the occupants of those roles do, and, most important, what effects those activities have on the members of the community.

Finally, community members need to see the value of the conventions. They need an understanding of how the activities of community members are beneficial, especially to themselves and those that they care most about. Of course, what community members receive from their society is beneficial not simply from the perspective of the isolated individual or even the family. Rather, it is beneficial according to the particular theory of the good that the community embraces. To appreciate the sense in which the community's traditions are mutually beneficial, then, each member must have some understanding of the community's theory of the good, especially as it applies to the conventions that most immediately affect his or her own life.

There can be some tension between the within-role socialization typical of communitarian societies and the more general education in how and why the community functions. Role socialization aims at enabling community members to perform the particular tasks that fall to them within the existing social order. Yet members do change roles throughout their lives, and the roles themselves may evolve as traditions are reinterpreted to overcome various imperfections. Thus, role socialization cannot be so effective that it leaves community members unable to cope with these potential changes. Knowledge of the community's theory of the good helps members understand and accept these changes because it provides a collective rationale for them. Yet this knowledge also provides a critical perspective on the community's existing conventions. It enables members to entertain doubts about the effectiveness of those conventions in meeting the community's broader purposes. Too great an emphasis on this general knowledge can, therefore, be potentially destabilizing to the community. Thus, communitarian education must strike a balance between effective role socialization and knowledge of the community's vision of the good.

Education for Interpreting Traditions

All community members must have a sufficient general understanding of their community to accept their current roles and to cope with possible changes in them. Imperfections in the community's conventions, however, require more than merely coping with change; someone must be able to initiate and implement the changes to which the deliberative reinterpretation of tradition leads. At least some members of the community, then, must possess the profound understanding of the community's theory of the good and the intellectual skills necessary for the wise interpretation of tradition.

The study of community purposes that interpretation requires is not limited to the application of those purposes to justify existing practices and conventions. Interpreters must be able to see behind the superficial effects of those practices to the principles that inform them. They are the philosophers of their community. And while effective interpreters must be committed to their community's basic values, they must be able and willing to criticize the status quo and imagine new ways of conducting the community's business. Interpreters are not wild-eyed revolutionaries, however; they must have a thorough knowledge of the sociology of their community, of how the community's institutions, roles, and practices interact to maintain the stability of the society. Thus, interpreters are also the social scientists of their community. They must be able to predict the ramifications of particular reinterpretations of tradition on the community's institutions so that they can ensure that the outcome of a proposed change will actually enhance the community's ability to achieve its central purposes.

Who should be involved in the process of interpretation? Although nothing in basic communitarian theory prohibits wide participation in this process, the potentially destabilizing effects and the rigorous intellectual requirements of interpretive thinking have led many communitarian thinkers to reserve the role of interpreter and the education that goes with it to a relatively small group of individuals. Thus, education for interpretation of tradition may be, and often is, provided to a select few of the community's members—sometimes to a priestly or aristocratic class—but in any case to a cadre of designated community leaders.

WE NOW HAVE a general account of how communitarian societies operate. Moral communities answer the basic question of political legitimacy— Why should their members obey a government's decisions when they disagree with them?—by noting that the community's traditions benefit its members in roughly equal measure according to some particular theory of the good. For this answer to be persuasive, a community's policies must actually maintain its traditions, either by enforcing existing conventions or by interpreting its traditions to overcome imperfections in those conventions. Children are full members of this community; all are socialized to the particular childhood and adult roles they occupy and are educated about the community's theory of the good and the way in which social conventions benefit its members according to that theory. At least some members of the society also are educated in the skills of interpretation of tradition so as to allow the community to respond intelligently to various imperfections in its conventions, roles, responsibilities, and practices. Let us now see how this perspective applies to a specific dispute in a multicultural and multilingual society.

As we have noted before, all ethnic and cultural groups display a wide diversity among communities and among the individuals that live within any particular community. This is especially true of Native Americans. There are now around 1.5 million Native Americans, over half of whom live outside of reservations or traditional villages. Nearly three hundred tribal entities are recognized by the U.S. government, and there are many other unrecognized groups (Prucha, 1984). Each community has a unique configuration of custom, language, and tradition, based upon its particular history, geography, and experience. As with other ethnic groups, then, there is little basis for generalizing about Native Americans. The following case is based, as it must be, upon the concrete realities of an actual community, the Big Cypress community of the Florida Seminole Tribe. Although the historical and anthropological background described in this case is based upon scholarly studies of this community (Garbarino, 1972; Garbarino, 1989; and, to a lesser extent, Weisman, 1989), the specific situation described here and the people involved in it are entirely fictitious. As is true throughout this book, this case is intended to illustrate multicultural issues in the United States, not to report on actual events.

THE BIG CYPRESS SEMINOLES

Samuel Billie is one of the few Seminole teachers at the Bureau of Indian Affairs day school on the Big Cypress Reservation; indeed, he is one of the relatively few reservation Seminoles to have graduated from college. He grew up at the small Hollywood Reservation on the eastern coast of Florida near Miami, where he attended state-sponsored public schools because there was no reservation school available. Unlike many of his Seminole friends and relatives, he did well in school and was able to receive financial aid at a junior college and later at a Florida university. Like them, however, Mr. Billie's first language was Mikasuki, one of the two mutually unintelligible languages of the Seminoles and the language spoken by the residents of Big Cypress. He also learned English at home because the members of his community were employed in tourism and agricultural work that brought them into frequent contact with whites.

Located deep within south central Florida, Big Cypress is, however, geographically isolated from white society, and children there have limited experience with English before they come to the reservation school. For this reason, the primary purpose of the federal school has been to give children an introduction to English to prepare them for the predominantly white public school in Clewiston to which they will be bused after completing the fourth grade in the day school. Big Cypress parents comply with the state requirement to send their children to school, but few of them see school education as significant to their children's future. Seminole homes rarely provide space and seclusion for children to do homework, and parents seldom assist their children with schoolwork or object when they choose to drop out to participate in adult life on the reservation.

In his three years at Big Cypress, Mr. Billie has become more and more dissatisfied with the role he is playing in his students' lives. At best, he finds his work irrelevant to those students; at worst, he fears that he is participating in the systematic dismantling of Seminole language and culture. Florida Seminoles have never had an especially strong tribal identity. Historically, the Seminole people originated from a series of dislocations of other native groups from South Carolina, Georgia, and Alabama. It is believed that "seminole" is a corruption of a native word for "runaway." These groups first settled in the fertile valleys of northern Florida but, as a result of the bloody Second Seminole War in the 1830s, were forced south into the interior swamplands for which the white colonizers had little use. Seminole communities were small and scattered, and they developed a strongly individualistic culture in which loyalty to the clan and locality was of greater importance than any commitment to a larger tribal heritage. Indeed, the Seminoles were not formally organized as a tribe until 1957. Seminole culture, Mr. Billie believes, is fragile, and he has come to the conclusion that a simple continuation of the status quo will within a generation or two produce further fragmentation of the Seminole people and the ultimate demise of their languages and traditions.

While in college, Mr. Billie learned of three developments that may help reverse this process of cultural disintegration. In his Indian Studies classes, he discovered that over the past thirty years many tribes have embarked on a concerted effort to reclaim their religious, linguistic, and social heritage. All over the United States and Canada, tribes have sponsored projects to revitalize their original languages, to collect and publish tribal legends and histories, and to revive native social and religious practices. Hand in hand with this renaissance of native culture, some tribes have developed their own schools, controlled by tribal boards of education and based upon the model of the Rough Rock Demonstration School, a Navajo experiment begun in 1966 in Chinle, Arizona (Fuchs & Havighurst, 1972/1983). Finally, the federal Indian Self-Determination Act of 1975 has made it possible for tribes to contract with the Bureau of Indian Affairs (BIA) to operate their own social programs, including schools (Prucha, 1984).

In light of these developments, Mr. Billie has proposed that the Seminole Tribe take over operation of the day school at Big Cypress. His plan calls for two significant revisions of the school program. First, instruction would be conducted in Mikasuki, not English. In the early grades, the curriculum would focus upon native language and culture study, using oral and, eventually, written materials that school personnel would assemble with the assistance of senior members of the tribe. Arithmetic, science, and other subjects would be taught in Mikasuki, utilizing wherever possible native concepts and materials. English as a second language would be taught to all children in the school beginning in second grade. Second, Mr. Billie wishes to expand the day school program to include grades five through eight. There would be two purposes for these four grades—to continue and expand the study of Seminole culture and to provide a transition to the public high school in Clewiston for those children who wish to attend. About half of the curriculum—focusing primarily upon social studies, physical education, art, and music—would continue to be taught in Mikasuki. By eighth grade, mathematics, science, and English classes would be conducted primarily in English, with a planned transition from Mikasuki in grades five and six. The school would be governed by an elected board of education and financed with BIA education funds now used for the day school as well as with federal impact aid and Florida per-capita public school funds that currently are paid to the Clewiston schools.

After preliminary discussions with a number of influential Big Cypress residents, Mr. Billie fully aired his proposal at a meeting of the Seminole

Tribal Council, an elected governing body representing all three Seminole reservations, Big Cypress, Hollywood, and Brighton, a reservation located in central Florida north of Big Cypress, on which Muskogee, the other Seminole language, is spoken. There was interest in the idea of a tribally controlled school, although representatives of the other reservations expressed some doubt about whether a school at Big Cypress would have any particular advantage for their residents. After considerable discussion, it was decided that if the Big Cypress community was in favor of pursuing the idea, the Tribal Council would assist in discussions with federal, school district, and Florida officials. After Tribal Council representatives from Big Cypress expressed their personal support of the proposal and their belief that most residents of their reservation would support it as well, the Council office set up a series of meetings with outside groups.

Discussions with the BIA produced mixed signals. On the one hand, federal officials expressed their acceptance of the idea of Indian self-determination. On the other hand, they were concerned about the Seminole Tribe's ability to govern a school efficiently and to satisfy the complex federal regulations that apply to such contracts. The Tribe, they said, was not especially effective in carrying out its current functions, especially given the lack of tribal unity. Turnout for elections was usually low, and the Council had had little success in generating enthusiastic support for past cultural and economic initiatives. The intense localism of the Seminoles, they suggested, was unlikely to provide a solid foundation for the important and demanding task of operating a school. The existing day school, moreover, was well run and reasonably sensitive to the realities of students' lives and their needs for an education to prepare young Seminoles for opportunities in the larger society. It was hard to understand, BIA officials explained, how an educational program based on Mikasuki and focused on Seminole culture would advance the economic and social interests of Seminole children.

The tribal delegation, although sharing some of the same concerns, responded that the leadership of Mr. Billie would ensure the efficient operation of the new school. Furthermore, most of the Tribe's other projects were marginal undertakings, with little effect on the day-to-day lives of many Seminoles and, therefore, unlikely to generate a great deal of enthusiasm from tribe members. This project had the potential to touch the lives of a significant number of Big Cypress residents and to create a sense of tribal identity and solidarity upon which real unity might be built. Big Cypress residents would be involved in the operation of the school not only through the school's governing board but also as employed classroom aides and sources of the cultural knowledge and materials upon which the school curriculum would be based. Indeed, that curriculum would recognize and legitimize the language, history, beliefs, and practices of the Seminoles. It would represent in concrete form the tribal identity that could help to unite the Seminole people and to give Seminole children a sense of the value of their culture and of themselves. Mr. Billie argued that, without this sense of self-worth, Seminole children would continue to do poorly in school and to lead economically and politically marginal lives as adults.

The reaction of school district and Florida state officials was even more pessimistic. First, they pointed to the consistently poor performance of Big Cypress children in the Clewiston schools. Seminole children entered the fifth grade with limited skills in English. Despite the best efforts of the Clewiston teachers, those children scored, on the average, a full standard deviation below the mean on standardized tests. They were retained in grade frequently. And they dropped out of school at twice the rate of other children in the state. More time on the reservation, the Clewiston superintendent asserted, was exactly what these children did not need. Second, state officials argued that the proposed curriculum for the new school did not meet state curriculum regulations. It provided much less English instruction than was required, and the emphasis upon Seminole history and culture meant that important objectives in social studies would necessarily be neglected. Finally, state and local officials argued that the proposed school would aggravate the segregation of Seminole children. It was not clear, they said, that the use of state funds for this purpose would be constitutional. In a state with a previous record of segregation, state and local authorities were extremely hesitant to support any program that might increase the separation of the races.

Meanwhile, informal conversations about the proposal were taking place on all three Seminole reservations. At Brighton, some community members expressed a concern that the proposed Big Cypress school would not meet their need to preserve and develop the Muskogee language. Brighton children attend Clewiston public schools from the first grade on, and as a result, Muskogee is, they believe, in far greater danger of extinction than Mikasuki. If the Tribe is to support an effort at cultural and linguistic preservation, it should focus on Muskogee. Discussions at Hollywood were far less heated. Few Hollywood residents found any personal advantage in the program, but they saw no reason why the Tribe should not support the Big Cypress community.

The greatest controversy was generated in Big Cypress itself. Most residents are satisfied with the proposal; in fact, some of the oldest and most respected community members see it as critical to reestablishing the traditions and values that they hold dear. A few families, however, have said that they would send their children to live with relatives at Hollywood if the Tribe takes control of the day school. They want their children to receive an education that will enable them to attend college or to qualify for work in white society, if they wish. They fear that the proposed school would limit these possibilities. These families will not, they say, speak against the establishment of the new school, but they will quietly seek other educational opportunities for their own children.

Mr. Billie and other proposal supporters have reacted strongly to these families. They see these families as disloyal to Big Cypress and the Seminole Tribe, as a potential threat to the cultural and tribal unity at which the new school aims. Some have even suggested that the Tribe should exercise its sovereignty to prevent reservation children from going to school elsewhere. Even worse, they believe that federal and state authorities will use these defections as a pretext for denying the request for the proposed contract and the financial support necessary to make the school a success. Any signs of community discord, they fear, will jeopardize chances for outside assistance and perhaps even weaken the support of the Tribal Council itself.

How should this complex set of disputes—between the Seminole Tribe and the U.S. and Florida governments, between the members of the Brighton and Big Cypress communities, and among members of the Big Cypress community—be resolved?

THE COMMUNITARIAN CONCEPTION OF CULTURE

Intuitively, this network of disputes over Mr. Billie's proposal has clear cultural dimensions. It involves conflicting beliefs and practices that are not only deeply personally important to the individual parties, but that also represent the shared convictions of the groups of which those individuals are members. The language, values, and ways of life that inform the existing BIA day school, the Clewiston public schools, and the proposed school represent fundamental and collective commitments of the United States, the State of Florida, and the Seminole Tribe. These shared convictions reflect, moreover, long-standing and pervasive traditions of those groups. These schools are based upon ideas that have evolved over many centuries, ideas about children's social roles and about the lives they will lead as adults. Let us see how the cultural dimensions of this dispute appear from the communitarian perspective.

As we have seen, communities are characterized by a set of relationships and interactions that are ongoing, pervasive, historically based, and socially prescribed. In a very real sense, then, culture is a necessary condition of community. Communitarian theory, however, distinguishes between morally legitimate and illegitimate communities. A moral community must, first, be based upon a conception of the good for its members that expresses roughly equal concern for all. Because some cultures may not necessarily include the requisite theory of the good for all, they may not be morally legitimate. In other words, culture is a necessary but not sufficient condition of a morally legitimate community. Communitarian theory thus permits an external moral critique of particular cultures; it provides a perspective from which the members of one culture may criticize another group's culture on the grounds that it does not possess an adequately inclusive and equitable theory of the good.

Some of the debate over Mr. Billie's proposal takes the form of such cross-cultural critique. Mr. Billie and the Seminole Tribe argue that the culture of the United States and the State of Florida makes inadequate provision for the welfare of Seminole children and adults. They point to the history of conquest, marginalization, and neglect that has rendered the Seminole people materially and educationally disadvantaged according to white society's own standards. The white community, they charge, has never recognized the dignity of Seminoles or other Native Americans and cannot, therefore, legitimately command their obedience to its political decisions. Similarly, BIA and Florida officials argue that the program that would be provided at the proposed school would unfairly limit some tribal members' opportunities to obtain the education they want for their children. As a result, Seminole culture, they claim, does not adequately represent at least some Seminoles' own values and aspirations.

Communitarian theory also requires a community to interpret and reinterpret its conventions in light of its own theory of the good for its members. In this way, communitarian theory permits an internal critique of particular cultures on the grounds that a community's prescribed practices, relationships, and responsibilities do not adequately fulfill the principles to which the community is committed. Some of the debate over the school at Big Cypress reflects such internal tensions within the involved communities. Seminole culture does have a long-standing commitment to individualism; Seminoles have not traditionally sought to enforce narrow tribal standards upon their constituent clans and members. Thus, the possibility that the proposed school might involve this sort of group imposition upon individuals raises the issue of whether that plan is an adequate interpretation of Seminole culture. The BIA's mixed reaction to the proposal reveals a similar conflict within the community of the United States as a whole. That community has, on the one hand, a traditional commitment to cultural self-determination, reflected generally in its constitutional protection for the freedoms of religion and expression, and particularly in its long-standing, if imperfect, recognition of tribal sovereignty. This commitment implies that religious and other groups have the right, within the boundaries of the law, to develop their own practices, beliefs, and identities and to govern their lives according to those shared traditions. On the other hand, the United States has a commitment to the freedom, opportunities, and well-being of individual community members, reflected generally in the Constitution's provisions for personal rights, equal opportunity, and the promotion of the general welfare of the nation, and in the federal government's particular role as "Great White Father" to Native Americans. This commitment is to ensure that individuals are to have the chance to live a life that is personally satisfying and not narrowly confined to the expectations of the particular families, ethnic groups, or religious communities into which they are born.

In sum, communitarian theory conceives of culture as the historically based and socially specified roles, practices, conventions, and responsibilities that define a bare community. However, culture is a necessary, but not sufficient, condition of moral community. The moral commitments of communitarian theory, furthermore, make two types of cultural conflict possible—conflict between cultures in which the moral adequacy of the cultures' theories of the good is at issue and conflict within cultures in which the adequacy of a culture's actual conventions to satisfy its own fundamental commitments is of concern.

THE DISPUTE IN COMMUNITARIAN PERSPECTIVE

Communitarian theory resolves disputes by assessing the moral legitimacy of conflicting communities and by applying the principles that are implicit in a community's traditions. Before determining what principles to apply to the dispute at Big Cypress, however, we must decide to what community the involved individuals belong. Are the residents of Big Cypress members of the Seminole tribal community, or are they more accurately seen as members of the political community of the United States?

The answer to this question is not simply a matter of ascertaining what the Big Cypress residents themselves think. After all, communities and their traditions prescribe roles and responsibilities to individuals. Thus, the communities' own conventions determine who is and who is not a member. From this perspective, we need to consider the rules for membership that the Seminole Tribe and the United States apply to the residents of Big Cypress.

Early in its history, the United States considered Native Americans as members of other nations. Wars with Indian tribes were not seen as civil wars, that is, as wars among the citizens of the United States, but instead as foreign wars. The U.S. government established treaties with Indian tribes in the same way that it did with the nations of Europe. And the U.S. Constitution did not originally confer full citizenship upon Native Americans. Over the past one hundred years, however, the situation has changed considerably. Although tribes and tribal lands have retained a special legal status, Native Americans now have full citizenship rights within the country. They may vote in elections, are counted in the census, are subject to military service, and have access to welfare and other programs available to citizens. The membership rules of the U.S. community clearly lay claim upon the residents of Big Cypress.

The Florida Seminole Tribe has since its formal organization in 1957 maintained explicit rules about tribal membership (Garbarino, 1989). Individuals must apply to the Tribal Council for recognition. To qualify, they must be at least one-quarter Seminole by birth. Beyond this, in order to vote and hold tribal office, individuals must reside on one of the three Seminole reservations. Based on these criteria, nearly all of the Big Cypress residents are members of the Seminole tribal community.

In sum, the individuals affected by the disputed Big Cypress school proposal are members of *both* the U.S. and the Seminole communities. Should the traditions of both these communities apply to this dispute, then? Communitarian theory regards such traditions as morally binding upon individuals only if the bare community that maintains the traditions also meets the requirements of moral community. At this point in our analysis, then, we must consider the external moral critiques of the communities involved. Do the U.S. and Seminole cultures and traditions possess a theory of the good for their members that expresses and promotes a roughly equal concern for the well-being of all?

Mr. Billie makes a very strong argument for the moral inadequacy of U.S. culture, especially with regard to Native Americans. Over the past century, federal and state governments as well as individual whites have repeatedly ignored treaty obligations with various tribes, shown contempt for tribal customs and beliefs, and neglected the welfare of Native Americans generally and Seminoles in particular. As a result, the average standard of living of Seminoles and other Native Americans today is significantly lower than that of other U.S. citizens. But before accepting these facts as evidence of the moral deficiency of the U.S. community, we must consider carefully the full implications of communitarian theory.

That theory holds that we must evaluate a culture's theory of the good on its own terms, and not from the perspective of an outside culture. The fact that one community does not value, and therefore does not strive for, the things that are important to another culture does not necessarily imply that that community's theory of the good is morally defective.

The significance of this communitarian principle can be seen in evaluating the critique of the Seminole culture offered by Florida and U.S. officials. They claim that the Seminole culture does not place sufficient value on material wealth and English literacy for the members of the tribe, even though some individual tribe members actually prefer them. This difference in the priorities of two cultures is not sufficient to condemn either one, however. Communitarian theory does not insist that all cultures must value the same things, but only that each culture must express roughly equal concern for the welfare of all its members *according to the culture's own definition of the good.* Therefore, Seminole culture cannot be regarded as morally deficient simply because it prefers Mikasuki to English or village life to an urban, industrial existence. But neither can U.S. culture be criticized for maintaining precisely the opposite priorities.

What about the claim that some Seminoles want things not valued by traditional Seminole culture? Once again, communitarian theory does not require a legitimate community to serve the actual desires of all its members, but only to define and provide goods for its members in a way that expresses equal concern for all. In other words, a morally legitimate community may define the good for its members in a way that is at odds with what some of them may actually want, as long as that definition does not treat some community members as inherently inferior to others. Thus, the fact that some Seminoles prefer their children to become literate in English rather than Mikasuki does not imply that the Seminole community is morally bankrupt because it does not satisfy that preference. But neither is it illegitimate for the U.S. community to promote English literacy among those who prefer Mikasuki.

Therefore, the facts that the U.S. and Seminole communities define the good in different ways and that some Seminoles, who are members of both communities, prefer one definition of the good to the other do not imply that either of those communities is morally illegitimate. All that really matters from the communitarian perspective is whether a community's theory of the good relegates some of its members to a patently second-class status, that is, whether the roles and well-being of some community members are clearly and openly regarded as subordinate to those of others. In other words, communitarian theory labels as morally illegitimate only those communities that maintain a patent caste society, like those that practice slavery. Do the U.S. or Seminole cultures fail this test?

This question is relatively easy to answer in the case of Seminole culture. As we have seen, traditional Seminole society is not at all hierarchical. Although it provides for different roles for men and women, children and adults, and, to a lesser extent, older and younger adults, Seminole culture recognizes and values individual and clan autonomy within the larger tribal community. In fact, this traditional Seminole value has made it difficult for the tribe as a whole to create and maintain a strong internal governing structure. As a result, the Seminole community simply is not a caste society and is therefore morally legitimate from the communitarian perspective.

However, the question of the moral legitimacy of the U.S. community is far more complicated. Mr. Billie argues that the history of the treatment of Native Americans demonstrates the second-class status to which they have been assigned in U.S. culture. What else could account for the past and present disregard of the agreements between tribes and the U.S. government, the exploitation of Native American lands and resources, the neglect of the education and welfare of those who reside on reservations?

A communitarian analysis of the moral legitimacy of a community requires a judgment about the principles upon which that community is based. After all, we are concerned with the question of whether the community's theory of the good demonstrates a roughly equal concern for all citizens. As we have noted, communities can sometimes engage in particular practices that may turn out to be inconsistent with their fundamental principles. Thus, the existence of a patently discriminatory practice in a society is not, on its own, sufficient to condemn that society from the communitarian perspective. That practice must be based upon the society's principled commitment to the inferiority of those community members who are the victims of the discrimination. As Mr. Billie observes, the history of the United States is rife with examples of discrimination against not only Native Americans but many other racial and ethnic groups as well. Are these past and present patterns of discrimination adequate evidence that the United States is *in principle* a caste society?

A defender of U.S. culture might respond that the explicit principles of the nation, as articulated in the Declaration of Independence and the Constitution, are universal in scope. The Declaration proclaims that all are created equal and that all are endowed with the rights of life, liberty, and the pursuit of happiness. The Constitution's Bill of Rights guarantees to all citizens the freedoms of speech, religion, and assembly and the right of due process. Nevertheless, Mr. Billie might argue, these ostensibly universal principles did not prevent the nation from practicing slavery and conducting bloody wars of conquest against the Seminoles and other Native Americans; despite their wording, those principles were really only intended to apply to white, Anglo Americans. However, the defender might reply, those practices no longer exist; they were the result not of the principles of U.S. culture but of older European attitudes and beliefs. As the nation matured, it was able to free itself from those beliefs and realize the full meaning of its founding principles through constitutional amendments and interpretations and through civil rights legislation that abolished not only slavery but more subtle forms of legal and social discrimination. One should judge U.S. culture not by the practices of any particular era but according to the pattern of change in those practices over time; that pattern has been toward a gradually more inclusive application of constitutional and civil rights to all U.S. citizens. Although Native Americans may have once been deprived of personal and political rights, they now enjoy those rights on an equal footing with everyone else. But, according to Mr. Billie, whatever the intent of those

changes may be, Native Americans remain as poor, disadvantaged, and marginalized as at any time in their history. Most recent improvements in the
lives of Native Americans, he claims, have come from an assertion of tribal
independence rather than their enhanced participation in mainstream U.S.
culture.

Which is the correct interpretation of U.S. culture, the defender's view
of a progressively inclusive application of universal principles, or Mr. Billie's
portrait of a society in which Native Americans have been permanently con-
demned to a second-class existence? It is not at all clear that communitarian
theory can resolve this controversy; the facts about the treatment of Seminoles and other Native Americans point plausibly in either direction. There
has been a change in the status of Native Americans over the past one hundred years. Nevertheless, Seminoles as a group, like other reservation Indians, remain at a clear disadvantage in comparison with most U.S. citizens;
their tribal culture has been weakened, but they have not been fully accepted
or assimilated into the mainstream culture.

This inconclusiveness in the external critique of U.S. culture leaves the
debate over Mr. Billie's proposal unresolved. From the communitarian perspective, education is to enable the members of the community to fulfill the
roles and responsibilities that their culture prescribes for them. If U.S. culture
is morally legitimate, both the U.S. and Seminole communities have a claim
upon the residents of Big Cypress, and their education should reflect both
cultural traditions. But those traditions seem to be in conflict with one another in that they prescribe educational practices and priorities that cannot
be simultaneously realized. Ironically, the arguments for the moral legitimacy
of each culture make a compromise over the education of Seminole children
difficult. If Seminoles are not provided with a mainstream education, the
moral legitimacy of U.S. culture would be called into question because a
group of citizens would thereby be denied access to what is valued by the
community. But a similar problem would arise if Seminole children were
denied the education prescribed by tribal traditions. Communitarian theory
does not seem to be of any real help when, as is frequently the case in multicultural societies, some individuals are members of two different but morally
legitimate communities.

If U.S. culture is *not* legitimate, then only Seminole culture has a binding claim upon the residents of Big Cypress, and the education provided
should reflect only Seminole traditions. There is not, however, a Seminole
tradition of formal, institutionalized education, whether of the type recommended by Mr. Billie or that now provided at the Big Cypress day school
and the Clewiston public schools. Formal schooling is more a U.S. than a
Seminole tradition. To be sure, the history and present reality of Seminole
contact with U.S. culture may mean that new, nontraditional educational

practices are now necessary. After all, communitarian theory implies that a culture's practices should evolve as novel circumstances arise. Is Mr. Billie's proposal the best interpretation of Seminole cultural values in the circumstances in which the tribal community finds itself?

At least some families in Big Cypress do not believe so. They argue that the very origin of the Seminole Tribe as a collection of the members of other tribes who fled from the invasions of English and American settlers and troops implies that the essence of Seminole culture involves an openness to the language, values, and ideas of other communities. This openness, they point out, has led to the considerable autonomy that individuals and families have traditionally enjoyed within the loosely organized Seminole Tribe. Combined, these principles of cultural openness and autonomy suggest at the very least that the tribe should not enforce upon the residents of Big Cypress a single model of childhood education even if a majority of community members favor such a model. Shouldn't those families who prefer mainstream U.S. schooling for their children have, on the basis of the Seminoles' own traditions, a right to such an education? In fact, shouldn't such an education be available in Big Cypress itself so that these families are not required to send their children away to school as white society once forced many Native Americans to do?

Mr. Billie and the tribal leaders interpret Seminole tradition and the current situation differently. The cultural openness that some Seminoles celebrate and the desire for white man's education are, Mr. Billie maintains, really reflections of the damage that has been done to Seminole culture by decades of white society's lack of respect for the Seminoles and their way of life. To repair this damage, it is necessary to reconstruct Seminole culture and to transmit it systematically to the tribe's young people. Giving Big Cypress residents access to mainstream U.S. education would only make the process of revitalizing Seminole culture more difficult, perhaps impossible. The superficial attractions of mainstream U.S. life that Seminole parents and children encounter on television and on their visits to relatives on the Hollywood reservation must be offset by an effective and mandatory education in Seminole language and values. Otherwise, Seminole culture will continue to disintegrate, and the distinctive traditions of the Seminole community will eventually vanish.

From the communitarian perspective, which of these interpretations of Seminole culture is more adequate—that which emphasizes a receptivity to new ideas and individual choice, or that which emphasizes the need to maintain protective boundaries around the Big Cypress community? Here, again, communitarian theory seems incapable of resolving this dispute over the internal interpretation of a community's culture. With some rare exceptions, most cultures include the two elements that have been separately emphasized in the debate over Seminole culture in this case—one that welcomes and utilizes external influences, and another that accentuates the internal self-sufficiency and coherence of the community. These two elements of a culture are often perfectly compatible; the first gives the culture access to new ideas, and the second enables the culture to assimilate those ideas to the traditional purposes of the community. But when contact between cultures is systematic and sustained, as it is in multicultural societies, these two elements of culture can produce internal tensions and conflict within particular cultures. The large-scale and long-term exchange of ideas, technologies, practices, and so on can overwhelm a culture's ability to retain its separate identity.

This same phenomenon is present in U.S. culture as well. U.S. culture does include traditional commitments both to permitting various religious and ethnic groups to live their lives as they see fit and to promoting a distinctive American identity. During, for instance, periods of significant immigration, the inability of the society to assimilate the cultures of new citizens to traditional American purposes has produced an internal struggle over the meaning of U.S. culture, a struggle often characterized by jingoism and cultural repression. As we have seen, this tension is present in the BIA's mixed reaction to Mr. Billie's proposal.

Communitarian theory says that internal conflicts of this kind should be resolved according to a deliberative interpretation of the community's most fundamental principles. But, as in this case, the fundamental principles of most cultures are self-contradictory when confronted with strong and sustained influence from other cultures. When this happens, communitarian theory provides little help in resolving internal conflicts over the most appropriate interpretation of particular cultures.

The communitarian perspective, then, produces inconclusive results about the most important issues in the Big Cypress case. The application of communitarian theory to cultural conflicts requires an interpretation of the cultures involved. For an assessment of the moral legitimacy of each community, their respective theories of the good must be reconstructed from the facts of their practices, beliefs, and histories. When, as in this case, a community is as large as an entire modern nation, those facts are so complex and disparate that it may be impossible to discover a single, authoritative answer to the question of whether the community does or does not have a principled commitment to an equal concern for all its members' well-being. If the conflicting communities both turn out to be morally legitimate, communitarian theory provides no principled way of deciding which community's values should have higher priority in the dispute; indeed, compromise on an issue as central to a culture as the education of children is likely to undermine either community's justification for its own moral legitimacy. Finally, communitarian theory resolves disputes internal to a community by seeking a deliberative interpretation of its culture. As we have seen, when a community is subject to pervasive and protracted external influences, as is likely in multicultural contexts, the tendencies of most cultures both to assimilate new ideas and to assert their self-sufficiency may produce contradictory, but equally plausible, interpretations of a community's character and priorities.

THE ADEQUACY OF COMMUNITARIAN THEORY IN MULTICULTURAL CONTEXTS

Our analysis of the situation at Big Cypress from the communitarian perspective has, unfortunately, provided no clear-cut resolution of the dispute over Mr. Billie's proposal. Our efforts to find a resolution have been frustrated because of competing interpretations of U.S. and Seminole culture, and because of communitarian theory's inability to establish priorities among the conflicting values of morally legitimate communities. Let us now consider how satisfactorily this perspective satisfies our four criteria for adequacy in multicultural contexts.

The Conception of Culture

Communitarian theory identifies culture with the complex set of roles, relationships, responsibilities, and practices that constitute a bare community. These characteristics of a community are understood to arise not just from individual preferences or political negotiation but from a concrete historical and social context that in large part defines the identities and beliefs of community members. This view of culture seems to meet the objections raised about liberalism's and democracy's conceptions. Unlike liberalism's portrait of culture as one's personal vision of the good life, communitarian theory acknowledges that culture originates outside the individual, in a community's theory of the good for its members and its social conventions, which themselves have been shaped over many generations. Unlike democracy's identification of cultures with political factions, communitarian theory acknowledges that culture penetrates more deeply into individuals' lives than mere opinion about how particular political decisions should be made; it involves shared fundamental principles and ways of life. In short, communitarian theory seems to capture the full range of our intuitive understanding of culture.

The Ethical Priority of Culture

Communitarian theory places the community's values and practices at the center of political morality. To be sure, the traditions of actual communities do not have absolute moral priority from the communitarian perspec-

tive. The community's theory of the good must display a roughly equal concern for the welfare of all its members, and the community must continually
interpret and, if necessary, revise its conventions to satisfy the requirements
of its theory of the good. But once a community passes the basic test of moral
legitimacy, its traditions, interpreted reflectively, are accepted as defining the
roles, responsibilities, and expectations of all its members. Thus, in communitarian theory culture has an ethical priority second only to the very general
demands for equal concern and deliberative interpretation, demands that a
wide variety of cultures may meet.

The Power to Resolve Disputes

This criterion demands two things of a theory of political morality—
that it is capable of dealing with the full range of disputes that arise in a
society and that it produces definitive resolutions for those disputes. Communitarian theory is not fully adequate on either of these counts.

That theory permits the resolution of some disputes between communities by assigning priority to the claims of morally legitimate communities,
and by holding that the conventions of each morally legitimate community
should govern the conduct of its own members only. The assessment of
whether a community is morally legitimate can be relatively straightforward
for small, homogeneous communities. But, as we have seen, when the community is a large and complex nation, the interpretation of the community's
theory of the good can be ambiguous, and a final judgment about its moral
legitimacy may be uncertain. Furthermore, when conflicting communities
are both morally legitimate, communitarian theory does not resolve several
sorts of disputes—when, for instance, some people are members of more
than one community, or when the effects of one community's social principles and practices create conditions in which another community's values
cannot be effectively realized. In these situations, communitarian theory does
not assign moral priority to either community's culture or prescribe external
principles or procedures according to which their differences may be resolved. Of course, such disputes may actually be brought to an end by the
use of coercion or, under the threat of mutual coercion, through an ad hoc
compromise in which neither community's fundamental principles are fully
realized. But these are courses of action to which a robust theory of political
morality is supposed to provide a peaceful and principled alternative.

Communitarian theory also provides guidance for the resolution of disputes internal to communities. It directs a community to interpret and revise
prevailing practices in light of its fundamental principles when disputes arise
from the advent of new circumstances, ambiguity of existing rules, and so
on. But, as we have seen at Big Cypress, a community's fundamental prin-

ciples may themselves come into conflict with one another, especially in the context of a multicultural society. Such basic conflicts require a different procedure than that necessary to resolve inconsistencies among existing practices or conventions, where the issue is settled by referring to the community's fundamental principles. When those principles are in conflict, to what higher authority can a community appeal?

The criteria for moral community may provide some guidance. If giving priority to one of the conflicting principles would render the community illegitimate, such a change in the community's theory of the good should be ruled out. However, the criteria of moral community are not likely to produce a definitive resolution of these fundamental conflicts. First, it may be that the community would still be morally legitimate no matter which principle is assigned priority. At Big Cypress, for instance, it is not clear that an emphasis on either cultural openness or self-sufficiency would violate the criteria of moral community. Second, there are many other ways in which the community might resolve the conflict among principles besides assigning priority to one principle or another. It might modify the old principles or even invent an altogether novel theory of the good. In any case, communitarian theory seems inadequate to resolve internal community disputes that reflect conflicts among the community's fundamental commitments.

The power of communitarian theory to resolve the types of disputes most likely to arise in multicultural societies—conflicts about the moral legitimacy of large and complex communities, conflicts between morally legitimate communities, and conflicts at the level of a community's basic principles—is seriously limited at best.

The Acceptability of Resolutions

The dispute resolutions that a theory of political morality produces should be understandable to the parties involved and, ideally, acceptable to them. In the types of disputes to which it most clearly applies—internal conflicts over prevailing practices and external conflicts over the moral legitimacy of small, homogeneous communities—communitarian theory meets both of these criteria. Internal disputes are resolved on the basis of the principles underlying the community's conventions. Accordingly, the reasons for a particular resolution will be cast in the language of the community's own values and social concepts. Because of their education in the community's basic structure, rationale, and conventions, community members should find those reasons not only understandable but acceptable, even if they are not fully in line with their own personal preferences. Disputes over moral legitimacy involve the application of criteria that are external to a community's own theory of the good, criteria that require the community's practices to reflect a roughly equal concern for all its members. Nevertheless, judgments about moral legitimacy rely on the community's own theory of the good to determine whether or not some community members have been relegated to a permanently second-class status. Communitarian theory does not define individuals' good outside of their cultural context, as liberalism does. Therefore, although many community members are not likely to be pleased with a judgment that their community is morally illegitimate, they will at least have the ability to understand and appreciate the reasons advanced for that judgment, namely, that some community members are denied that which the community's traditions regard as most important.

There are, however, many types of disputes to which the principles of communitarian theory do not readily apply—disputes about the moral legitimacy of large communities, between morally legitimate communities, and about a community's fundamental commitments. Communitarian theory provides no principles or procedures for resolving these disputes. Therefore, any outcome of such disputes will appear to community members as entirely arbitrary, based neither upon the community's own theory of the good nor upon superordinate principles of political morality. As such, those outcomes will be hard to understand because they will not be structured by the community's concepts and standards of reasoning, and hard to accept because they will not be informed by internal or external moral precepts. They will, to use Ronald Dworkin's (1986) phrase, lack integrity. Because many, if not most, of the socially significant and complex disputes that arise in a multicultural society will be of these types, communitarian theory will prove particularly inadequate in producing acceptable resolutions for the conflicts of such societies.

A REVIEW OF THE ADEQUACY OF COMMUNITARIAN THEORY

The central commitment of communitarian theory is to the morally legitimate community, a social entity whose members are bound together by ties of tradition; a theory of the good that reflects equal concern for all; and a commitment to interpret those traditions so as to overcome any imperfections in existing conventions and practices in order more fully to realize the community's fundamental purposes and principles.

This conception of political morality recognizes and utilizes communities' own values in the resolution of controversies between and within communities. Its conception of culture includes all the characteristics that we intuitively ascribe to that concept, and it assigns a very high moral priority to the traditions of individual communities. It provides clear and widely acceptable guidance for the resolution of disputes about a community's conventions and about the moral legitimacy of some communities. However, it fails almost entirely to resolve the most intractable problems of multicultural societies: disputes about the moral legitimacy of large nations, disputes between morally legitimate communities, and disputes about a community's fundamental commitments.

REFERENCES AND FURTHER READING

Bellah, R. N.; Madsen, R.; Sullivan, W. M.; Swidler, A.; & Tipton, S. M. (1985). *Habits of the heart: Individualism and commitment in American life*. New York: Harper & Row.

A sociological study of Americans' attitudes toward their work, personal relationships, and communities that argues that the lack of a social and political tradition of community in the United States is a primary source of a widespread sense of incompleteness and dissatisfaction.

Dworkin, R. (1986). *Law's empire*. Cambridge, MA: Harvard University Press.

An attempt to show how the Anglo-American legal tradition is grounded in a theory of moral community.

Fuchs, E., & Havighurst, R. (1983). *To live on this earth: American Indian education*. Albuquerque, NM: University of New Mexico Press. (Original work published 1972).

A report on a national study of Native American education funded by the U.S. Office of Education. This document had an important influence on federal legislation on Native Americans during the 1970s.

Garbarino, M. S. (1972). *Big Cypress: A changing Seminole community*. New York: Holt, Rinehart, & Winston.

An anthropological study of the Seminoles living on the Big Cypress reservation in the 1960s.

Garbarino, M. S. (1989). *The Seminole*. New York: Chelsea House.

An introduction to the history and contemporary lives of the Florida Seminoles.

Marx, K. (1972). Critique of the Gotha program. In R. C. Tucker (Ed.), *The Marx–Engels reader* (pp. 382–398). New York: Norton. (Original work published 1875).

A compilation of Marx's critical notes on a proposal to form the German Social Democratic Party. Includes Marx's discussion of the goals of communism and of the organization and nature of advanced communist society.

Marx, K., & Engels, F. (1972). The communist manifesto. In R. C. Tucker (Ed.), *The Marx–Engels reader* (pp. 335–362). New York: Norton. (Original work published 1848).

The founding statement of Communist Party in France, including an analysis of the class system of capitalist society and the communist revolutionary program.

Nisbet, R. A. (1953). *The quest for community: A study in the ethics of order and freedom*.

New York: Oxford University Press.

   An effort to reconceptualize democratic theory to encompass the value of community.

Prucha, F. P. (1984). *The great father: The United States government and the American Indians*. (2 vols.). Lincoln, NB: University of Nebraska Press.

   A wide-ranging history of the relationship between the U.S. government and Native Americans.

Rawls, J. (1971). *A theory of justice*. Cambridge, MA: Harvard University Press.

   A statement of modern liberal theory that attempts, in part, to show how a well-ordered liberal society can reflect and support the value of community.

Sandel, M. J. (1982). *Liberalism and the limits of justice*. New York: Cambridge University Press.

   A critique of liberal theory based significantly on its inability to recognize the sources of human identity and value available in genuine communities.

Weisman, B. R. (1989). *Like beads on a string: A culture history of the Seminole Indians in north peninsular Florida*. Tuscaloosa, AL: University of Alabama Press.

   An archaeological study of the culture of Florida Seminoles prior to their forced evacuation to south Florida in the 1830s and 1840s.

CHAPTER 5

Concluding Reflections on Political Morality in Multicultural and Bilingual Contexts

We have thus far developed three influential theories of political morality and examined the way in which each is able to deal with the difficulties and complexities of concrete cases of cultural and linguistic conflict in education. This concluding chapter will summarize and compare the success of those three perspectives in meeting the criteria for an adequate response to the realities of cultural and linguistic difference developed in the first chapter. As may already be obvious, none of these perspectives is wholly satisfactory. It will be a second purpose of this chapter, then, to attempt to understand just why these approaches are inadequate to the task we have set for them. Finally, we will consider what thoughtful responses to this inadequacy might be possible.

A COMPARISON OF THE PERSPECTIVES

One aim of the preceding three chapters has been to delineate three different answers to the fundamental question of political morality: Why should people accept and obey the decisions of a political system, especially if some of them disagree with those decisions? The liberal answers by saying that a political system is legitimate when it produces results that are just to all concerned. The democrat answers by saying that a political system is legitimate when it decides controversial questions according to a procedure that is fair to everyone. The communitarian answers by saying that a political system is legitimate when its decisions accord with the morally justified relationships that exist among its members. From each of these starting places, the three perspectives go on to define and explain the basic moral concepts that each takes to be most important in establishing the legitimacy of a political order. Liberalism argues that just outcomes are those which take neutrally and equally into account each person's self-defined interests. Democracy argues that a fair decision-making procedure is one in which all citizens have fully and actively participated. Communitarianism argues that justified relationships are those which maintain traditions that reflect an equal concern for all community members.

The second purpose of the first three chapters was to examine how well each of these perspectives might deal with the educational issues that arise in multicultural and multilingual societies, with the hope that at least one of them would prove reasonably adequate or at least conclusively better than the others. In particular, we want an adequate theory to conceptualize culture in a satisfactory way, give a high moral priority to culture in the making of social decisions, produce clear resolutions to conflicts between cultures, and provide resolutions that the parties to the conflicts can find mutually acceptable. Let us review each of these criteria in turn.

The Conception of Culture

We have seen that our intuitive understanding of culture includes at least three important characteristics: First, a culture is of deep personal significance to its members; indeed, a culture can be seen as defining to a large extent the personhood of individuals. Second, a culture is a collective phenomenon, consisting of shared convictions, aspirations, understandings, and behavior. Finally, a culture reflects a larger historical and social context that helps to define the roles, beliefs, and practices of its members.

Liberalism identifies culture with individuals' visions of the good life, with their personal, autonomously chosen self-definitions. Obviously, this way of understanding culture meets our criterion of personal significance. But its emphasis on individuality completely neglects the collective and contextual character of our intuitive understanding of culture.

Democracy sees a culture as a political faction, a group of people with a shared vision of the society's present and future. From the democratic perspective, however, this vision is simply a shared opinion about one's society; it may or may not reflect beliefs that are fundamental to one's identity. Moreover, democratic theory does not distinguish those political factions that are rooted in historical and social traditions from those that are not so rooted.

Communitarianism identifies cultures with bare communities, those social groups bound together by pervasive patterns of mutual interaction that reflect continuing and shared traditions that in turn define the identities, roles, and responsibilities of their members. This conception of culture seems to meet all three of our criteria. Because a bare community defines the identities of its members, it is of real personal significance to individuals. Culture, according to this view, is inherently a collective phenomenon. Finally, a bare community is defined by a shared historical and social context.

Plainly, then, of the three theories of political morality communitarianism has the most adequate conception of culture. Insofar as democracy's conception includes the idea that culture is shared, it seems marginally preferable to liberalism's, but neither is especially robust or attractive.

The Ethical Priority of Culture

This criterion requires us to consider how important cultural values are in the political decisions that a society makes. Let us consider first whether anything is of greater value than culture in the three theories of political morality. The answer to this question is positive for all three theories. Liberalism's premier political value is substantive justice; thus, any cultural practice that denies liberty or equal opportunity to individuals is prohibited in a liberal society. Democracy's basic commitment is to procedural justice; here, too, a cultural practice that interferes with all citizens' free and full participation in the political process is ruled out. Communitarianism requires bare communities to meet the requirements of moral legitimacy; a culture that fails to demonstrate a roughly equal concern for all its members is not worthy of preservation or protection.

Each theory takes a critical moral perspective on culture, and all, therefore, regard certain possible cultural values and practices as morally illegitimate. For example, slavery fails to meet the moral requirements of all three theories because it involves a denial of basic personal liberty, the rights of universal political participation, and equal concern for the welfare of all.

Thus far, then, all three perspectives make some moral and political values—neutrality, participation, or equal concern—more important than culture. In other words, culture does not have absolute moral priority in any of the three perspectives. Nevertheless, these perspectives do assign different secondary values to culture. We can see these differences by considering two questions. The first might be called the question of scope: How many cultures can meet the primary test of moral legitimacy imposed by each of the perspectives? The second might be called the question of relative value: Once a culture has met the test of moral legitimacy, how secure and significant a role does it have in determining the decisions of the society?

SCOPE. The tests of moral legitimacy for culture imposed by these theories are not equally stringent. As we have noted, the requirement for equal concern need not imply that all citizens be given an equal role in social decision making; indeed, it is consistent with reserving the task of cultural reinterpretation and modification to a limited class of community leaders. Nor does equal concern require that all community members must be granted the opportunity or the resources to develop their own individual visions of the good life; here, too, equal concern can permit a morally legitimate community to prescribe individuals' social roles in a way that would be impermissible in a liberal society. As a result, communitarianism will rule out fewer cultural values and practices than either liberalism or democracy.

On similar grounds, we can see that democracy's tests for the moral legitimacy of culture are less stringent than liberalism's. As we have noted, democracy requires freedom of opinion and expression, but it does not, as does liberalism, actually require that individuals be given the right to live according to the opinions they profess. Thus, democracy is compatible with some cultures that liberalism is not, namely, those that permit individuals to express their preferences but deny them the liberty to live their lives as they see fit.

In summary, then, the basic moral commitments of communitarianism are consistent with more cultures than those of liberalism or democracy, and those of democracy are consistent with more cultures than liberalism's. But the simple fact that a culture does not violate the basic moral principles of a society does not necessarily mean that its values will have a prominent role in the society's political decisions. To put the matter on a personal level, someone may believe that reading books is a morally permissible activity, yet he or she may place such a low value on reading that it never figures significantly in any personal decisions. In other words, we must consider what relative value each perspective places upon the cultures that meet its test of legitimacy.

RELATIVE VALUE.   Communitarian theory holds that, if a community is morally legitimate, then its traditions, reflectively interpreted, are the appropriate basis for decision making in that society. Thus, a morally legitimate community both can and should define its members' roles, rules, and responsibilities in accordance with the traditions of its culture. To the adherents of the cultures that meet its test for moral legitimacy, a liberal society also provides certain guarantees. Indeed, since those morally permissible cultures are understood to define those individuals' personal visions of the good, a liberal society is obliged to facilitate their efforts to live their lives as their culture requires, as long as others are able to do likewise. The guarantees provided by democracy are less clear, however. Members of morally legitimate cultures in a democracy are given the right to express their cultural values and to persuade others to permit them to live their lives according to those values. But a political majority in a democracy may negotiate and enforce a collective vision of their society that may prohibit the practices of some morally legitimate cultures, as long as they do not thereby deny the members of those cultures the right to participate in the democratic decision-making process.

OVERALL ETHICAL PRIORITY. Communitarianism assigns the clearest ethical priority to cultural values in the making of social decisions. It is consistent with more cultures than the other theories, and it recognizes and protects the rights of the members of morally legitimate cultures to live their lives as their culture requires. The other two perspectives fare less well on the tests of scope and relative value. Culture is important in a democracy insofar as it is a legitimate source of opinions about the society, but a democracy guarantees only that the members of a legitimate culture will have the opportunity to have their opinions heard, and not that they will be able to live their lives in full compliance with their culture. Liberalism recognizes as legitimate fewer cultures than either communitarianism or democracy, but it does guarantee that the members of legitimate cultures will have the liberty and access to a fair share of the society's resources necessary to fulfill the vision of the good life that the culture includes. Despite their shortcomings in comparison to communitarianism, both democracy and liberalism do assign a reasonably significant role to culture in social decision making; they clearly regard culture as an important, if not exclusive, source of value in a morally legitimate society.

The Power to Resolve Disputes

Different cultures, as we have seen in the various cases we have considered, often want different things for the adults and children who comprise a society. Ideally, we would like a theory of political morality that would produce clear and unambiguous decisions when these differences lead to social conflict. The three perspectives we have surveyed provide significantly different strategies for resolving these cultural disagreements.

Liberalism specifies a set of substantive principles for resolving the disagreements among citizens; it directs a society to consider which alternative most clearly meets the requirements of liberal education, personal liberty, educational opportunity, economic opportunity, and material welfare for those affected by the decision. Liberalism's principles of substantive justice provide for clear and unambiguous resolutions of nearly all social disputes. First, those principles are hierarchically arranged so that if a dispute involves two different types of values—personal liberty versus economic opportunity, for example—liberalism assigns clear priority to one of those values. Second, even if the conflicting alternatives involve the same value, liberal principles establish clear social preferences—for more personal liberty rather than less, for instance. Finally, when alternatives involve equal outcomes of the same value, liberalism directs that the dispute be resolved by private negotiation among the disputants, within the boundaries established by its principles.

By specifying a set of fair procedures, democracy also establishes a way of resolving social disputes: A decision that affects the society's political process must be made in a way that enhances universal participation; otherwise, the decision is to be made by means of that political process. Unfortunately, democracy produces ambiguous results in some conflict situations, for it is unable to establish definite jurisdictions based on democratic principles within which fair procedures should operate. When different decisions would be reached by using fair procedures in larger and smaller jurisdictions—a school district as opposed to a single school's attendance area, for example—democratic theory produces ambiguous guidance for social decisions.

Communitarian theory approaches cultural conflicts in two stages. Initially, one is to determine whether the communities involved are morally legitimate—that is, whether they express a roughly equal concern for the well-being of all of their members. Subsequently, communitarianism directs the parties to the dispute to act in accordance with the traditions of the legitimate community or communities. There are several sources of ambiguity in the communitarian approach. First, it is often difficult to make a clear determination of the moral legitimacy of large and complex communities like modern nations. A nation's history and traditions usually include such a wide range of events and ideas that an uncontroversial interpretation of its basic theory of the good for its members, and therefore of its moral legitimacy, is impossible. Second, even when one can reasonably ascertain the moral legitimacy of the contending communities, communitarianism may still produce ambiguous results. On the one hand, more than one community may turn out to be legitimate, in which case communitarian theory does not assign clear moral priority to any community's traditions. On the other hand, when only one community is legitimate, that community's fundamental commitments may themselves be in conflict. As long as those commitments are all consistent with the community's moral legitimacy, communitarian theory does not specify which fundamental commitment is to take precedence over the others and, thus, which course of action is justified.

Liberalism clearly has more power to resolve disputes than either of the other perspectives because it is able to produce conclusive results for most cases of cultural conflict. Democracy sometimes fails to generate unambiguous resolutions when, as is frequently the case in multicultural societies, democratic procedures produce different decisions in larger and smaller jurisdictions. Communitarian theory seems to fare worst of all because of the difficulty of assessing the moral legitimacy of complex cultures and because of its inability to assign clear moral priority to equally legitimate communities or to only one of a community's conflicting fundamental commitments.

The Acceptability of Resolutions

All three perspectives provide individuals with reasons why they should accept the political decisions of their society. Liberalism tells its citizens that those decisions reflect the fundamental interests of all parties. Democracy says that those decisions reflect the will of the majority. And communitarianism asserts that the society's decisions reflect the traditions of a morally legitimate community. How much moral authority do these reasons carry in situations of cultural conflict?

The ambiguity about resolutions that we have already noted in the democratic and communitarian perspectives can undermine the moral authority of the justifications that they offer for accepting political decisions. Suppose that it is a tradition in Marie's school that children are to start each year with the study of nature. Suppose further that Marie's art teacher instructs her to draw a picture of a tree for her first art project, but Marie would rather draw the mountain she and her family had visited on their summer vacation. The teacher justifies her decision by saying that the project is supposed to depict something from nature. That, of course, *is* a reason to draw the tree, but it is equally a reason to draw the mountain. Even though Marie accepts the teacher's reason in this situation, that reason does not make the teacher's decision acceptable. When a reason points equally to two or more alternatives, the selection of any one alternative is capricious, and the reason will simply not provide someone who prefers one of the other alternatives an acceptable justification for the selection.

As we have seen, democracy's inability to define jurisdictions in a principled manner and communitarianism's inability to establish priorities among morally legitimate cultures imply that they cannot definitively resolve many of the disputes that arise in multicultural societies. When a political decision is made from among the justified alternatives, that decision will not seem morally authoritative to those whose preferences lie elsewhere. For communitarianism, this problem is compounded by the difficulty of applying its principles to complex societies. Sometimes the moral legitimacy of a culture is simply uncertain, and a decision based upon the premise that a culture is either legitimate or illegitimate will appear capricious and therefore will be difficult for some parties to a cultural dispute to accept.

Although the moral authority of a liberal society's decisions is not undermined by this sort of ambiguity and uncertainty, those decisions may be hard to accept for two other reasons. First, liberalism's principles abstract from the real concerns and motivations of its citizens. Because a liberal society must be neutral to the concrete visions of the good that define the individual lives of its citizens, its decisions are based upon what it takes to be their more fundamental interests—in liberty, opportunity, and so on. Consequently, the reasons that it offers to justify its decisions may be so disconnected from its citizens' actual motivations as to be unpersuasive to them. To recall the case presented in Chapter 2, how important will the liberal education of his children seem to Reverend Creasey when he is primarily concerned with the salvation of their souls? To be sure, democratic and communitarian theories sometimes render decisions that do not coincide with citizens' concrete motivations. After all, democracies must guarantee the fairness of their decision-making procedures, and communitarian societies must ensure the moral legitimacy of their cultures. Nevertheless, democratic political debate and deliberation, at the very least, provide citizens with the opportunity to make their case in the terms most meaningful to them. And communitarian judgments of moral legitimacy begin from a culture's own conception of the good for its members.

The second reason why a liberal society's decisions may be hard to accept is that liberal principles often imply that there are no grounds for the reversal of a particular decision. When a decision is based correctly on the equal consideration of citizens' fundamental interests, that decision marks a permanent constraint on the lives of those who oppose it. This immutable character of liberal decisions means that such decisions will be harder for opponents to accept than those made by democratic majorities, where there is always the possibility that political negotiation and persuasion may produce a different result in the future. Communitarian decisions face a similar, though less extreme, problem. Traditions can change, but they usually do so over a long span of time. Opponents to a decision can direct their energies toward a change of fundamental commitments or the interpretation of existing commitments in their community, but the pace and likelihood of change are more limited than in a democracy.

None of the perspectives produces clearly acceptable outcomes in a multicultural society. Democracy's problem with ambiguity and communitarianism's with both ambiguity and uncertainty seem most serious because they provide those who do not wish to accept a decision a reason not to do so based upon the moral principles of the perspectives themselves. Democracy redeems itself to some extent by fostering public debate in the opponents' own terms and by allowing the possibility for rapid change. Communitarianism also conducts its analysis in terms of the community's own values but faces the same problem with change that liberalism does. The immutability of liberal decisions and their justification in terms of abstract interests renders their acceptability less than fully satisfactory.

WHY THE PERSPECTIVES ARE INADEQUATE

Table 5.1 summarizes our comparison of the perspectives in terms of the four criteria. As we have already noted, this comparison of the perspectives gives us at least one cause for satisfaction; all three of these views of political morality do place a reasonable value upon culture in the principles they prescribe for political decision making. Nevertheless, this assessment is deeply disappointing. In the end, we would like a system of political morality that would give the members of various cultures such a compelling reason for its decisions that they would be willing to acquiesce in those decisions even when those decisions are not entirely consistent with the dictates of their cultures. Unfortunately, none of the perspectives seems capable of producing resolutions of multicultural conflicts that the parties can find fully acceptable. In fact, it appears that there is a trade-off between the moral significance that a perspective assigns to culture and the acceptability of its resolutions. Similarly, there also seems to be a trade-off between the adequacy of a perspective's conception of culture and its ability to generate any sort of proposed resolution to multicultural conflicts. Thus, although liberalism's view of culture is seriously flawed, it is able to provide a solution to most cultural disputes. Just the opposite is true for communitarianism. Although its conception of culture is robust, communitarianism just does not produce clear solutions to the most difficult problems of cultural difference. Why do these apparent trade-offs arise? Are they avoidable, or must we simply accept that any theory of political morality is doomed to prove inadequate on some of the criteria for multicultural conflict that we have proposed?

Political Legitimacy as Autonomy

In an attempt to answer these questions, it will be helpful to develop a slightly different view of our three theories of political morality. Although we have been emphasizing the differences among the three perspectives, it is possible to understand each of them as providing an interpretation of the

TABLE 5.1 The Adequacy of Three Perspectives on Political Morality

Criteria	Liberalism	Democracy	Communitarianism
Culture	Weak	Moderate	Strong
Significance	Moderate	Moderate	Strong
Resolutions	Strong	Moderate	Weak
Acceptability	Moderate	Moderate	Weak

traditional political ideal of self-government, the idea that a political order is legitimate if it enables its members to define and regulate their lives according to their own lights. To be sure, each perspective applies self-government at a different level of human organization. Liberalism takes as its ideal the self-governing individual, the person who lives according to his or her own conception of the good. Communitarianism aims for the self-governing community, a human association that regulates itself according to its own traditions. And democracy seeks the self-governing society, a society that constructs and reproduces itself according to the opinions and judgments of its own citizens.

Although each perspective values independence for individuals, communities, or societies, none defines that independence only as simple freedom from external control. Thus, for example, liberals do not see self-government as authorizing individuals to do unlimited harm to themselves and others. Rather, in all three cases, self-government is understood as living according to self-imposed constraints. For liberalism, those constraints are implicit in each person's conception of the good; for communitarianism, the constraints consist of the community's traditions; for democracy, the constraints derive from the decisions of the political process. Moreover, each perspective requires these self-imposed constraints to meet certain standards. In a democracy, for instance, the political process must be universally participatory. It is these additional requirements that make the constraints morally legitimate.

Immanuel Kant defined *autonomy* as the ideal of living according to self-imposed moral principles. For Kant, the principles that govern one's life qualify as morally legitimate when they meet two requirements—the criteria of equality and reason. As we shall see, each perspective meets these criteria in a different way, and each aims, therefore, not just at simple self-government but at moral autonomy. Thus, liberalism seeks the autonomous individual, communitarianism the autonomous community, and democracy the autonomous society.

The criterion of equality expresses the idea that morally legitimate actions and interactions must respect the inherent value each human being possesses; an action cannot be moral if it assumes that some people are just another natural resource to be used to satisfy the purposes of others. The commitment to neutrality is liberalism's way of recognizing this requirement, for neutrality holds that each person and his or her vision of the good life is at least as good as other persons and other visions (Ackerman, 1980). Democracy's principle of universal participation similarly acknowledges each citizen's value because it guarantees everyone a role in the society's decision-making process. And communitarianism recognizes each community member's value through its requirement that the community's traditions express an equal concern for all.

The criterion of reason holds that moral action requires the exercise of human intelligence; thus, the behavior of animals or the insane cannot be judged either moral or immoral because they lack the capacity for reason. In assessing the interests of its citizens, liberalism considers what it would be individually rational for each person to want given his or her vision of the good life, not what that person actually happens to want. Thus, a liberal society prohibits its members from selling themselves into slavery even if some might be willing to do so. Liberalism therefore interprets the criterion of reason to mean individual rationality. Similarly, democracy demands that society's decisions be based on the thoughtful reflection of all citizens upon the evidence and opinions available in the society. Here democracy is committed to an interpretation of reason as collective deliberation. Finally, communitarianism requires that the traditions of a community be thoughtfully reinterpreted when new circumstances or apparent conflicts among the traditions arise. Thus, communitarianism is committed to reason as reflective interpretation.

As Table 5.2 shows, each perspective, then, offers an account of the morally legitimate society based upon an alternative conception of autonomy. This table also suggests that each perspective portrays the political inadequacies of a society in significantly different ways. When a commitment to equal-

TABLE 5.2 Three Perspectives on Political Morality as Alternative Conceptions of Autonomy

	Liberalism	*Democracy*	*Communitarianism*
Moral Ideal	Autonomous Individual	Autonomous Society	Autonomous Community
Interpretation of Equality	Neutrality	Universal Participation	Equal Concern
Interpretation of Reason	Individual Rationality	Collective Deliberation	Reflective Interpretation
Lack of Equality	Authoritarianism	Tyranny	Exploitation
Lack of Reason	License	Mob Rule	Blind Traditionalism

ity is wanting, the liberal sees a society governed in the interests of those whose conception of the good becomes illegitimately authoritative for all. In the absence of equality, a democracy becomes tyranny, where the opinions of some determine the policies for all. Without equality, a community is exploitative, a society in which some members become mere servants of others. In the absence of reason, liberal freedom becomes license, and society degenerates into an enterprise devoted to the satisfaction of individuals' temporary whims and desires. Democracy without reason is mobocracy, in which political majorities use their power to achieve ill-considered ends. And communities that do not interpret their traditions in the light of new circumstances or internal conflicts become blind adherents to traditional roles and customs.

How Trade-offs Result from the Conceptions of Autonomy

This analysis of the perspectives shows that all three are committed to the idea that morality consists of autonomy, that is, independence constrained by equality and reason. The differences in the perspectives arise, then, from the alternative ways in which each applies this basic commitment.

Communitarianism holds that morality is internal to a legitimate cultural community. Thus, each such community defines the precise meaning of reason and equality for itself. Of course, some actual communities may fail to be committed to *any* conception of reason or equality or both, in which case they would be morally illegitimate. But within very broad limits, each community has the prerogative to specify its own standards for equal concern and reflective interpretation—what the good for each member of the community is and how the community will enable each to realize that good; what principles of judgment apply to the interpretation of tradition and to whom the responsibility to apply those principles will fall. As a result, communitarianism takes culture extremely seriously. The community's history and the social relationships that exist among its members help to define right and wrong, good and evil. In this way, communitarianism's conception of culture is robust, and the ethical significance it assigns to culture is central.

The conflicts that arise in multicultural contexts, however, are *between* the members of various cultures or within individuals who are members of more than one culture. One problem, as we have found, is that communitarianism provides no substantial, external standpoint from which to fashion a resolution for such conflicts. And because reason and equality are internal to a culture, any justification that a communitarian can give to the members of one culture for accepting a particular way of resolving a multicultural conflict will not necessarily turn out to be acceptable to the members of another. For, in the first place, that justification may not adhere to the accepted standards of judgment of the other community, and, second, it may be based on a conception of equal treatment that is foreign to the other community's conception of morality. For the communitarian, there are no universal norms of reason and equality according to which the differences between morally legitimate communities can be judged. As a result, there can be no guarantee that a mutually satisfactory resolution to a conflict between such communities exists. The trade-off between, on the one hand, the conception of culture and its ethical significance and, on the other hand, the power to resolve disputes acceptably arises from communitarianism's vision of autonomy as internal to each cultural community.

Liberalism avoids these difficulties by proposing conceptions of equality and reason that are external to culture. To the liberal, the rights and responsibilities of one person are the same as those of any other, no matter to what cultural group that individual may belong. Similarly, the same standards of reason apply to all. As a result, liberalism is able to produce moral resolutions to nearly all conflicts that arise among individuals, including conflicts based upon cultural differences.

However, the liberal's strategy for resolving conflicts exacts three prices. First, its view of culture is limited to those elements that individuals actually incorporate into their personal conceptions of the good. Second, the history and social relationships necessary to the flourishing of a culture are morally important only to the extent that they are direct objects of living individuals' aspirations and values. And, third, although a liberal society is able to produce reasons why people should accept its proposed resolutions, those reasons are based upon a purportedly universal code of rationality and equality that, at best, is an abstract representation of what its citizens care most about. Thus, liberalism's commitment to standards of reason and equality that are external to culture enables it to generate reasoned resolutions for cultural conflicts at the sacrifice of conceptual adequacy and, to a lesser extent, of ethical significance and acceptability.

Democracy takes yet a third tack. For the democrat, reason and equality are both internal and external to culture. Democracy imposes a certain form upon the decision-making procedures that a society must use, but it tolerates any results to which those procedures may lead (except results that undermine the procedures themselves). Thus, participation guarantees to all a formal equality in the political process, and deliberation ensures that a formal process of wide public debate will occur. But democracy does not prescribe the standards of judgment to be utilized in that process; indeed, those standards are likely to be whatever the society's citizens find to be reasonable based upon their cultural backgrounds. Moreover, as we have seen, the results of the democratic process may favor one cultural group over others. Here, too, what is good for the society is likely to depend upon its citizens' cultural orientations. In other words, for the democrat the form of reason and equality is external to cultures, but the substance of these concepts—the standards of judgment and the society's social priorities—is determined by the cultures embraced by the society.

These dual conceptions of reason and equality are both democracy's strength and its weakness in dealing with multicultural conflicts. By recognizing local and collective standards of rationality and value, democracy portrays culture more adequately than does liberalism. In contrast to communitarianism, however, the requirement that the society's decision-making processes take a particular form prevents democracy from reflecting the fact that particular cultures may differ as to the procedures they employ to make social decisions as well as to the standards of judgment they apply to those decisions. As a result, democracy's conception of culture is not fully adequate.

This mix of externally determined form and internally determined substance has precisely the opposite consequences for democracy's power to generate definitive resolutions of multicultural conflicts. The democratic process is in theory capable of resolving any conflict. However, the formal requirements of democracy simply do not specify the size of the jurisdictions within which decisions are to be made. That is, a decision-making process at the local level can be just as participatory and deliberative as that at a state or national level. To assign particular decisions to particular jurisdictions, then, democracies must rely upon their citizens' convictions and traditions for making such assignments, which, in turn, are likely to depend upon those citizens' cultural orientations. When the actual decisions that are made depend upon the jurisdiction to which they are assigned, those decisions will seem arbitrary and therefore unacceptable to some citizens.

Although all three perspectives are committed to political morality as autonomy, as independence constrained by reason and equality, each characterizes these constraints in a different way—as defined internally by cultures, externally to them, or externally in form but internally in substance. The ability of each perspective to meet the four criteria for adequacy in multicultural conflicts flows directly from the way that they conceptualize autonomy. In particular, the apparent trade-offs among the four criteria can be explained as the result of these perspectives' alternative conceptions of political morality as autonomy. Given this way of understanding morality, in fact, these trade-offs begin to seem inevitable. It appears that the only available alternatives are to see reason and equality as internal, external, or a mix of the two in relation to culture. Yet each way of thinking about these moral constraints leads to inadequacy on one or more of the criteria. The important question now is whether and how these apparent trade-offs can be overcome.

STRATEGIES FOR OVERCOMING THE INADEQUACIES

Our overview of the three perspectives has left us with two related problems. First, for dealing with differences and conflicts among cultures, especially those that are reflected in disputes about the education of children, we need a better theory of political morality than those provided by any of the perspectives we have surveyed. But, of course, the educational issues presented by multicultural and multilingual communities are present realities, both in the U.S. and in nearly every other nation. Teachers, administrators, and concerned citizens cannot defer thinking and action on these issues while civilizations, ours and others, evolve more satisfactory political theories. Thus, our second problem is how we can use our current political and intellectual resources to respond to the immediate need to cope sensitively and intelligently with concrete situations of cultural and linguistic difference as they arise.

The Search for a Better Perspective

Contact between cultures—whether in inner-city New York, between ethnic groups in eastern Europe, among the tribes of Nigeria, or between religious factions in India—has long been the source of profound human suffering as well as mutual enrichment. In simplest terms, one crucial task of a theory of political morality is to enhance the likelihood for such enrichment without risking the suffering that often accompanies it. It would be presumptuous to suppose that we could here solve the problems of political and moral theory that have plagued civilizations around the world for thousands of years. But our reflections on the three perspectives can at least help us understand the nature of the problems we face and suggest some of the resources that might be helpful in our continuing search for a more adequate approach to them.

Our exploration of the three perspectives in this chapter has revealed a potentially troubling source of the difficulty that Western theories of political morality may have in solving the problems of multiculturalism, namely, that there may be a conflict—some might call it a contradiction—between the concept of political morality upon which those theories are based and the criteria we have for an adequate response to multicultural differences. As we have seen, all three perspectives are committed in different ways to the ideal of political legitimacy as autonomy. Yet we have also found that those different interpretations of autonomy are responsible for the varying patterns of inadequacy displayed by the perspectives. In other words, it may not be logically possible for a theory based upon the ideal of autonomy to produce clear and acceptable resolutions of cultural conflict that reflect a robust and morally significant conception of culture.

This would not be the first time that our political ideals proved to be internally incoherent. For example, Kenneth Arrow (1963), a Nobel Prize–winning economist, showed that no system of social decision making could meet five widely accepted conditions. Utilizing a strategy similar to Arrow's, we can see graphically how the criteria of autonomy and multicultural adequacy might be inconsistent with each other. The large box in Figure 5.1 represents all imaginable theories of political morality. Each time we place a requirement on such a theory, we select from this universe of possibilities some limited set of theories that meet the requirement. The smaller boxes in Figure 5.1 represent the theories that meet the requirements of autonomy. As the figure suggests, only some of these possible theories meet autonomy's requirement to treat people equally. Others meet the requirement to use reason in the making of political decisions. And some smaller number still, represented by the shaded area in Figure 5.1, meet both of these requirements. As we have seen in this chapter, all three perspectives do in fact satisfy these two criteria for autonomy.

Similarly, Figure 5.2 shows how the criteria for multicultural adequacy also apply to the universe of possible theories of political morality. The shaded area in Figure 5.2 represents the number of theories of political morality that meet all four requirements of a robust conception of culture, attributing ethical significance to culture, generating clear resolutions to cul-

FIGURE 5.1 The Criteria of Autonomy

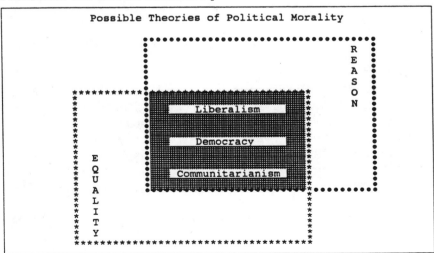

FIGURE 5.2 The Criteria of Multicultural Adequacy

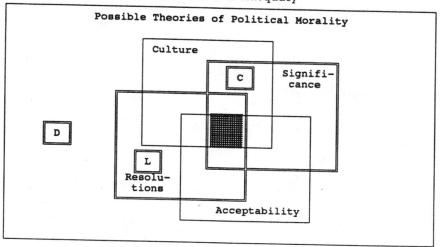

tural conflicts, and producing resolutions that are acceptable to all the parties. Our analysis shows that neither liberalism, democracy, nor communitarianism satisfies all of these requirements. The small boxes in this figure indicate the proper placement of the three perspectives. Liberalism, indicated by the boxed L, fully meets only the requirement for clear resolutions. Communitarianism, indicated by the boxed C, meets the criteria for a robust conception of culture and attributing ethical significance to culture. And democracy, indicated by the boxed D, does not fully meet any of the four criteria.

Finally, Figure 5.3 combines both sets of requirements. This figure shows how the two criteria of autonomy and the four criteria of multicultural adequacy would narrow even further the range of possibilities for a political theory that would do everything we want it to do. We do know that none of the perspectives studied in this book falls into the shaded area in Figure 5.3, the class of theories that meet all six of our requirements. What we do not know, however, is whether *any* possible political theory meets these requirements. Our quest is for some theory that does, but our analysis at least raises the possibility that no such theory of political morality exists.

If this proves to be the case, we will have to give up one or more of the requirements we have imposed on the ideal political theory. If such a sacrifice is necessary, it is not at all clear which portion of our ideal is expendable. Would we be satisfied with a political theory that fails to treat human beings equally? Or would it be better to give up our aspiration for a theory that produces mutually acceptable resolutions to multicultural conflict? If we examine them one by one, each of our criteria seems to be essential.

FIGURE 5.3 The Criteria Combined

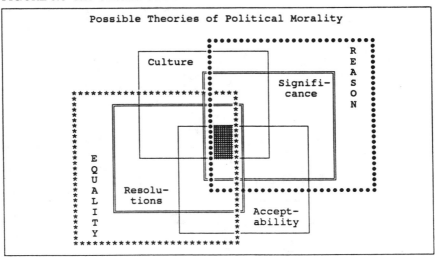

It is clear, then, that the solution to the issues posed by the presence of multiple cultures and languages within a single society will be difficult. At the very least, it will require us to think beyond the political traditions now available in the West. Even worse, it may require a painful sacrifice of one or more of our most prized expectations for an ideal political system.

Several contemporary philosophers have helped to make us acutely aware of the current problems of political morality, especially the difficulties of attempting to reconcile our desires for community and cultural coherence, on the one hand, and for autonomy, on the other. Alasdair MacIntyre (1981), for example, traces the origin of this tension to the inconsistencies between classical and enlightenment intellectual and moral traditions. Richard Rorty (1989) attributes these problems to philosophers' efforts from the time of Plato up to the present to establish an unshakable foundation for science and morality. And Kenneth Strike (1991) explores the difficulties that this tension poses for the moral education of children in schools.

Some other contemporary thinkers have sought ways to relieve or dissolve this tension. In the last chapter, we noted the efforts of John Rawls (1971) and Robert Nisbet (1953) to find a place for communitarian values within the liberal and democratic perspectives. Robert Nozick (1974) is another philosopher who has attempted to create a space for robust communities within the liberal state. And Jürgen Habermas (1987) has attempted to combine democratic and Marxist perspectives to portray the ideal political state as an unconstrained conversation among the members of cultural and other groups within a society. Although it would be inappropriate here to summarize and assess these efforts to deal with the problems we have noted in this book, we can at least recognize that these issues are receiving serious attention today.

One final note on the search for a more adequate theory of political morality is in order. The perspectives we have examined have all been developed in the West; they are the product largely of European and North American intellectual and political traditions. But because multiculturalism is not an issue unique to the West, and given the shortcomings we have found in these perspectives, it would be unwise to limit our search for more adequate ways of thinking about and responding to these problems to those with an exclusively European pedigree. Progress on the problems of multiculturalism may, in other words, demand that we ourselves become more multicultural in our search for alternative moral and political concepts, patterns of reasoning, and modes of action. The moral and religious thought, the systems of social organization, and the lives of important political and cultural leaders from non-Western civilizations may provide important resources in the international enterprise of creating more productive responses to multiculturalism. These resources are not likely to provide ready-made solutions for the problems we seek to overcome; after all, the West is also not unique in its failure to cope with cultural and linguistic differences. But by casting a wider net than we have done in the past, we as members of the international community may improve our collective understanding of, and response to, the issues that arise when cultures collide.

Coping with the Realities of Cultural and Linguistic Difference

The difficulties we have encountered throughout this book in finding permanent and satisfactory resolutions to the problems of multiple cultures and languages in our schools and elsewhere are profound. No single political perspective on its own can meet all of our expectations. And minor or superficial adjustments of those perspectives seem unlikely to overcome the difficulties we have found, in that they seem to originate from the fundamental interpretations that each perspective gives of the ideal of autonomy. The prospect for an immediate corrective for these inadequacies is therefore remote. What, then, should teachers, principals, school board members, parents, and other citizens do about the very real problems of cultural and linguistic difference that arise almost daily in the conduct of our schools' affairs? Is the exercise of naked coercion—civil war, whether open or covert, whether on a large scale or a small one—the only alternative we have in the current circumstances?

Such a pessimistic conclusion is not necessary. For although all the perspectives we have surveyed are imperfect, each is still able to accomplish some of our goals. As a result, it may be possible to choose a perspective to guide our thinking and action in a particular situation where the strengths of the perspective seem intuitively to fit. There are at least two different ways of thinking about how to choose a perspective that is best for a particular situation.

THE NATURE OF THE CONFLICT. The perspectives have different strengths, first of all, because of the way they portray conflicts. Liberalism sees conflict as the result of differences among different individuals' personal aspirations. Communitarians see conflict as arising from the fundamental ways of life and values of identifiable and distinct cultural groups. And democrats see conflict as the consequence of differences of opinion about how the future of the society as a whole ought to be constructed. Thus, we can select a perspective based upon our judgments about the nature of the conflict in a particular situation.

Let us recall the conflict, as outlined in Chapter 2, between Reverend Creasey and the school board over the proposed change in the school curriculum in the town of Hardy. At least within that school district, Reverend Creasey represents a very small minority. Thus, it seems intuitively right to see this dispute as a conflict between the Reverend's personal aspirations for his children and those of the other citizens of the town, rather than as a collision between two large cultural groups. Therefore, of the three perspectives, liberalism may fit this situation best. Moreover, liberalism, with its emphasis on individual rights, is likely to provide stronger support to Reverend Creasey's position than either democracy or communitarianism would.

By contrast, the conflict at Big Cypress, as described in Chapter 4, seems intuitively to involve large-scale differences between the traditions of distinct cultural groups. Mr. Billie's proposal for the elementary school program appeals to a traditional way of life shared by a significant proportion of the families in Big Cypress, a way of life that is dramatically different from that experienced in the mainstream U.S. culture. In situations of this type, communitarianism seems likely to represent the real nature of the conflict more adequately than either of the other two perspectives. For here the conflict seems clearly to involve more than mere individual differences or the opposition between political factions.

Chapter 3 presented a disagreement over a proposed Spanish-language alternative program in San Pablo. This problem here is not just a matter of a dispute between individuals; after all, substantial groups of citizens are involved on both sides. Even though there are clear cultural elements in the conflict, it is not obvious that there are wide gulfs in fundamental beliefs and ways of life between the supporters and opponents of the alternative program. This dispute has a more traditionally political character, in which the opinions of one faction are in conflict with those of another. Therefore, the democratic perspective seems most appropriate to situations of this sort.

In sum, our intuitions about the basic nature of the conflict in particular situations can be one guide to selecting a perspective according to which we may analyze and act. When confronting a case of multicultural conflict, like those reported in the final chapter of this book, the thoughtful and concerned professional can ask, first, exactly what kind of conflict seems to be present. The simple fact that cultural differences are present in a conflict does not necessarily mean that the conflict is best understood as fundamentally cultural. Is the conflict, perhaps, primarily among individuals and their personal visions of the good life? Or is it really between various political factions that see the future of the society in different ways? Or is it, after all, between the members of different cultures whose traditions and fundamental beliefs are so disparate that we can reasonably conclude that they live in significantly different worlds? How these questions are answered in concrete situations can suggest the most appropriate moral perspective to apply to them.

THE MOST DESIRABLE OUTCOME.   The four criteria for multicultural adequacy each specify a desirable consequence of how a perspective on political morality treats conflicts between culturally and linguistically different groups. In general and in the abstract, all four of these criteria are important. But in particular situations, our intuitions may tell us that some of these outcomes are more important than others. As our analysis has shown, the three perspectives have varying abilities to meet these criteria. Hence, our judgments about which outcome is most desirable in a particular situation may indicate which perspective we should use in thinking about that situation.

Combined, the first two criteria permit us to appreciate the cultures that are in conflict. If a perspective on political morality has an adequate conception of culture, it enables us to see, first, how the beliefs and practices of the parties are attached to existing human relationships that help to define their identities, and, second, that those relationships are not entirely objects of individual choice, but are given to the parties by the historical and social circumstances in which they find themselves. If a perspective assigns ethical significance to culture, it enables us to recognize that culturally based beliefs and practices demand a degree of respect from those who do not happen to share them. Together, these two criteria can help us to understand and value—in other words, to *appreciate*—the profound importance that cultures have in the lives of the parties to a conflict. As we have found, communitarianism and, to a lesser extent, democracy are able to satisfy these two criteria better than liberalism is.

The last two criteria permit us to settle disputes between the members of different cultures. If a perspective on political morality is able to generate resolutions of conflicts, it enables us to determine a definite course of action for which there is clear moral justification. If such a perspective produces resolutions that are acceptable to the parties in conflict, it enables us to provide reasons for the course of action that the parties themselves can understand and live with. Combined, these two criteria allow us to bring a reasonable conclusion to—in other words, to *settle*—a conflict between the members of different cultural groups. Although none of the perspectives we have considered is entirely successful in this regard, liberalism and, somewhat less satisfactorily, democracy meet these criteria better than communitarianism does.

When faced with a concrete situation of cultural or linguistic difference, the thoughtful professional can, in light of this analysis, ask a second question: Is it more important in this case to promote an appreciation of the cultural nature of the conflict or to find a reasoned settlement of it? Here, too, our judgments about the most appropriate answer to this question can help us decide which perspective to use in thinking about and acting upon particular instances of cultural conflict.

To see how this question might be answered, let us consider once more the conflict at Big Cypress described in Chapter 4. In this situation, there are specific decisions that need to be made: whether the Seminole Tribe will take charge of the Big Cypress day school, whether the school's program will be extended to the eighth grade, whether the proposed native language and culture curriculum will be instituted, and whether dissatisfied families will be allowed to send their children to another school. At the same time, the culture and language of the Big Cypress Seminoles have been the object of longstanding denigration and neglect from white society. In fact, there is little recognition among Florida's white population that the Big Cypress Seminoles possess a robust culture; instead, whites tend to view Big Cypress residents as primitive and backward, not possessed of a real culture at all. Is it more important in this situation to make the necessary decisions in a reasoned and justifiable way, or to foster an enhanced appreciation of the culture and language of the Big Cypress Seminoles?

Here it seems that a recognition of the Seminole cultural heritage and an acknowledgement that this conflict is between Seminole and white cultures are of more immediate importance than a reasoned settlement. Intuitively, the moral wrong of continuing to deny cultural status to the beliefs and practices of the Big Cypress Seminoles seems graver than denying them a clear and consistent basis for making decisions in this particular dispute. And, to be pragmatic, civil war is not a probable outcome in these circumstances. As a result, the communitarian perspective seems more appropriate to this situation than either democracy or liberalism.

Using this perspective implies, as we have seen, that whatever decisions are made are likely to be ad hoc and to some extent unjustified. There is, in fact, no reason to suppose that such decisions will be fully supportive of the position that the Seminole Tribe has taken. Many, if not all, of the parties to the dispute are likely to be dissatisfied with those decisions and the reasons that are given for them. Nevertheless, encouraging the public discussion to be conducted in communitarian terms will promote a respect for Seminole culture as morally legitimate; such a recognition is not possible to derive from the liberal view that Seminoles are simply individuals with unusual personal visions of the good, or from the democratic view that they are a minority political faction.

Despite the difficulties with the available perspectives on political morality, then, it may still be possible to use them as resources for thinking about and acting upon concrete cases of cultural conflict over education. Depending upon whether we judge the conflict to be between individuals, cultural groups, or political factions, or whether we find the appreciation of culture or the reasoned settlement of a particular dispute to be of greater immediate importance, we may be able to select one of these perspectives over the others as more appropriate to the problem we face. Of course, this is not a completely satisfactory result. We do need to work collectively to evolve more adequate theories of political morality than we now have. In the meantime, however, our efforts to make pragmatic use of our current political and intellectual resources offer an alternative to the deployment of naked coercive force that has all too often characterized our responses to cultural and linguistic conflict in the past.

REFERENCES AND FURTHER READING

Ackerman, B. (1980). *Social justice in the liberal state*. New Haven: Yale University Press.

See references for Chapter 2.

Arrow, K. J. (1963). *Social choice and individual values* (2nd ed.). New Haven: Yale University Press.

A classic demonstration that no social decision procedure or rule can meet five reasonable conditions, including the requirements that the decisions reached must reflect the preferences of society's members and that no individual society member should be allowed to be a dictator.

Habermas, J. (1987). *The philosophical discourse of modernity* (F. Lawrence, Trans.). Cambridge, MA: M.I.T. Press.

A complex analysis of modern European philosophy, in which the author advances a conception of political morality based upon full and free communication.

MacIntyre, A. (1981). *After virtue*. Notre Dame, IN: University of Notre Dame Press.

> A wide-ranging and challenging history of, and reflection upon, the evolution of European conceptions of morality; argues that modern liberalism and individualism are incoherent, and that an ethics of virtue based on Aristotle's philosophy is preferable.

Nisbet, R. (1953). *The quest for community*. New York: Oxford University Press.

> See references for Chapter 4.

Nozick, R. (1974). *Anarchy, state, and utopia*. New York: Basic Books.

> A liberal argument for a minimal state that operates as a political framework in which alternative communities flourish by competing for the allegiance of citizens.

Rawls, J. (1971). *A theory of justice*. Cambridge, MA: Harvard University Press.

> See references for Chapters 2 and 4.

Strike, K. (1991). The moral role of schooling. In G. Grant (Ed.), *Review of research in education* (Vol. 17, pp. 413–483). Washington, DC: American Educational Research Association.

> A comprehensive review of the recent literature on the political and moral function of schools from liberal, democratic, and communitarian perspectives; exposes some of the contradictory expectations that modern society places upon the moral education of the young.

CHAPTER 6

Using and Analyzing Cases

The purpose of this book is to reveal the ethical dimensions of educational issues in societies that embrace many different cultures and languages and to explore some of the intellectual resources available for coping with those issues. As has been clear from the beginning, we have not sought to propose any comprehensive solution to those issues. Instead, we have attempted to stimulate the reader's sensitivity to, and thinking about, educational issues.

The seven cases included in the following chapter present more challenges to the reader's thought. Each of these cases introduces new situations, ethnic groups, and issues that demand perceptiveness, knowledge, and reflection. They, like the other cases in this book, are intended to illustrate the range of cultural and linguistic differences in this society, not to provide an exhaustive list of all the groups or issues, and certainly not to convey general or stereotyped representations of the groups with which they deal. There are many cultural groups not included in these cases that deserve the careful attention of the student of education. And many members of the cultural and linguistic groups included have different experiences and viewpoints from those of the characters in these cases.

The number of different uses to which these cases might be put is limitless. But to focus the imagination of readers and instructors, we will make a variety of suggestions about the purposes they might fulfill, the questions that might be asked about them, and the activities in which they might be used. Finally, we will provide a brief sample analysis of one of the cases that might be used as a model for the reader's reflection, discussion, or writing.

PURPOSES FOR USING THE CASES

In approaching each of these cases, there are at least three goals that the reader might keep in mind. The first is to *understand* the people who are included in the case; the beliefs, especially about education, that they hold; the positions they take on the specific educational issues they confront; and the meaning and importance that those issues have in their lives. The second goal is to *apply* the three perspectives on political morality to the situation; to see how the basic concepts and values of each perspective are represented in the case; and to determine whether, and how, each perspective's principles would resolve the issues presented there. A third goal is to *evaluate* the resolutions proposed by the perspectives, to determine which perspective seems to work best and why, and to consider whether other ways of approaching the issue might be more fruitful.

Of course, not all of these purposes will be appropriate for all readers at all times. If, for example, the reader is attempting to learn about the democratic perspective, it may be most important to focus on the application of that perspective to one or more of the cases.

QUESTIONS FOR REFLECTION AND DISCUSSION

In the effort to reach these goals, it is useful to consider questions that focus on particular dimensions of each goal. Below, we list a variety of questions, organized around each of the three goals, that are intended to help the reader think more deeply and precisely about various aspects of each case. We should note that this list is long and perhaps a bit overwhelming. As a result, we do not recommend that every reader answer every question. Instead, the questions should be selected to meet the needs of each reader. If one is most concerned with learning about the beliefs, values, and attitudes of one of the cultural groups represented in the case, for instance, one should focus on questions included in the first category. Even here, not all of the questions may be appropriate to every case. We should also note that none of these questions is easy; they all require careful thought and may have more than one equally plausible answer. Therefore, it is important to entertain alternative answers and to examine what justification can be offered for any particular answer, that is, the evidence and the logic that support it.

Understanding the Parties and Positions

- What decision or policy is to be made in the case?
- What basic values concerning children's lives and their own lives do the various parties in the case hold?
- What experiences have the parties had that lead them to hold these values?
- What do the parties understand the purposes of education to be, and how is this understanding related to their basic values?
- What position on the decision or policy do the parties take—about who should make the decision or what it should be, and how is that

position justified by their basic values and understanding of education?

- What do the parties think about others' positions, and why do they reject those positions?

Applying the Perspectives

LIBERALISM

- Which individuals have interests that are affected by the decision or policy?
- What effects would the decision or policy have on these individuals' interests?
- Would the decision affect some individuals' right to a liberal education, an education that enables them to become their own persons?
- Would the decision affect some individuals' basic liberties, their freedoms of conscience, of expression, of association, or of the person?
- Would the decision affect some individuals' opportunities to acquire the knowledge or skill necessary to pursue their vision of the good life?
- Would the decision affect some individuals' opportunity to be employed in positions to which they aspire?
- Would the decision affect some individuals' access to a fair share of the society's material resources?
- Of the individual interests affected, which are more basic or important from the liberal perspective?
- What decision or policy should be made according to liberalism's principle of equal advantage, that the parties to the dispute are to be neither relatively advantaged nor disadvantaged in their pursuit of the good life as they see it?

DEMOCRACY

- Which political groups or factions have opinions about the policy or decision to be made?
- Would the decision affect the fairness of the society's political processes?
- Would the decision affect some individuals' right to a basic political education, an education that would enable them to participate fully in the processes of democratic decision making?
- Would the decision affect some citizens' basic political rights, their freedoms of opinion, political association, or voting their conscience?

- Would the decision limit some citizens' access to information relevant to political decisions, or their opportunities to deliberate about those decisions?
- In which political jurisdiction should the decision be made? Why?
- What is the opinion of the majority of citizens in that jurisdiction?
- Do the decisions of the majority create opportunities for societal education or employment to which citizens deserve equal access?
- What decision or policy should be made according to democracy's principle of pure procedural justice, that any decision made according to a fully fair decision-making process is morally binding upon all citizens?

COMMUNITARIANISM

- Which distinct communities are affected by the decision or policy?
- Is each of these communities morally legitimate?
- Does each community have a conception of the good for its members that demonstrates a roughly equal concern for the well-being of all, or are there some community members whose welfare is clearly secondary to that of others?
- Does each community have a system for interpreting the community's traditions reflectively, a system that enables it to overcome inadequacies or conflicts in those traditions?
- What decision or policy should be made according to communitarianism's principle of deliberative interpretation, that the alternative chosen should most fully advance the traditional purposes of the morally legitimate community?
- Which decision or policy do the traditions of each community say is correct?
- To which communities do the parties belong, and which decision should they accept?

Evaluating the Outcomes

- Which of the perspectives' resolutions best reflects the cultures of the parties, gives culture a significant ethical priority, produces definite guidance for action, and will be easiest for the parties to accept?
- Do the differences between the parties in this case seem most to reflect different individual interests, different opinions of political factions, or different beliefs and practices of distinct cultural groups?
- Is it more important in this case to promote the mutual apprecia-

tion of cultures, as communitarianism and, to a lesser extent, democracy do?

- Is it more important in this case to reach a definite and reasoned resolution, as liberalism and, to a lesser extent, democracy do?
- All things considered, does any one of the perspectives' proposed resolutions seem clearly better than the others?
- Are there any moral principles not included in the perspectives that produce an alternative course of action in the case that seems better than those suggested by the perspectives, and if so, why is it better?

ACTIVITIES INVOLVING THE CASES

These cases can be used to promote individual thinking or collaborative work. Because of their complexity, these cases often invite more than one interpretation, and their analysis therefore frequently benefits from interactive discussion and group work. We will suggest a few individual and group activities that we have found helpful in our own experience.

Individual Activities

GUIDED REFLECTION. Readers can, either on their own or at the request of an instructor, use the appropriate questions from the previous section to stimulate their understanding of the case itself or the perspectives they are learning about. It may also be helpful to talk with someone else while attempting to answer the questions—a friend, a classmate, or a family member. It is often valuable to provide a chance to share these reflections in class.

GUIDED INFORMAL RESPONSE. Readers simply write out their guided reflections on appropriate questions, perhaps in a journal kept for the class or in short papers to be shared with the instructor or other members of the class.

FREE RESPONSE. Readers write spontaneously in class about a case that they have just read. These responses are often best used to help readers clarify their thinking for subsequent class discussion.

Group Activities

SMALL GROUP ROLE PLAYS. After the class is divided into an appropriate number of small groups, each member of each group takes the role of one of the parties in the case. They articulate and explain the positions they hold on the central issues in the case. Obviously, this activity is designed to promote readers' understanding of the parties and the positions in the case.

STRUCTURED SMALL GROUP DISCUSSION.   Small groups of class members answer an appropriate set of questions drawn or adapted from those suggested in the previous section. Depending on the questions selected, this activity can be used to develop understanding, application, or evaluation skills. It is often most effective for representatives of the groups to report their conclusions to the entire class. Sometimes structured discussion can also be used to initiate some more formal group activity, such as a presentation based on the case.

CLASSROOM DEBATES.   Teams of readers can engage in a debate before the entire class over the way in which a case should be resolved. If each team represents a different party in the case, the debate can help promote understanding of the parties and their positions. If each team represents a different perspective on political morality, the debate can foster skills in applying the perspectives to the case. Finally, if teams simply develop and defend what seems to be the best resolution to the case, they will develop skills of evaluating outcomes. A consideration of the questions outlined previously can help teams develop their arguments and ideas for these assignments.

Individual or Group Activities

ESSAYS OR PRESENTATIONS.   Cases can provide an opportunity for readers to demonstrate, in formal papers or class presentations, their learning about the ethics of multicultural and bilingual education. These products may be focused on understanding, application, or evaluation, and the questions suggested above can therefore be adapted as stimulus materials for these formal projects.

RESEARCH PAPERS.   Readers can investigate and write about the ethnic and language groups discussed in a case or the educational issues that the case raises. The references for the various chapters and cases can provide a starting place for library research, and interviews with members of various ethnic communities or educators can often provide new insights and ideas.

DEVELOPING NEW CASES.   Probably the most difficult and rewarding way to develop an understanding of cultural groups is to develop one's own case of cultural conflict over an educational issue. Although library research is a good starting place for developing new cases, it is usually crucial to check one's perceptions through interviews and discussions with members of the communities about which one is writing.

CHOOSING A PRINCIPAL
A Sample Analysis of a Case

As we have seen throughout this book, dealing intelligently and sensitively with the ethical issues that education in a multicultural situation may present is a demanding task. Let us consider another such case and then attempt briefly to understand the issues, apply the perspectives, and evaluate the alternatives. This analysis is not by any means complete; rather, it is intended to illustrate some of the approaches we recommend and the difficulties to which they may lead.

Mrs. Shimada is one of five members of a search committee that is screening and interviewing applicants for a principal's position at one of the newly designed middle school programs in Honolulu. The number of candidates has been whittled down to two top contenders. Two of the five committee members voted for Mrs. Shields. The other two, however, preferred Mr. Fukuyama. It is now up to Mrs. Shimada to break the tie. She has asked for a day or two to think the matter over carefully.

As a *sansei,* or third-generation American of Japanese ancestry, Mrs. Shimada was reminded by her close friends that, with due respect to Mrs. Shields, she was nevertheless expected to favor one of their own. The Japanese Americans of Hawaii have secured a strong foothold in all areas of the social, political, and business world today, but this was not always the case. Their success was achieved by surmounting hardships and discrimination during their very early years on plantations. The rise of Japanese Americans to prominence was not only hard earned but attributable, in their minds, to an enviable loyalty to Japanese values and to the tradition of group solidarity.

Mrs. Shimada pulled the applicants' folders from her desk. Both candidates met the minimum requirements, although Mrs. Shields has had three more years of experience as an administrator than her competitor. Both candidates' commitment and enthusiasm were evident to the committee. In addition to their credentials, both Mrs. Shields and Mr. Fukuyama come highly recommended by their peers and previous supervisors as popular and effective administrators. Mrs. Shimada, who was impressed with the candidates' dossiers and their interviews, has grown uncomfortable at having to choose one over the other. She remembers her own experiences in applying for various jobs over the years. How did she manage her own steady and progressive rise to her present position as assistant superintendent of the state's public educational system?

Mrs. Shimada had started out with five years of classroom teaching in the first grade, and an additional four years of teaching with fourth graders. During these years, she got married, had two children, and earned a master's degree. She taught for two more years after receiving her advanced degree before being selected for the position of resource specialist in one of Oahu's four school districts.

The resource specialist's job was difficult to secure because there were few such positions available, and many experienced teachers who were interested in, and qualified for, those positions. She was fortunate to be helped by friends, and friends of friends. The network of contacts, primarily with other Japanese Americans in Hawaii, was useful in getting information about a job soon after it was available within the Department of Education. Furthermore, these contacts helped her find out about the particulars of these positions and to make the appropriate connections. This informal assistance was to be expected since Japanese Americans were found at every level of the state's school system. At a crucial time in the state's development, the teaching profession provided an opportunity for Japanese Americans to gain economic and social mobility. Finding a niche in a service-oriented governmental agency such as education was so compatible with their traditional values that the number of Americans of Japanese ancestry employed in the state's education system grew rapidly. Today, they dominate the field despite the fact that they are less than one-fourth of the state population. In 1983, 60% of Hawaii's 9,000 teachers were Japanese Americans (Oda, 1983). In the past ten years, the Department of Education has been criticized for this enormous overrepresentation of Japanese American personnel in the system. The ethnic imbalance has been more difficult to correct than the underrepresentation of women administrators in a system where the teaching faculty are overwhelmingly women. In 1982, 73% of the administrators were male, although 74% of the teachers were female (Verploegen, 1983). At the time of her appointment as assistant state superintendent, Mrs. Shimada was one of the few women occupying a top leadership position.

Mrs. Shimada remembers that she once believed she could not come close to realizing her ambition to become the state's school superintendent. With two growing children, and a husband who needed his wife to be actively involved in the many social activities he was expected to attend as a junior executive on his way up, she put her own career goal on hold. In the Japanese culture, a good wife is expected to place her husband's career ahead of her own. An unexpected event, however, changed her life. Her husband died in a plane crash. Partly to keep herself busy and distracted from the tragic and sudden personal loss, she enrolled in a doctoral program. After attending two semesters of classes in Hawaii, she decided to continue and finish her program at a mainland university. Leaving her two children with their grandparents, and encouraged by friends and other relatives, she put all her energies into completing the doctoral program as early as she possibly could. With two sets of grandparents, aunts, and uncles, she knew her children were in good hands. Still, as a mother, she knew she was expected to be with her children. This often left her anxiously wondering about what her friends might say even if they were not saying it aloud. During the three years needed to finish her degree, she maintained contact with her large circle of family and friends by telephone and letter. They repeatedly assured her that her success would be worth the sacrifice because, after she finished, they could all share in her honor as well.

Recalling those years brought many memories to Mrs. Shimada, particularly of the periodic stresses that accompanied her graduate study. Could she really have attained her goals through her individual efforts alone? Circumstance and strong family and community support combined to help her achieve her goal. To this day, she feels indebted to all who helped her. Always, those who helped the most would simply say, "Help your people in return." Her friends and family encouraged her when she felt discouraged. They would remind her that the Japanese spirit is like that of the carp—strong, gracious, and persevering. Besides, she was constantly reminded to look beyond her own plans and realize that in attaining the highest degree in her profession, she would be able, in turn, to assist others who would come after her.

Remembering this, Mrs. Shimada realized that her whole life was a continuous series of well-orchestrated exchanges of assistance, and the giving and receiving of favors. From a very early age, she was taught to be dutiful and to reciprocate graciously at all times. The maintenance and manipulation of social relationships was not just accepted, it was cultivated. This way of acting paid off. After all, group cohesiveness and ethnic solidarity were two powerful factors in the collective success of the Japanese Americans in Hawaii. Her family's story was told over and over to the children and grandchildren so that the next generation would not forget.

Mrs. Shimada's fraternal grandfather came to Hawaii ten years after the 1885 contract between the Japanese Government and the planters of Hawaii to provide the island with labor for the sugar plantations. Her grandmother, who followed seven years later, was a "picture bride." As the Japanese men who came as laborers became farmers, many sent for their wives or ordered brides by mail.

The selection of a bride was arranged by family members in Japan with the use of a go-between, who matched couples on the basis of *ken,* or prefecture of residence, and suitability and similarity of family background (Takaki,

1989). The betrothed then joined the bridegroom after satisfactory arrangements were completed. Both parties prior to meeting one another would know little more about the other's attributes than what photographs revealed. Her grandfather had originally intended to return to Japan after fulfilling his contract and had talked often about it. After the birth of their fifth child, however, the couple, like many of their contemporaries with growing families, thought less and less of going home. Instead, they concentrated their efforts on succeeding in their adopted land.

Hawaii's Japanese Americans initially established themselves as farmers. To obtain land, they used different approaches. As contractors, some farmed others' land and received payment after the harvest. Others shared farm land and got a percentage of the crop's profit. Still others farmed leased or rented land. The goal of these Japanese Americans was eventually to own some land themselves. Alone, each person had limited opportunities to advance economically. But collectively, with the spirit of entrepreneurship and family and racial pride, they strengthened their resolve to succeed in a foreign land. And succeed they did. By 1930, 74% of the state's farmers were of Japanese ancestry. At that time, they also operated 49% of the retail stores in Hawaii (Lind, 1946).

For the Japanese immigrants, the decision to stay in Hawaii was a momentous turning point. It meant making a substantial commitment to another way of life. To fulfill their needs to preserve some of the Japanese traditional values, as well as to participate fully in a cultural environment that differed from their own, the Japanese established language schools. Offered after the regular school day and on Saturdays, these schools provided an opportunity for teaching the basic ideals of the Japanese culture (Okahata, 1971).

The Japanese schools were closed down during World War II, and when they resumed, many had lost their following. Succeeding generations of Japanese Americans felt less pressure to speak Japanese. Mrs. Shimada knows about these schools only from her parents' stories. She does recall the many times when her grandparents fervently instilled in her the importance of loyalty to the family and close relations for promoting harmony, unity, and cooperation.

Mrs. Shimada's mother's parents, unlike her father's parents, met and grew up as neighbors in one of the plantation camps. Although different ethnic groups in the plantation camps mingled at work and celebrated social events together, each ethnic group generally remained clannish. Mrs. Shimada's mother's parents were a young married couple when the Japanese Exclusion Act of 1924 was passed. Not only was there resentment toward the Japanese then, but there was also the antagonism and hostility initially directed at the Chinese (who preceded them in this country) but that the

Japanese inherited. Within this context of ethnic discrimination, the Japanese developed group reliance and shared group identity. For the Japanese, it was unthinkable to consider marriage to a non-Japanese during those years. Opportunities for the young to meet one another were provided. One of these occasions was the annual *ken* club picnic.

Coming from different prefectures in Japan, the first Japanese immigrants formed clubs that identified their particular places of origin. Every year, members of the *ken* club gather for a family picnic. This usually is an all day social event at which families from the prefecture mingle. Sitting on gaza mats under huge tropical shade trees, these events serve as opportunities for reaffirming Japanese ethnic solidarity. These reunions bring everyone together under pleasant and festive circumstances to renew and encourage camaraderie. Children play while the adults visit.

As members of the *ken* club, Mrs. Shimada's parents took her and the rest of her family to many picnics in the city park when she was young and, even throughout most of her teens. She has seen changes over the last generation at these gatherings. She vaguely remembers that previously families were grouped strictly according to their prefectures in Japan; today, however, there is less consciousness of families' places of origin. Now even non-Japanese friends are welcome to enjoy this favorite event.

Mrs. Shimada very rarely attends these picnics anymore. She had used every excuse possible to miss these events while she was in college. She started attending the picnics again when her two children were very young, partly from an occasional pang of guilt that she might fail to give them a sense of community with other Japanese Americans. Mrs. Shimada was pleased at that time that the groups welcomed others without regard for their belonging to a given prefecture, and even without regard for their ethnicity. Due to the intermarriage among the members of different *ken* clubs and between the Japanese and other ethnic groups, there is less demand for adherence to the old distinctions. Mrs. Shimada wanted to encourage her children to accept and enjoy the greater ethnic and cultural mix of their generation. Not only did Mrs. Shimada, like her mother, welcome the social interactions among different ethnic groups, she actively encouraged it.

As a third-generation Japanese American, Mrs. Shimada has grown to accept ethnic diversity in Hawaii; she is not as sensitive as her parents about having to establish her ethnic identity. Her recent experiences on the job have made her receptive to the interplay that this diversity has brought to the workplace. She has to admit, however, that her sense of security was founded on knowing, respecting, and understanding her roots. Her grandparents made it clear that she belonged to a group that mattered and cared. Her own parents, especially her mother, were more relaxed about the rules of the group.

Mrs. Shimada's grandfather had strong feelings about his daughter's wish to become a doctor. It just was not right for women, he would say. Furthermore, he believed his daughter, as a Japanese, would face insurmountable discrimination and hardships. He suggested nursing. Nursing and teaching were two professions *nisei* (second-generation Japanese American) women were encouraged to pursue. Although her mother believes to this day that he was mistaken, she harbors no resentment toward her father. She believes that he misjudged her ability to persevere and succeed against the odds. At the time, she did not even discuss the matter with her father. She would not contradict, much less argue with, her parents, even on an important decision affecting her future. However, she quietly made up her mind that her own children would be allowed to choose their careers.

Mrs. Shimada's mother wholeheartedly believed that one should aspire to the highest position and succeed. Success, or *seiko,* would be achieved through education. As Yori Wada has said, "We *nisei* were told over and over about the importance of school and education—how knowledge in one's mind could never be taken away and that learning could be the ladder toward success and security and equality" (Takaki, 1989, p. 217).

The *issei,* or immigrants who decided to stay, were determined that the *nisei* would become highly educated citizens. They were to become the *kakehashi,* or bridge, between the Japanese community and the larger American society. By 1940, approximately 65% of Americans of Japanese ancestry had, at the age of 25, completed eight or more years of schooling, compared with only 30% of the entire population of the Territory (Lind, 1946). Education was and continues to be of great importance to Japanese Americans.

So determined and so successful are Americans of Japanese ancestry that today they are considered by many to be a "model minority." They survived the animosities caused by World War II and grew beyond the unskilled status of farm laborers to become powerful contributors to the political and social life of Hawaii. The agreement from one generation to the next has been the promotion of group cohesion. Whenever and wherever possible, loyalty to group members would reaffirm ethnic solidarity. Mrs. Shimada never questioned this perspective—until recently. In the last few years, the voices of concern in the state have grown louder, raising questions about equal access for all ethnic groups to the jobs in the public sector in which Japanese Americans are now predominant. Lately, she has begun to wonder if preferential treatment, as others have called it, needs reexamination, although some of her most trusted friends find it just and even admirable. The case before her today is just another instance of a kind of decision that she finds increasingly difficult to make. The problem nags at her sense of fairness. She feels a strong need to support one of her own, but must it be at the expense of another qualified individual? The most obvious difference between the two candidates lies in their gender and ethnicity. On what basis should Mrs. Shimada make her decision?

Understanding the Issues

Mrs. Shimada's thinking in this situation is informed by a number of different values. She clearly has made a commitment to seeking a highly qualified principal, someone whose education and past experience makes him or her likely to perform well in this position. The value that Mrs. Shimada places on professional competence stems in part from her own upbringing, the emphasis that her parents and grandparents placed on educational and career achievement. It also comes from the institution in which she works, the state's public school system. Such civil service systems are publicly predicated on the idea that jobs should be allocated on the basis of what one knows rather than who one knows. The difficulty here is that Mrs. Shimada's commitment to competence does not tell her whether she should choose Mrs. Shields or Mr. Fukuyama. Both have excellent records. And while it may be possible to find differences in the candidates' experience and skills, those differences do not seem to rank one conclusively superior to the other. Mrs. Shimada is forced to consider other factors in making her decision.

One such factor is the loyalty that she feels to other members of the Japanese American community in the state. That loyalty has been partly responsible for the general success that Japanese Americans have had in overcoming a history of economic disadvantage and social discrimination. Such loyalty has also worked specifically to Mrs. Shimada's own advantage. The family and community support she received enabled her to complete her education. The advice and assistance she has obtained from other Japanese Americans throughout her career have helped her to attain her current position. As a result, Mrs. Shimada feels that she owes a debt to other members of her ethnic community, a debt that implies that she should choose Mr. Fukuyama.

But Mrs. Shimada's reflections and experiences lead her to have certain doubts about this implication of her ethnic affiliation. Unswerving group loyalty was perhaps a necessity for survival and success in an era when Japanese Americans experienced overt discrimination. Now that such discrimination has been significantly overcome, wouldn't a preference for Mr. Fukuyama represent the same type of ethnic bias that Japanese Americans have struggled against? Mrs. Shimada has come to appreciate cultural diversity in her work and personal life. She has also experienced the difficulty that women in the United States face in their efforts to attain the most responsible and respected positions based on their own merits. These considerations suggest that Mrs. Shimada has a responsibility to promote ethnic and gender diversity in her profession, a responsibility that implies a preference for Mrs. Shields, despite the obligations she feels to her own ethnic group.

Applying the Perspectives

LIBERALISM. This perspective emphasizes the interests that individuals have in their efforts to live according to their own conceptions of the good. It identifies a number of interests as crucial to that effort—liberal education, basic liberty, equal educational opportunity, equal employment opportunity, and material welfare. As a result, we need to consider the possible effect of Mrs. Shimada's decision on those interests in the order of priority that liberalism assigns to them.

We do not know enough about the approach to the education of children that Mr. Fukuyama or Mrs. Shields would take to tell whether one of them would be more likely than the other to promote a liberal education in the school at which they would be principal. From the liberal perspective, then, Mrs. Shimada should further investigate the candidates' specific educational plans and priorities before she makes her decision. In the absence of such an investigation, however, there is no way of determining which candidate should be preferred in the interests of liberal education.

Similarly, basic liberty does not seem to be an issue in this case. All three parties—Mrs. Shimada, Mr. Fukuyama, and Mrs. Shields—are agents of the government, and the decision to be made here concerns how the power of the government should be used to affect people's lives. Thus, Mrs. Shimada's freedom to live her personal life as she sees fit does not give her the right to ignore the interests of the two candidates in this case. Nor do Mr. Fukuyama's or Mrs. Shields' basic liberties of conscience, expression, or association give either one a right to the job.

From the liberal perspective, this decision is best understood as giving one of the candidates the opportunity to realize his or her own aspirations. It is an opportunity not to acquire new skills or knowledge but to exercise abilities that have already been acquired. In other words, this case concerns the candidates' employment opportunities, and Mrs. Shimada should use the principle of equal economic opportunity in making her decision. That principle states that economic opportunities should be allocated to those whose potential productivity on the job is the greatest.

The problem in this case is that from everything Mrs. Shimada has seen, the two candidates are equally promising as potential principals. Given this fact, many liberals would simply say that either candidate is acceptable and that Mrs. Shimada would be ethically justified no matter what choice she makes. Other liberals, however, would argue for a further analysis of the situation. What equal economic opportunity requires, they maintain, is not just that any particular job decision be fair, but that the opportunities that each person experiences across his or her lifetime be equal. Thus, if a person has experienced unfair discrimination at one point in life, he or she has a right to be compensated for that discrimination by being given a preference for jobs later on. This is often known as the principle of affirmative action.

We do not know the details of either Mr. Fukuyama's or Mrs. Shields' employment history, but we do know certain general facts that can help us apply the principle of affirmative action to this case. We know, for example, that despite the fact that the vast majority of teachers are women, most of the principals in the system are men. We also have no reason to believe that men are inherently better principals than women are. Together, these facts suggest that in general women have suffered unfair discouragement or discrimination in their efforts to realize their aspirations to be administrators, which Mrs. Shimada's own experience confirms. We also know that Japanese Americans are heavily overrepresented in the school system, both as teachers and principals. The network of contacts and support that Mrs. Shimada experienced seems to be at least partly responsible for this situation. A case can be made, therefore, that Mrs. Shields, like other Caucasian women, has been disadvantaged by her gender and ethnicity in the past. And the principle of affirmative action thus implies that she should be preferred for this particular job.

But we are still missing a great deal of the information necessary to make this conclusion certain. Are the underrepresentation of women and the overrepresentation of Japanese Americans the result of individuals' preferences and hard work rather than unfair discrimination? Has the principle of affirmative action already worked to Mrs. Shields's advantage? Is it fair to penalize Mr. Fukuyama for the unfair actions of others? Despite these uncertainties, however, liberalism seems to suggest tentative support for a decision in favor of Mrs. Shields.

DEMOCRACY. This perspective emphasizes the use of fair procedures for making political decisions in a society. It, too, establishes a set of moral priorities to which a procedurally just society must adhere—a basic political education for all, universal rights of political participation, a decision-making process that includes information and deliberation, the application of majority rule, and equal access to the educational and employment opportunities created by majority decisions.

It is not clear that any of the first three democratic values is implicated in this case. We do not know enough about the type of education that either candidate proposes to determine which one is more clearly committed to a basic political education for all students. Nor do we know what type of decision-making process the candidates plan to use within their schools.

Clearly these are matters into which Mrs. Shimada needs to inquire before she makes her decision. But the situation as described gives us no reason to prefer one candidate over the other according to these priorities.

We do have evidence that applies to the last two democratic values, majority rule and equal access. Japanese Americans are in a minority in Hawaii, and Mrs. Shimada has seen clear indications that the state's citizens are dissatisfied with the dominance of Japanese Americans in the state government, including the public educational system. Although we do not have a great deal of information on this subject, it appears that a majority of citizens would prefer a broader representation of cultural values and ideas among public servants than is now the case. The Japanese American hegemony over the educational system, even though it has been achieved by means of the existing decision-making procedures, seems inconsistent in this case with the will of the majority. As a result, those procedures may not be consistent with the requirements of democracy. The rules that give current employees of the system a relatively free hand to choose their colleagues seems to permit the perpetuation of over- and underrepresentation despite the political majority's preference otherwise.

Given this analysis, the solution to this problem is not for Mrs. Shimada to choose one of the candidates, but instead for the system of decision making for education to be reformed to permit greater popular participation in the selection of principals (and perhaps other school employees as well). Hawaii is unique in that its Department of Education and Board of Education, rather than individual school districts, are charged with operating all of the state's schools. This centralized system of decision making may be partly to blame for the schools' apparent lack of responsiveness to the preferences of the majority. This is not the place for a detailed analysis of the best way to change Hawaii's system of decision making, but the current literature on the reform of school governance suggests some of the available alternatives—from popular election of boards for individual schools as in Chicago (Hess, 1991), to school-based management plans like that in Miami (David, 1990), to parental choice programs as in the East Harlem school district in New York City (Chubb & Moe, 1990).

Although reform of the system of decision making is the basic democratic strategy for resolving this case, we should briefly note the implications of a second democratic value in this situation. Democracy is committed to a principle of equal access to employment opportunities. As in liberalism, this principle implies that jobs should be allocated to the most qualified candidates. Even if the system of decision making were decentralized in this case, the decision makers would still need to follow this principle. We should also note that the democratic perspective on equal access is probably less concerned about affirmative action than is the liberal perspective. Liberals favor equal opportunity as a way of being fair to individuals, but democrats' support of this principle is based on the idea that equal opportunity makes more efficient use of a society's resources, which in turn enables the society to carry out the wishes of the majority more completely. From the democratic perspective, compensating victims of past discrimination is not likely to be efficient; therefore, democratic theory is probably less committed to affirmative action than liberal theory is.

COMMUNITARIANISM. The focus of the communitarian perspective is upon maintaining the roles, responsibilities, and relationships established by morally legitimate communities. There seem to be at least two different communities involved in this case. The most obvious is the Japanese American community in which Mrs. Shimada grew up. She has strong ties to this community through her family and through the personal and professional support she has received throughout her career.

But Mrs. Shimada also feels ties to a larger community, the community that has embraced members of many different ethnic groups in Hawaii, that has developed an eclectic set of values drawn from the cultures of those groups, and that actively supports diversity. Although this community is not very clearly defined, Mrs. Shimada has found herself drawn into it in a number of different ways. Her experience of her mother's acceptance of friends from other ethnic groups, Mrs. Shimada's quest for a broad cultural experience for her own children, her quiet rebellion against some of the traditional expectations and practices of the Japanese American community, and her relationships with a wide variety of friends and colleagues in her social and professional lives all reflect her membership in this wider and more diverse community.

Thus, we can understand Mrs. Shimada's dilemma as a conflict that arises from her affiliation with these two different communities. The traditional Japanese American community emphasizes loyalty to other members of the community and leads Mrs. Shimada to feel an obligation to choose Mr. Fukuyama. The wider community emphasizes an appreciation for many cultural and ethnic backgrounds and values diversity. It leads her to accept and perhaps even to prefer the appointment of Mrs. Shields.

Communitarianism attempts to resolve conflicts between communities, first, by assessing whether they are morally legitimate. Both of these communities seem to pass this test. Japanese American traditions in Hawaii stress the obligations that members of that community have to one another. To be sure, those obligations are often demanding, but they are predicated on the equal value that each person has within the scheme of cooperation that exists within the community. Although there may be different roles for men and women, and for older and younger persons, those roles emphasize the responsibilities that community members have for each other's well-being; they do not create a caste of people whose welfare is to be sacrificed for others.

Similarly, the culture of the wider community also seems to respect the value and well-being of all its members, despite their differences in origin or ethnicity. It shows this respect by assimilating a variety of linguistic customs, social events, and cultural practices from Native Hawaiians, Japanese, Chinese, Filipinos, Europeans, and other groups, and by promoting a mutual appreciation of those original cultures. Although there may still be inequities among the various groups included in the wider community, there is a growing sense that those conditions are in need of correction through enhanced respect, educational opportunities, and involvement in government and business.

Both communities appear to meet the requirement of roughly equal concern for all their members, but communitarianism also requires that morally legitimate communities interpret their traditions deliberatively in order to meet new conditions or to overcome inadequacies in those traditions. The larger community seems to meet this requirement; after all, that community is in the process of emerging from a reinterpretation of several older cultures. The Japanese American community seems also to meet this criterion. The practices and values of that community are evolving in a variety of ways as the social conditions surrounding it change. The community's acceptance of Mrs. Shimada's position as assistant state superintendent is only one significant instance of this evolution of values between her grandparents' generation and her own. Thus, communitarianism's commitment to deliberative interpretation of tradition does not justify a finding that either is morally illegitimate.

Since both communities appear to meet the requirements of moral legitimacy, is there any other reason from the communitarian perspective for Mrs. Shimada to give priority to one community's values over the other? One might argue that the larger community is so new that it does not have any real traditions and so fails to be a genuine community at all. However, that community has roots both in the various ethnic traditions that it includes and in the older generations' experiences of, and accommodations to, cultural contact during the nineteenth and early twentieth centuries. In any case, communitarianism does not rank communities according to their age. One might also argue that the Japanese American community in Hawaii is less inclusive than the larger community and thus less worthy of moral recognition. Whether this observation is true or not, communitarianism does not require a community to demonstrate an equal concern for all human beings but only for its own members. A community that fails to respect the moral legitimacy of other communities would be subject to moral censure and constraint from the communitarian perspective, but the modern Japanese American community does not seem to assume that other ethnic communities are inherently illegitimate. At most, it expects those other communities to look out for their own just as it does. Here, too, communitarianism does not rank communities according to their inclusiveness.

From the communitarian perspective, then, both communities' traditions are worthy of respect. And, as a member of these two communities, Mrs. Shimada has an obligation to adhere to both communities' values. When those values lead in conflicting directions, as they do in this case, communitarianism can only reveal and accentuate the dilemma; it cannot resolve it.

Evaluating the Alternatives

In considering which of the perspectives might provide the most appropriate approach to particular conflicts in multicultural societies, there are at least two factors to consider. The first is whether it seems most appropriate to characterize the conflict as one between individual interests, political factions, or cultural groups. Although the individual interests of Mrs. Shields and Mr. Fukuyama are at stake here, those interests do not seem to be the fundamental basis of Mrs. Shimada's problem. Rather, she is pulled in different directions by her association with different groups within her society. Is it more satisfactory to characterize those groups as political or cultural? It is a bit difficult to characterize the larger community in Hawaii as a cultural group; its boundaries are so indeterminate and its membership so diverse that it is easier to see what unites it as a confluence of political opinion than as a sharing of a particular way of life. The Japanese American community has a more definite cultural character, but the speed at which its values are evolving and its increasing inclusion of non-Japanese people through intermarriage and occupational affiliations have begun to give it some of the hallmarks of a political faction rather than a self-contained cultural enclave. Intuitively, then, we might best classify this conflict as more political than individual or cultural.

Next, we need to consider whether it seems more important to achieve a reasoned resolution of this conflict or a mutual appreciation of the cultures of those involved in it. While these are both worthy aims, two elements of this situation may make the appreciation of cultures a less important outcome. First, as we have noted, it is not clear that the ethos of the larger community is actually a culture. Second, it is not clear that those involved in this case lack a basic understanding of the conflicting ideas and traditions. The emergence of the Japanese American community as an important influence in the state's government and economy means that, to some extent at least, the citizens of the state have had the opportunity to become acquainted with the nature of Japanese American culture and experience. And the inclusiveness of the larger community means that many citizens have had the opportunity to participate in and shape its commitments.

When the political nature of the conflict and the need for a reasoned resolution are recognized, the democratic perspective seems more appropriate to this situation than either of the other two approaches to political morality. And the resolution proposed by that perspective—a reform of the educational system's procedures for making decisions—tentatively seems to be preferable. We have not considered whether another perspective on political morality would meet the criteria for adequacy better than this resolution does. We leave that difficult problem as an exercise for the reader. What are the major difficulties with the democratic resolution? What alternatives might correct those difficulties?

REFERENCES

Chubb, J. E., & Moe, T. M. (1990). *Politics, markets, and America's schools.* Washington, DC: Brookings Institution.

David, J. L. (1990). Restructuring in progress: Lessons from pioneering districts. In R. F. Elmore (Ed.), *Restructuring schools* (pp. 209–250). San Francisco: Jossey-Bass.

Hess, G. A., Jr. (1991). *School restructuring, Chicago style.* Newbury Park, CA: Corwin.

Lind, A. (1946). *Hawaii's Japanese: An experiment in democracy.* Princeton, NJ: Princeton University Press.

Oda, L. (1983, February 18). Employment patterns. *The Hawaii Herald,* p. 1.

Okahata, J. (1971). *A history of Japanese in Hawaii.* Honolulu, HI: The United Japanese Society of Hawaii.

Takaki, R. (1989). *Strangers from a different shore: A history of Asian Americans.* New York: Penguin.

Verploegen, H. (1983, May 28). DOE's Chief circulates proposal to bring about ethnic balance. *Honolulu Star Bulletin,* p. A3.

CHAPTER 7

Cases for Reflection and Discussion

BEYOND DESEGREGATION IN TAYLOR CITY

Taylor City, founded by early midwest pioneers, consists of a set of distinctive areas that radiate in concentric semicircles from an industrial center fronting on one of the Great Lakes. Adjoining the industrial center is the old downtown area, surrounded by neighborhoods of sturdy but aging homes originally occupied by immigrant laborers from Eastern Europe. Currently they are almost entirely occupied by African-American families whose parents and grandparents migrated from the South during and after World War II. Railroad tracks and an expressway effectively isolate this area, called Eastside, from Westside, which is an older residential area of quiet streets with larger homes surrounded by trees and grass. Here the occupants are the middle- and upper middle-class grandchildren of the earlier European immigrants and other white Americans whose families have "always" been there.

During the 1970s, restrictive real estate covenants were no longer effective in keeping black middle-class professionals from moving into Westside neighborhoods. Increasingly they are joined by black working-class families. During the 1980s, white Westside residents moved into nearby suburban areas that have been carved out of what was once farmland. A new suburban shopping mall has made it unnecessary for Westside and suburban residents to travel to the now declining downtown area.

For ten years a voluntary busing program, part of a larger desegregation plan, has brought African-American students from crowded Eastside schools to Westside schools where enrollment has declined with the continuous white migration to the suburbs. These children, unlike those of the African-American families who first moved to Westside, are from lower-income, mostly single-parent families. Mandatory and two-way busing were ruled out when it was predicted that these would only accelerate white flight. Because there was no evidence that suburban governmental or educational policy was willfully generated to produce or enhance segregation between school districts, the suburbs never were included in any larger desegregation effort.

The almost all white Westside teaching force, however, remains in Westside schools. These aging faculty members view themselves as professional educators and are proud that they have master's degrees (and a few doctorates) from major universities throughout the Midwest. They are increasingly dismayed by what they view as a decline in the high standards of respect, courtesy, and academic achievement that existed when they began teaching, a decline they believe to be accelerated now by the influx of African-American children from Eastside.

Dr. Jack Brent, a Caucasian in his early forties, is a longtime resident of a neighboring community who earned two of his three degrees from the state university and was recently hired to be superintendent of schools by the Taylor City Board of Education. The Board of Education is composed of six white males, one white female, one African-American male, and one African-American female. Seven of the board members, including the African-American female, are professionals or managers with ties to local business and industry. Dr. Brent is the first Taylor City superintendent of schools with a doctorate in educational administration. His last position was as assistant to the superintendent of schools for a predominantly white school district with a stable, established minority population of middle-class African-Americans and Asian immigrants. Since his days as a university undergraduate, Dr. Brent has been a strong supporter of the civil rights movement and civil rights legislation. His family, relatives, and friends are often ambivalent about his stand.

Dr. Brent knows that he was hired, in part, as one board member told him in private, "to keep a lid on things" and to reassure the faculties of Westside schools that they have his (and the board's) unqualified support for quality education at all levels, including the vocational, business, and college preparatory programs at Westside High School.

Although desegregation laws, integration initiatives, and white guilt have in the past brought children of differing racial, ethnic, and social class backgrounds under the same roof, Dr. Brent believes that additional action is warranted. He is concerned about whether all the children under that one roof are receiving equal protection and equality of educational opportunity through equal exposure to excellent education.

This Saturday morning, Dr. Brent is meeting with Ms. Marie Cross, the principal of Eastside Junior High School, and Mr. Bill Wills, the principal of Eastside Elementary School, the schools from which students are being bused to the Westside. After this meeting, Dr. Brent will meet with the corresponding principals from Westside schools. The principals know the city and their individual schools better than he does. The Board of Education has given him a relatively free hand and expects him to make some recommendations for future policy and planning. First, he must assess the effects of the voluntary busing program and elicit suggestions about how an increasingly integrated Westside system might better benefit the parents, teachers, and children it serves.

Ms. Cross, an African-American in her late forties, is a former social worker and teacher. She has been a principal for fifteen years and is respected and liked by both the parents and the students. She and her husband, a social worker, live in Eastside, where she enjoys informal encounters with students and their parents outside the school. Mr. Wills, also an African-American, is in his middle thirties. He has been a principal for ten years and, like Ms. Cross, is respected and liked by parents and students. He and his wife, an officer in the local education union, live in Westside near other African-American professionals. Both Ms. Cross and Mr. Wills favored the hiring of Dr. Brent and they have looked forward to working with him.

Ms. Cross and Mr. Wills agree that, up to this point, the busing program has had a modest but positive effect on the achievement of the black students and no observable negative impact on the achievement of the white students. Ms. Cross and Mr. Wills are both troubled by the disproportionate number of African-American students at all grade levels who drop out of school and receive disciplinary suspensions. They also find evidence of continued tracking, in-class ability grouping, and limited expectations by Westside teachers for Eastside arrivals. They are aware of Westside teacher claims that the majority of these students come largely unprepared for the more rigorous academic programs. Ms. Cross, in particular, is also acquainted with the many Eastside families whose children have successfully completed the Westside High School program. Although many African-American parents would like to be more involved in their children's education, they often find it difficult to get to meetings at Westside schools.

As the discussion proceeds, Dr. Brent sees two different positions emerging. Mr. Wills's position is that real equal opportunity and social justice will be achieved only if African-Americans attain greater political power than they have had in the past. Then the political system will provide for the equal facilitation of individual goals and provide equal advantage in resolving conflicts. The failure of American society to act with the "deliberate speed" mandated by the U.S. Supreme Court makes it even more imperative for the black community to press for change through the courts and other forms of confrontation.

White people talk about a system open to all where progress depends upon individual effort, but African-Americans still experience the effect of very real structural barriers and white ignorance about black people and their aspirations. The limits of what can be accomplished by the enforcement of law have yet to be reached.

Mr. Wills identifies resegregation in Westside schools as a very real problem and points to what he calls "racially identifiable outcomes" in discipline referrals, suspensions, expulsions, program assignments, and extracurricular activities. It is these outcomes that prevent the majority of African-American students from having effective, stimulating, and enriched learning experiences.

It is not enough, he declares, for most Westside teachers to take pride in their color-blind thinking and their efforts to treat everyone the same. These teachers refuse to see the significant differences between African-American and white children and do not understand that black children's identity as African-Americans is crucial to promoting their development and achievement (Sheeter, 1990, p. 38). The culture of the school is alien to African-American children, and standardized tests are invalid for them because both are grounded in mainstream values (Banks, 1983, pp. 584–585). There is intrinsic value in the home and neighborhood culture that the African-American child brings to school, a value that often goes unrecognized by white middle-class teachers. Westside teachers have failed to use the children's home culture to create relevant learning situations. The obvious conclusion is that African-American children must be taught differently from white children because of their different values, language, and motivational styles.

Mr. Wills emphasizes the need for restructured schools and for faculty development programs that promote a multicultural perspective that shows the strength and value of cultural diversity, promotes respect for cultural differences, and enables teachers to match their teaching styles to students' unique learning styles. He recommends hiring more African-American teachers because they share the cultural background of black children and understand existing structural barriers, and because they can serve as positive role models.

Ms. Cross is not in total agreement with Mr. Wills. She agrees that it is still necessary to demand legislation, seek court decisions, and mandate programs to combat segregation within schools and to promote a multicultural perspective. But these alone, she says, are not sufficient for coping with the adversarial relationships that often accompany such activities. Such relationships are destructive to the very intergroup relations that the multicultural perspective should nurture. Litigation, she believes, may sometimes be ineffective in achieving the ultimate goal of raising the quality of education provided to African-American children (Bell, 1983, p. 572). Ms. Cross's commitment is to effective schooling and greater parent participation in the educational process, even if they come at the expense of less commitment to the ideal of racial integration (Bell, 1983, p. 572). Despite racial obstacles, Ms. Cross is convinced that lower-income parents want the same things for their children that most middle-class parents want for theirs—good mainstream social and academic skills that make for the kind of success that breeds further success and confidence (Comer, 1988, p. 221). The real issue, for her, is not racial or structural, but relational (Comer, 1988, p. 216). Effective schooling results from a commitment to creating a condition of community with relationships, roles, and obligations that the participants recognize as mutually and individually beneficial. Such relationships reduce the necessity for persons to be coerced by guilt or by legal mandates. Instead, people will more readily accept and obey political decisions because it is in their interest to do so, and because they stand in a special relationship to each other.

Eastside African-Americans can take the initiative in creating this condition of community. It begins with facing the fact that most Eastside black families are at risk for educational pathologies like dropping out and underachieving. These problems are significantly and frequently the result of the disintegration of the African-American family and the loss of its function as a channel for transmitting sound values (Wharton, 1986, p. 24).

Ms. Cross believes (and she thinks many Eastside parents share this belief) that the school alone is not responsible for providing all of a child's academic training (Clark, 1983, p. 122). Many of the problems that show up at school have their origins (and solutions) outside the schools, in the quality of parent–child relationships that result in differential preparation of children to deal with the challenges of school (Clark, 1983, p. 1).

Ms. Cross wonders aloud why so many in her generation choose to ignore the traditional role of the family and values that in the past have generated patience, love, hard work, ambition, sacrifice, and discipline. These are values that certainly contributed to her success and (she assumes) to the success of Mr. Wills and many African-Americans with whom they both are acquainted (Wharton, 1986, p. 24). No law or mandate can motivate teacher interest like children who responsibly pursue knowledge, attend class, listen and evaluate carefully, participate actively, accept and respect the teacher, and adhere to the standards, ideas, and codes of the school (Clark, 1983, p. 124). While Mr. Wills emphasizes ethnic and racial differences, Ms. Cross emphasizes similarities in psychosocial communication patterns within the families (regardless of occupational, income, ethnic, or other structural differences) of children who achieve academically (Clark, 1983, p. 12). Parents can be taught to create family environments where consistent expectations for learning are discussed, understood, and generally accepted by the child as part of a personal set of values. These parents can also learn to work within the school structure and, in the process, increase the probability that they and their children will be eligible for the opportunities available to all Americans.

It is assumed by Ms. Cross that teachers of both Eastside and Westside schools want to be successful professionals. But children who have not been read to, learned how to think, and achieved confidence and competency in problem solving keep teachers from achieving their professional goals. Teachers find it hard to have high expectations for such children and to create positive emotional bonds with them. In response, the children often fail to embrace the values of the school (Comer, 1988, p. 215). Children who can "present themselves as well-behaved, bright, and able" will in turn elicit from competent teachers behaviors that show caring, acceptance, and high hopes for their success (Comer, 1988, p. 221). Ms. Cross points to improvements in standardized test scores for children from specific families in her school where the parents, the children, and their teachers have achieved such a positive relationship.

Mr. Wills rejects Ms. Cross's "at risk" designation and her concept of community. The former he rejects because it is just a resurrection of the thoroughly discredited concept of "culturally deprived," and the latter he rejects as nothing but the equally discredited assimilation model that historically devalued the cultures of people of color and forced them to accept the behaviors, values, and characteristics of the dominant society. He also accuses her of "blaming the victim"—of failing to see that it is the low expectations that teachers generally have of African-American students, and their ignorance of African-American culture, that are the causes of the problem. Finally, Mr. Wills dismisses standardized test scores as having little to do with intelligence, as biasing teacher expectations of children, and as only showing "the degree to which a child is assimilated into the dominant culture" (Gollnick & Chinn, 1990, p. 106).

Ms. Cross reiterates that she is talking about relationships and patterns that are neither racially nor structurally specific, but are the outcomes of a particular kind of human community. She also suggests that to identify mainstream cultural values as "white culture" is a red herring. Blacks and whites alike hold and benefit from these values. To identify such values as "white culture" is to create a bias against them in the very persons who would benefit the most from them, young African-American males. She emphasizes again the empowerment and involvement of parents in the educational process and argues that the academic success of children is the real goal of education.

Dr. Brent wonders if he can or should attempt to serve equally the interests of all concerned parties—the Board of Education, the principals and faculties of the Eastside and Westside schools, and the Eastside parents and children. He retains his strong sense of social justice and believes that the African-American community has borne the largest share of the disruption and inconvenience of the desegregation process up to this point. Although he wants to do what is fair, he also wants to be certain that African-American children have equal access to the best education available to any other student in the Taylor City school system. What are the best policies to meet the needs of African-American and white children now that past efforts at desegregation have not produced fully satisfactory results? How should Dr. Brent develop and implement those policies?

WHO SPEAKS FOR THE NGUYENS?

Located in the southern half of a large western state, Balboa Central High School has for fifty years served a racially and culturally diverse community. Originally it was a stable community of Anglo and Latino families, but after World War II the student population began to include children of African-Americans who came from the south to work in wartime industry and children of whites who migrated from all over the United States to the West Coast.

In the late 1960s and 1970s, beneficiaries of the Revised Immigration Act of 1965 were added to the student mix. Finally, the late 1970s and 1980s brought two waves of refugees. Those in the first wave were persons escaping from conflicts in Latin America and those Vietnamese, mostly urban residents and ethnic Chinese, who left immediately at the war's end in 1975. Those in the second were the so-called Boat People—later Vietnamese refugees fleeing the country for political and economic reasons who had often spent time in overseas refugee camps before settling in the United States.

Balboa Central benefits from a relatively stable staff and administration composed of Anglos, African-Americans, and Latinos. They have acute cultural sensitivities and a nurturing approach to education but still are unprepared to participate in the "demographic and cultural revolution" in a state where "one in six students is foreign born" (Cannon, 1989b, p. A1) and where, despite their best efforts, too many frustrated students drop out, and even those who graduate may still experience a life of substandard wages and unequal citizenship (Cannon, 1989b, p. A8).

The school's principal, Ms. Sara Jane Kato, grew up poor in Appalachia. Aided by scholarships and student loans, she successfully completed college and then married Robert Kato, a classmate of Japanese ancestry whose parents and grandparents were interned during World War II. He is a teacher in a nearby elementary school.

After two years as principal, Ms. Kato has begun to have doubts about the way schools, including her own, have tried to meet the needs of students and their families, especially those who fall in one way or another outside the mainstream. The 1960s and 1970s brought many special programs and regulations, promulgated by federal and state governments and aimed at particular populations—racial minorities, the poor, those whose first language was not English, females, and the handicapped. As well intentioned as these efforts may have been, they have placed schools like Balboa Central—where exceptionality is the rule—in what seems to Ms. Kato like an increasingly untenable position. The curriculum at Balboa Central has become a patchwork of special programs, each serving particular and overlapping constituencies and each governed by externally imposed rules. As a result, the total school program, and the experience of most students within the school, seems to lack any real coherence—a consistent philosophy of, and approach to, learning. Even worse, Ms. Kato fears that the external control of these programs is fostering an atmosphere of dependency among students at the school, a sense that life is a matter of being done to instead of actively doing.

Conversations with some of the teachers and parents at Balboa Central have convinced Ms. Kato that the solution to these problems has to start with greater parent involvement in the school's decisions. The members of the school community must, she thinks, develop a sense of ownership in the school in order to create a coherent vision of how the school can meet the needs of its diverse student body. To this end, she has sponsored a series of public forums on particular issues in the school—bilingual education, vocational training, the social studies curriculum, and so on. After a somewhat reluctant beginning, these meetings have become lively, well attended, and provocative discussions, genuine opportunities for parents and teachers to air their concerns and frustrations and to consider together what might be done about them. Ms. Kato believes that the trust, honesty, and participation developed in these forums have prepared the way to establish a more permanent system of shared decision-making at Balboa Central.

As she draws up the plans for an elected parent and teacher school council, one issue nags at her. Members of the African-American, Latino, and Anglo communities have become actively involved in the forums, but participation from the Vietnamese community, and especially the Boat People, has been limited. Only a few self-styled community leaders, most from the first wave of Vietnamese immigrants, have spoken out. When questions have been directed to other Vietnamese parents, usually through a translator, they only smile, nod their heads, and repeat the Vietnamese word for "yes." Ms. Kato wonders why it is that they respond in almost the same manner to often contradictory proposals. The more animated other parents become while stating and defending their positions, the more withdrawn these Vietnamese parents seem to be. She wonders how this group can be effectively involved in the school's decision-making plan. These parents' participation, she is convinced, is crucial to their children's success precisely because she and the other members of the school community know so little about their needs and expectations. She has heard that, of all American ethnic groups, they are likely to have the highest rates of poverty and to be receiving some form of public assistance (Gardner et al., 1985, p. 34). Their needs are very real.

The only second-wave Vietnamese refugee Mrs. Kato knows at all well is Mrs. Nguyen. Mrs. Kato's church sponsored, first, Mrs. Nguyen and her elder son and daughter to come to the United States from a refugee camp in the Philippines and, two years later, Mrs. Nguyen's husband, younger son, and daughter from a camp in Thailand.

Ms. Kato knows little about the Nguyens' decision to leave Vietnam or about how they became separated. But when Mrs. Nguyen and the two oldest children first arrived, their church sponsors arranged for them to receive public assistance and live in public housing. Shortly thereafter, Mrs. Nguyen, out of necessity, found a job assembling electrical components. It was routine work that required minimal spoken English, and she learned it quickly. When necessary, she was instructed in Vietnamese by one or two other Vietnamese women who had worked there longer.

When Mr. Nguyen arrived, the two youngest children, despite their long stay in the camp, began to adjust well to school. For Mr. Nguyen, who knows only farming, it has been harder to find work than it was for Mrs. Nguyen. He is reluctant to accept an opportunity for vocational training offered him, and talks about getting a college education. On several occasions, Mr. Nguyen roughly restrained his wife when she wanted to go out with female friends in the evening. And he has struck his children in a futile attempt to reassert his authority, which has waned with the years of separation from his wife and older children, his wife's working, and his children's greater proficiency in English and familiarity with the community.

Ms. Kato knows the two oldest Nguyen children. Their daughter, Lan, finished high school last year, got married, and went to work. She and her husband live in the same small apartment with her parents and siblings. Huy, the elder son, is something of a puzzle to his high school teachers. They report that during some weeks he is the model of a hardworking student. At those times, he reminds them of some of the Chinese and Korean immigrant students they have in class who also come from countries strongly influenced by the teachings of the ancient Chinese philosopher Confucius. Confucian teachings emphasize an appreciation of education, self-improvement through study, and the need for children to repay the sacrifices of their parents by bringing honor to the family name through academic achievement. On other occasions, however, they observe that Huy appears indifferent to his studies and unmotivated. During these times, he is seen hanging out at the nearby shopping mall with other Vietnamese youths, many of whom have dropped out of school and are not gainfully employed. The Nguyens say they hope Huy will be able to attend college, but his teachers worry that he may not be prepared for the demands of college.

Ms. Kato has tried to learn what she can about the Boat People from books and from some of her school's Vietnamese parents. Vietnam is a nation with a history of occupation and war. It was a French colony in the nineteenth century, occupied by the Japanese between 1940 and 1945, reoccupied by the French until 1954, and, finally, torn by civil war and the intervention of the United States from the 1960s until 1975. Even before the French occupation of Vietnam, the Vietnamese had struggled on and off for over a thousand years against political domination by the Chinese. The culture and national character of the people bear the imprint of the philosophical and religious systems that came to Vietnam from China (Confucian ethics, Taoism, and Buddhism) and the West (Christianity and Marxism).

The Nguyens, like most of the Boat People, are rural in origin. Until the 1960s, their village was an island of peace and security where life flowed with the rhythm of the seasons. Families experienced an unbroken continuity from the past to the present and on to the future as they tended the graves of the ancestors whom they consulted in times of crisis (Fitzgerald, 1972, pp. 429–430). In village life, work, suffering, success, and sacrifice were not for oneself but "for the home, the nuclear family, the extended family—including the dead and the unborn, for the village, for the nation" (Tran, 1989, p. 602). Ms. Kato believes that this village experience is at least partly responsible for the Nguyens' behavior at the school forums.

The web of interaction in this Vietnamese family, extended family, and village was characterized by well-defined, hierarchical roles. These roles, a legacy of Confucian teaching, reflect a preoccupation with the preservation of interpersonal harmony. Those in power are not to abuse their positions since they reflect a divine mandate that is subject to withdrawal. The powerful are to provide advice, guidance, and encouragement in paternalistic fashion to those beneath them (Liem & Kehmeier, 1980, p. 211). And subordinates are to respond with politeness, obedience, and acceptance while trying to achieve a balance between being cared for and being exploited (Fitzgerald, 1972, p. 113).

By the end of the Vietnamese War, 40% to 50% of the population lived in and around towns and cities, compared with only 15% before the war (Fitzgerald, 1972, p. 427). Great personal and collective trauma accompanied the American wartime strategy of relocating and resettling villages in the south in order to deny the Vietcong a source of supplies and recruits. Mr. and Mrs. Nguyen remember both their own and their parents' grief as they became "refugees within their own land" (Liem & Kehmeier, 1980, p. 202). The death of friends and relatives meant the death of the village, and the death of the village meant the death of their own identity, which was inexorably tied to multiple generations, extended families, and the graves of the ancestors (Fitzgerald, 1972, pp. 429–430).

Mrs. Kato is not sure whether she should try to encourage the Nguyens and others like them to become involved in her plan for shared decision making at Balboa Central. She worries that the more outspoken Vietnamese from the first wave of immigrants may not understand the special concerns and problems of the Boat People. At the same time, many Americans choose not to become involved in civic activities. Don't the Nguyens have the right to leave school decisions to others as long as they are willing to accept the results?

Besides, what could she do to involve them, anyway? It does not seem possible to reserve elective positions in the shared decision-making plan for these people in particular. Perhaps that plan might provide for appointed committees on issues likely to be of special interest to this group of parents. Then, she could arrange to have some of them appointed to those committees. But would these people be any more active on a committee than they were at the public forums? What should she do, or with whom should she consult to resolve this dilemma? What more does she need to find out about the Nguyens and their culture? What other possibilities for involvement might she consider?

A LANGUAGE OR A THINKING PROBLEM?

Mr. Russ Narido just taken up the principalship of his third school in the last eleven years. His new elementary school is in Honolulu, at the center of a community with a large population of immigrant families. One of the notable differences between this and his two previous communities is that here most of the newly arrived immigrants move within two or three years to other communities where they have found jobs.

The students at Mr. Narido's new school, though not all immigrants, are representative of Hawaii's multicultural community. Filipinos, Koreans, Vietnamese, Samoans, and a few Japanese and Caucasian students all combine to challenge any teacher who is new to the Hawaii public school system. Data from the 1990 U.S. Census show that Hawaii has one million residents and that there is no one ethnic group that is a majority of the state's residents. Caucasians are the largest group at 33.4%, followed by the Japanese at 22.3%. Filipinos comprise 15.2% of the population, Hawaiians 12.5%, Chinese 6.2%, Blacks 2.5%, and other races 2.4%. Smaller Asian-Pacific groups that include Koreans, Samoans, and Vietnamese constitute 5.6% of the state's population. In the past decade, the greatest percentage increases have been in the Asian immigrant groups (Glauberman, 1991).

Among the students from immigrant families, Filipinos are now the largest group in the state's program for students of limited English proficiency (SLEP). In the 1989 school year, 42% of the almost 9,000 students in the SLEP program were Filipinos (Hawaii Department of Education, 1989).

Many immigrant children have limited or no proficiency in English. For this reason, the school continues to receive assistance from the district office through its compensatory education program. Federal and state funds allow the schools to hire community resource people who help the schools to respond to the language needs and other needs of ethnic minorities. The schools also provide assistance for other children with special needs. There are, for example, classes staffed by specially trained teachers for children who teachers identify as having learning disabilities.

Today, Mr. Narido is reviewing a teacher's recommendation to transfer Benito to such a learning disability class. Benito, who came from the Philippines, has been in Hawaii for seven months. Because he is seven years old, he has been placed in a second-grade class. The recommendation came from Mrs. Honda, who teaches Benito language arts. It has been six weeks since school started. During this time, Benito has been given tests to assess his English language ability and number skills. His scores on these tests were so low that Mrs. Honda kept close watch of Benito's behavior in other subjects as well. According to her report, she has tried everything. She has talked to him, but he simply hangs his head. When she insists that he look her in the eye, he stares up at her, with jaws slightly opened, seemingly with little or no comprehension.

Mr. Narido asked for a few days to study this referral to the learning disability class. He is not exactly unfamiliar with the problems Filipino children experience in school. He has learned over the years, for instance, that Filipino children are taught not to look directly at older people or those in authority when speaking. However, he can also sympathize with the teacher's frustration in not getting any response. And he now wonders if Benito's lack of response and apparent uneasiness were really due to his unfamiliarity with this mode of interaction or to the child's intellectual deficiency in understanding what was communicated to him.

He cannot be sure that sending Benito to a class of children with various learning disabilities will be of any help to him. Although the boy would presumably get more attention in a smaller class where teaching is more individualized, Mr. Narido knows that when children are sent to these classes, they rarely leave. Furthermore, the label of learning disabled usually follows the child for the rest of his student years. What if Benito's language difficulty has been misdiagnosed as a lack of intelligence? Would placing Benito in a learning disability class help Benito or further compound the problem? If it were later discovered that Benito had been erroneously placed in the special class, what damage might already have been done to him—socially, psychologically, and academically?

Mr. Narido turned to another section of the report in which the teacher noted that the boy does not appear to take any initiative, that he relies almost entirely on other children, even to ask if he may go to the bathroom. Benito always brings another Filipino boy to speak for him, the report says. So dependent is he, observed the teacher, that Benito is almost always the last student to begin his work. He seems first to watch what his friends do before he himself acts. In his favor, Mrs. Honda acknowledged that once the boy began an activity, especially when the task was not especially language dependent, Benito's performance was average. In these instances, he finishes his work, and although it is not always perfect, his errors are no worse or more frequent than those of his classmates. It isn't that he does not understand. Benito just seems too slow.

On a few occasions, Mr. Narido has observed Benito from a distance during recess. The boy seemed able to hold his own within his small circle of friends. However, he interacted mostly with other Filipino children. Mr. Narido reflected a bit on his own shyness when he started school. Everyone seemed bigger and better informed. He was taught rules, and he had expectations of himself and others. He wondered what rules guided Benito as he tried to make sense of his present world. Mr. Narido sometimes wishes he could recreate the school environments of his immigrant students' home countries. How would Benito act in his home town of Lawag, Philippines, where he could converse in his own language? But then, this is not a province in the Philippines, and the sooner Benito learns about how things are done here, the better for everyone, he thought.

What harm is there, really, in insisting that children perform within acceptable standards and limits established by the school? In truth, Benito is performing far below grade level. Yet, the situation is disquieting. Filipino children tend to model behavior before they are allowed to venture out independently on their own. What if Benito is just going through a necessary stage of transition? Would daily interaction in a class with learning disabled children facilitate, prolong, or even block his adjustment?

Mr. Narido's mind turned to Mrs. Honda. She has had considerable experience with children at this age, and her qualifications are unquestionable. She is one of the more serious and dedicated teachers of children with language difficulties. Mrs. Honda has been in the Chapter I program for eight years, whereas most teachers move to regular programs or other schools after about five years or when the opportunity arises. Mrs. Honda has voluntarily chosen to remain in the program because of her strong belief in starting the children on the path to success from a very early age. Over the years she has demonstrated her ability to predict with enviable accuracy how well or poorly a student may function later in school. Her assessment of Benito's situation is only one instance of her characteristic way of alerting the student and the administration early that help is needed. She is a concerned, critical, and responsive teacher. Other teachers respect her evaluative skills.

Mr. Narido has learned to depend on her judgment as well. In the case of Benito, she seems sure of herself. Would denying her request to transfer him to a learning disability class undermine the trust that has been established between them? Furthermore, Benito's family is likely to move to another community in a year or two, where Benito could then start anew. What is Benito's family like? What are their aspirations? How much do we really know about Benito, his family, and immigrant Filipinos in general, Mr. Narido wonders.

Mr. Narido gazed out of his window and watched the children outside. With the growing school population it was harder than ever to get to know all of his students and their families. In this school as in his previous schools, Mr. Narido made it a practice to go out to the area where children were picked up after school in order to have some informal contact with their parents. In this school, however, the children are picked up not only by either parent but sometimes by a variety of relatives. For Mr. Narido, there is no longer the predictable meeting of familiar faces. His relationship with parents here is too often limited to open houses or advisory committee meetings that a disappointingly small number attend. Those who do come are generally parents whose children rarely need assistance. This is disturbing because when problems like Benito's occur, the principal and the teachers have little knowledge of the students' lives beyond what school records, test scores, and the teachers' classroom observations reveal. Mr. Narido just does not know Benito or his family very well, yet the decision he is to make has far-reaching consequences for the boy's educational future.

Mr. Narido thought through what he had learned about the Filipinos' experiences in Hawaii (Teodoro, 1981). Arriving in 1900, Hawaii's first Filipino immigrants followed the Chinese and Japanese as recruits to work on the plantations. Although the first immigrants were carefully screened to make sure they would stay on the plantations, those who came after World War II were less strictly bound. As a result, the Filipino population continued to grow and diversify.

The liberalized U.S. immigration law adopted in 1965 brought immigrants from the Philippines of an entirely different type. They came as professionals or students, or because they were immediate family members of naturalized citizens. Although still underrepresented in the state's university, and despite an average income below that of several other ethnic groups, Filipino participation in politics, the business world, and government jobs has increased considerably in the last ten years. Slow as this movement may appear, Filipinos are an upwardly mobile ethnic group. Most Filipinos see education as a vehicle for their social and economic progress. Filipinos often cite their pursuit of a better economic future through education as a reason for immigrating to the United States or for making great personal sacrifices to put their children through college.

Mr. Narido is aware of how deeply the Filipinos place their faith and trust in education. As a third-generation Japanese American, he personally understands this faith. Mr. Narido does not want to betray the Filipinos' trust, so he particularly wants to be certain about his judgment of Benito. Would he be shortchanging Benito if he were to keep him in the regular class when it seems obvious that he is not able to cope with the demands of that class? Would he progressively be denied a meaningful education? On the other hand, if transferred to a learning disability class, would Benito be denied his right to an education commensurate with his true capability? Is Benito's real academic ability masked by his lack of familiarity with English and the social conventions of American schools, or does he have a thinking problem? What course of action should Mr. Narido take?

TWO LETTERS OF RECOMMENDATION

Mr. Burns, the mathematics teacher, stops to talk with Ms. Ames, the school counselor, about a letter of recommendation that Wai-Lin Cheng, a student in his trigonometry class, asked him to write to accompany her applications to several well-known universities. Ms. Ames tells him that Wai-Lin also asked her to write a similar letter.

Mr. Burns has taught for twenty years at a high school located in a middle- to upper-middle-income suburban school district outside a large northern California city. Mrs. Ames has been employed at the same school for ten years. Within the school district there are a substantial number of first- and second-generation parents of Chinese ancestry. Most of the Chinese and non-Chinese parents in this district are upwardly mobile and see the school as a means for extending that mobility through the next generation. The recently arrived Chinese immigrant parents, in particular, believe that here their children have the opportunity for an education that will enable both the children and their parents to participate in the American dream. There seems to exist a satisfactory congruence between the expectations of the parents and the mission of the school as it is expressed in policy and practice.

Recently, however, Ms. Ames has argued for new programs and activities to counter what she and some of the younger faculty see as the school's narrow preoccupation with academic achievement and preparation for college admission. This preoccupation, she says, results in the neglect of other equally important knowledge and experiences that contemporary students need for enhanced self-esteem, self-actualization, and self-worth based upon something more than academic achievement. Other faculty, including Mr. Burns, argue that greater attention to these so-called needs will divert energy and resources from the school's academic mission, which is overwhelmingly supported by its constituency.

The issues embedded in this debate become concrete and personal as Mr. Burns and Ms. Ames discuss Wai-Lin's request. Mr. Burns, who has nothing but praise for Wai-Lin, finds that Ms. Ames does not share his unqualified praise for her qualities. She does not agree with him that more non-Asian families would do well to emphasize academic achievement and the current mission of the school to the extent that Wai-Lin's family does.

Eight years earlier Wai-Lin's father, the youngest of three sons, brought his wife and three daughters—who were then nine, seven, and four years old—to the United States from Hong Kong. The family was sponsored to come to the United States by Mr. Cheng's older brother who had come here twelve years earlier. Their eldest brother remained in Hong Kong, where he manages a small import-export business started by their father and cares for their elderly parents.

Mr. Cheng had always wanted a son who, by tradition, would care for him and his wife in their old age, but with the birth of his third daughter he decided that there would be no sons. Still, Mr. Cheng is committed to providing a better life for his family and the best education possible for his daughters. For those reasons, he brought his family to the United States. Now he works in a small business started by his brother. Mrs. Cheng was a nurse in Hong Kong, but after their first daughter was born she gave up her career to work part-time for her father-in-law, and to spend more time raising her children. Now in the United States, she works part-time for her brother-in-law.

Mr. Cheng was happy that the community where his brother lives has a reputation for good public schools. Mr. Cheng believes that education will provide a bright future for his daughters. He was also relieved to see other Chinese families in the neighborhood because their children are likely to have values similar to those he emphasizes for his own children.

For a year after they arrived in the United States, the Chengs lived with Mr. Cheng's brother. Then Mr. Cheng made a down payment on a home in the same community, which depleted most of his savings. Meeting the monthly mortgage payments would require sacrifice and careful budgeting. But this is only one of the sacrifices that Mr. and Mrs. Cheng are willing to make for their children.

Relationships in the Cheng family have their basis in mutual dependence, a tendency for family members to rely extensively upon each other. This, in turn, is the basis for both individual and family security (Hsu, 1981).

It is a dependence that is nurtured—the adults do not find it onerous and the children do not desire to escape from it as early as possible in order to make their own way in life. Mr. and Mrs. Cheng make every effort possible so that their daughters will get the best available education and become accomplished adults who will bring honor to the family name and eventually care for their parents when they grow old.

For the daughters, these family relationships and expectations are a given. If, on rare occasions, the daughters' behavior suggests that they have forgotten or do not fully appreciate these sacrifices, the parents—especially Mrs. Cheng—remind them and appear wounded that they would forget. Both Mr. and Mrs. Cheng have given up the possibility that they themselves will experience a high level of material success, but they look forward to the success of the next generation. Mr. Cheng is comfortable in the knowledge that his self-esteem is secure since its source is the respect shown him by his wife and children. His life is made purposeful by the continuing opportunities offered him to meet the obligations he has to his wife and children, his older brothers, and his parents in Hong Kong (Hsu, 1981, p. 309).

Over the years the Chengs' daughters have better understood these sacrifices; they respond to their parents with unquestioning obedience. When Wai-Lin is asked to play the violin for company, she does so without hesitation. When Mr. Cheng suggests to his daughters that they take those classes at school that will prepare them to enter the best universities, they do so.

The children have grown up accepting the wisdom of adults in general, and of their parents in particular. In their family, childishness, while tolerated when the daughters were young, was never rewarded. The world of the adults is the standard. When they were young, the Cheng children were never left with a baby-sitter unless it was their aunt. Usually, however, they were included in any adult gatherings attended by their parents.

Such gatherings, however, are almost always with Mr. Cheng's brother's family or other Chinese families. At these gatherings, the daughters usually visit with each other or with their cousins while the adults talk. Family celebrations, even those where the occasion is a child's birthday, always provide an occasion for the adults to discuss business, their children's educational progress, and the affairs of friends and relatives.

The few non-Chinese friends that the Cheng daughters had in elementary and junior high school were carefully screened by their parents. Mrs. Cheng used to drive her daughters to and from elementary school so that there would be little opportunity for them to fall into the company of children who might prove to be a bad influence or whose family values were at odds with those of the Chengs. The Chengs are preoccupied with their daughters' school achievement, rather than with their popularity among their peers (Hsu, 1981, p. 119). Boy–girl relations are discouraged. Such relations should take priority only after college when one is ready for marriage, not now when such relations would compete with school work. The Chengs do not openly boast of their daughters' school achievement; they do mention it with quiet pride at family gatherings when the adults discuss their children's grades and college plans.

Mr. Cheng views most extracurricular school activities as frivolous, especially if they are not academically oriented or supervised by adults. Such activities compete with homework and classroom achievement. After an appeal by the school orchestra director, whose opinion Mr. Cheng respects because of the good reputation of the orchestra in the community, Wai-Lin was allowed to play violin in the orchestra and practice with the orchestra after school. This in turn motivated the Chengs to make additional financial sacrifices so that Wai-Lin could take lessons from a private teacher rather than just from her mother.

There is very little money for extras in the Cheng household, but it can be found for those things deemed by the parents as worth the sacrifice. Recently Wai-Lin and her sister, Wai-Fun, approached their parents for permission to work part-time after school and to baby-sit on the weekends, as many of their peers do, in order to earn extra money to spend on clothes and other teenage preoccupations. Mr. and Mrs. Cheng said that employment would interfere with schoolwork; they feel that they already provide their children with all that is really necessary. When Wai-Lin suggested that, by working, they could earn and save some of the money needed for their college education, her parents replied that any money they earned would be but a drop in the bucket. It is their obligation as parents to pay for their children's education, but Wai-Lin and Wai-Fun can help by studying hard and earning scholarships. When Wai-Lin suggested that she and Wai-Fun need money to purchase special gifts for birthday and Christmas presents for their parents, the parents replied that the greatest gift that a child can give a parent is to be a respectful child who honors the family. The parents point out that most of their leisure time is spent in family activities and gatherings with friends and relatives and such activities cost the children nothing. The parents can always provide pocket money when the children go on trips sponsored by the school.

The Chengs interpret the present in terms of a concrete past, rather than an imagined future (Hsu, 1981, p. 383). Mr. Cheng believes that children are first and foremost family members and that the family is the basic unit of society. Things work out best if the community at large supports the parents in what they believe is best for the child. The security that the family provides its members through mutual dependency requires that each member knows and occupies his or her proper place vis-à-vis the other members. Mr. Cheng often refers to the belief, attributed to the ancient Chinese philosopher Confucius, that order is Heaven's first law. If the members of families are rightly oriented to each other, then all is right under Heaven in a society composed of such families (Moore, 1949, pp. 26–29).

Mr. and Mrs. Cheng are distressed when they read about the rising rates of delinquent and rebellious behavior among American children—both boys and girls—who reject their families for the values and company of their peers. Mr. Cheng, however, is certain that his own children, "secure in the shadow of their ancestors," have no great need to substitute the company of their American peers for their own family in particular and other Chinese in general (Hsu, 1981, p. 115). Self-reliance, much less rebellion, would come hard to the Cheng daughters after living in a family where security is the certain outcome of mutual dependence and its related obligations.

Mr. and Mrs. Cheng do not directly involve themselves in their children's education at the school. Both work long hours at Mr. Cheng's brother's business and, in addition, they are embarrassed by what they consider to be their poor spoken English. However, they do what they can to support the efforts of the teachers by seeing to it that their daughter's have all the necessary home resources for doing their best on school assignments. The girls have a good set of encyclopedias, a quiet place to study, and time unencumbered by chores and telephone interruptions in which to complete their schoolwork. Recently, Mr. Cheng invested in a computer–word processor that his daughters convinced him was essential to their schoolwork.

While all adults are to be revered, the Chengs have a special regard for teachers. Because Mr. and Mrs. Cheng view education as the means by which their daughters will become humane and moral persons—a credit to both their family and the ancestors—they expect teachers to be role models of truly humane and moral persons. They tell their children that the teacher is always right. When Wai-Lin and Wai-Fun first entered school, they spoke and understood almost no English. Mrs. Cheng had instructed them to pay close attention, whether or not they understood what the teacher was saying. This was hard for them to do because there was often much in the behavior of their peers to distract them. But by obeying their mother and observing the teacher, they quickly learned English and how to excel in their studies.

Mr. and Mrs. Cheng expect that the teachers, like themselves, will champion effort over ability, will emphasize in class that there is almost nothing that cannot be achieved through increased increments of effort, and will emphasize that success comes with being better, not feeling better (Krauthammer, 1990, p. 78). For Mr. Cheng, the basis of self-esteem lies in hard work, effort, high achievement, and being a credit to the family name.

By enrolling their children in a school district with a good academic reputation and by supporting the efforts of the teachers, the Chengs are satisfied that they have been accountable to the ancestors and have effected their own future happiness and security. They are, after all, revered and respected by their children who, as they attain success through their education, will most certainly fulfill their obligations to their parents to care for them in the years to come.

Although she knows something of Wai-Lin's background, Ms. Ames does not share Mr. Burns's enthusiasm for Wai-Lin's achievements and his admiration and respect for the Cheng family. Neither does she feel that the preoccupations of such families should guide school policy. She observes that there are days when Wai-Lin appears tired and overworked. She sees Wai-Lin as an overachiever and supports this observation by citing Wai-Lin's standardized test scores that show her achieving beyond her measured ability. Ms. Ames also notes that Wai-Lin and Wai-Fun do not seem to have many friends and are usually seen together, or in the company of other students of Chinese ancestry or one or two of the few female Korean immigrant students who attend the school. Wai-Lin and Wai-Fun, she declares, are too dependent upon adults for advice and appear to be overly preoccupied with the details of assignments and with making high grades. She is also critical of what appears to be an inordinate desire by Wai-Lin to please her father at the expense of learning to think for herself and to make her own intelligent choices. She thinks it is a shame that Mrs. Cheng never returned to her profession as a nurse.

Mr. Burns suggests that perhaps there are cultural factors involved here to which they need to be more sensitive as professional educators. Ms. Ames agrees that the school should encourage students to retain and maintain their cultural heritage, but not at the expense of their mental health, their social development, and a self-actualization that is freely chosen.

Mr. Burns says that Ms. Ames does not seem to appreciate the Chengs' support of the schools' academic objectives and their respect for teachers. Ms. Ames worries that the deep emotional needs of the Chengs' children for unconditional acceptance are neglected by their parents. Rather, the Chengs' regard for their children seems to be conditional on their school achievement, and there seems to no limit to their expectations for them. To deny children freely given love, esteem, and other positive responses will certainly have severe consequences (Rohner, 1975, p. 166). Mr. Burns walks away wondering how he and Ms. Ames can see this student and her parents so differently. Which of these two evaluations of Wai-Lin seems to be the most justified? To be honest with the colleges to which she is applying and to be fair to Wai-Lin, what should a letter of recommendation say?

GLORIA'S CAREER DECISION

Gloria stared for a long time at the letter she was holding in her hand. It was an invitation to apply for a two-year scholarship to attend graduate school in public health. This invitation seemed like the best thing that could have come her way except that it came from a university that would take her away from where she has lived almost all of her twenty-two years. Acceptance of the application is practically guaranteed. Although she is not the only Puerto Rican working at the U.S. State Department of Health, she is the most promising young bilingual woman. As an intern for the last eighteen months, she had demonstrated dependability and dedication, qualities that have not been lost on her supervisor and on the professor who recommended her to the agency. On the job, Gloria must constantly respond to a variety of situations that call for knowledge of Spanish and of her Puerto Rican traditions. Because of her vitality, her youth, and her commitment to help, Gloria is appreciated by her unit and the other units within the department that call on her for assistance. Gloria's internship is coming to an end, and both her supervisor and her professor have encouraged her to continue her studies. They are convinced that she should further develop her skills and so enhance her career.

The scholarship opportunity comes at a crucial time in Gloria's life, but the decision is not going to be easy. In fact, it is not really hers to make alone. Major decisions never are, for one in her situation. Many others will need to be consulted and involved. If she does attend graduate school, she will be the first in her family of six brothers and sisters to complete an advanced degree. Right after high school or college, her sisters and most of her friends married and are now raising families. If she accepts this scholarship, her life will be very different from those of her older sisters and close friends.

Gloria looked again at the forms. She only had a month to reply. She mentally reviewed what needed to be done. How would the decision to complete the degree affect her other goals and responsibilities in life? Who would support her? Her first and immediate concern is her family. Like most Puerto Rican families, hers is a tightly knit unit. Families define the roles of their members by sex, age, and kinship relations. As a young, unmarried woman, Gloria is obliged to get the family's approval. Obligation to the family governs every outside endeavor. And in her case, because she is officially engaged, her fiancé, Ricardo, and his family are also involved in her plans. Gloria thought of Ricardo's ambivalence.

Her boyfriend since high school days, Ricardo is also Puerto Rican and a year older. Gloria and Ricardo, both members of large families, realize that their older siblings have had to forgo various career opportunities to help their families. Their brothers and sisters have had to cut their education short to help relieve the pressure on their parents, who are not only supporting a large family in the United States but also helping relatives still living in Puerto Rico. Gloria and Ricardo are fortunate. As the youngest members of their families, they have not felt as much pressure as did their siblings. They each were able to concentrate upon and finish their college studies in four years.

After getting his degree a year ago, Ricardo has just completed his first year of teaching at a high school in their neighborhood. He and Gloria had already agreed to postpone marriage until after Gloria graduated from college. But because the opportunity to earn an advanced degree promises to make life so much better for them in the long run, Gloria is inclined to ask Ricardo to postpone marriage for another two years.

Gloria is aware that some of her Anglo friends have been able to combine marriage and graduate studies. Of course, these friends have also postponed starting a family until after completing their advanced degrees. However, in Gloria's culture, the more acceptable arrangement is to begin a family soon after marriage. After all, marriage is considered to be consummated only at the birth of the first child (Hatt, 1952). Although there has been some acceptance of a postponement in raising a family in recent years, Ricardo and Gloria's situation would still remain awkward. They would almost certainly have to live apart. It does not seem fair for Ricardo to quit his job and look for another so they can live together. The uncertainties of finding the right job, earning enough to support them with Gloria not working, renting a new apartment—everything seems so difficult. Furthermore, Gloria knows that Ricardo would be worried about what his friends might say if he were to marry someone who has more education than he. Ricardo has never discouraged Gloria's interest in pursuing graduate study. He himself wants to pursue an advanced degree for the same reason as Gloria. It seemed like something they could both aim for in the course of their married life. However, the possibility that Gloria might start her graduate studies immediately and finish before him has caught him by surprise. He is happy for her but also a little worried. He is just not sure that this is a wise thing to do. His doubts, which recently have come to occupy most of their conversations, make Gloria wonder if she might lose him were she to follow the advice of her professor. Will she be able to persuade Ricardo to wait another two years?

Ricardo is not the only person Gloria needs to persuade. She knows her father will object to her departure from family traditions. Gloria will have to be convincing so as not to alienate herself from him and the rest of her family. Without her family's and even her friends' support, she isn't sure that what lies ahead will be worthwhile. The loss of family harmony would be too high a price to pay. At twenty-two, Gloria is still living with her parents, and until she gets married, she is expected to do so. Most of the unmarried Puerto Rican women she knows live at home. Although her Anglo friends shared rented apartments in college, Gloria knew this was not an option for her, and she had no desire to live away from home. None of her sisters have lived away from home while single, except when with relatives in Puerto Rico.

How will Gloria meet her father's concerns? How can she keep from alienating the people most important to her? Harmony and support, she realizes again, are central values of her Puerto Rican heritage.

Puerto Rico became a U.S. colony as a result of the Spanish American War in 1898. Travel between the mainland and Puerto Rico has been easy since 1917 when, through the Foraker Act, the United States granted Puerto Ricans limited citizenship status (Rothermund & Simon, 1986). Gloria's parents, like many Puerto Ricans living and working in the United States, maintain strong ties with relatives and friends on the Island. They had arranged for all of the children to visit Puerto Rico at least once every three years. If they could have afforded it, the whole family would have commuted more often.

The Commonwealth Agreement also has served to support the use of Spanish as the official language of government, commerce, and public life in Puerto Rico, although the U.S. government has expressed its strong preference for English to be the language of instruction in the schools (Santiago, 1984). This language policy has proven to be a mixed blessing. When Puerto Ricans spend some years in the United States and then return to the Island, they face an educational handicap. Their Spanish, discouraged in the schools on the continent, is not really adequate for participating effectively in the schools in Puerto Rico. Gloria's two oldest siblings frequently commuted between the Island and the mainland, spending one year in the United States and another in Puerto Rico. Each time they returned from a year in Puerto Rico, they experienced real difficulties in the U.S. schools as they struggled with the level of English required. By the time Gloria started attending school, her parents were more settled, and visits to the Island were not as frequent. Still, Gloria is well aware that family ties and responsibilities extend far beyond her immediate environment. Her cousins, uncles, and aunts have come for visits in the United States even when her family couldn't always reciprocate. These ties have worked to Gloria's advantage, in that she sees herself as a bridge between two cultures, in part because of her knowledge of each culture's most obvious manifestation, its language. Whether at work, at school, at community meetings, or in church-related activities, Gloria has become a reliable and valued translator for members of both cultural groups.

Even if she succeeds in convincing her immediate family that traditions have changed enough for her to accept this scholarship, there are all of the close relatives who almost certainly will not understand. The frequent contacts among family members cannot be ignored, nor should their concern for members of the extended family be taken lightly.

The easy access to the mainland and its opportunities for employment, even on a short-term basis, have attracted many Puerto Rican families like Gloria's to the United States. Many eventually immigrate. Almost all of those who move to the mainland experience some degree of displacement. Often it is one of the parents, mother or father, who leaves the Island first to take a job in the United States or to live with relatives while seeking employment. The frequently large families must usually send for the children one or two at a time. The process of adjustment to the new culture and of readjustment to one another has proved to be a major challenge to almost every newcomer. During this process, each family member tries to find strength from parents, siblings, and others outside the family circle.

For many, the church has helped in the adjustment, especially for those who find solace in the guidance of a spiritual leader. Gloria's family turned to their parish priest. Father Rivera has proved himself to be particularly reassuring because of his hope in, and trust of, the younger members of the Puerto Rican community. He has been sensitive to the fears and anxieties of his people and has organized various committees to assist community members. His role as mediator and translator seems to be especially important. Gloria's father has been grateful to him for the many hours of time and wise counsel he has provided during the difficult teenage years of his four daughters. It was to the church that Gloria's family turned to find a sense of belonging and identity when frictions surfaced. On issues like the practice of "chaperons," the choice of marriage partners, and questions about community obligations, Gloria's parents have consulted Father Rivera.

Gloria hopes that Father Rivera will support her decision to take advantage of the scholarship. Surely, he would be an important ally in convincing her father in particular that the scholarship should be accepted. He may be able to help with other relatives, too, and perhaps even with Ricardo. Gloria has frequently turned to him as the longtime confidant of her family. She has always been able to count on his support, and she surely needs that support in this situation.

Gloria wonders if Father Rivera will be willing to give her his blessing in this endeavor. Finding a replacement for her in the parish will pose a challenge to him because she has been a valuable assistant in much of his community work. Will he support her as enthusiastically as her professor and supervisor do? Will he worry that Gloria may not return to the community?

As Gloria ponders these questions, she realizes that her professor and her supervisor will not be able to help her much with her family, relatives, and friends. She can count on them to help her in moments of self-doubt about her abilities to compete and achieve academically. But her success in graduate school is worth celebrating only if it is shared with, and appreciated by, her friends and family. Perhaps there are too many problems, and Gloria should just not press the issue. But then there is the possibility that she can make a real contribution to her own people by her increased competence as a health professional and by being even more capable as a bridge between

Puerto Ricans and other members of the society. Finally, she and Ricardo will have a better life and an easier time starting a family. Her children, too, would have greater opportunities, and she and Ricardo could help her parents assist the extended family even more.

Gloria sits before the typewriter and carefully begins to fill out the form. As she moves from one item to the next, it dawns on her that she will be committing herself to at least two full years of continuous and intensive studies to complete the degree. If she cannot finish in that time, she will need to reapply for continuation of financial assistance. At that stage, she would be competing with students just starting on their master's studies. The questions that had gone through her mind earlier crowd her thoughts once more. Is the chance to help her people as a professional and to have a better life down the road worth the risks of possibly losing her fiancé, disrupting family harmony, causing misunderstandings with members of the extended family, and incurring Father Rivera's disappointment? Gloria's dilemma is not an easy one, for it involves breaking new ground in the traditions of Puerto Rican culture. Shouldn't she really settle down, start a family, keep her job as long as she can, and just fit in, as her sisters and Puerto Rican friends have done? What should Gloria do?

SOON-YOUNG'S DIVIDED LOYALTIES

This Friday afternoon only Soon-Young Kim and four other students remain in the high school library after classes. Ms. Carol Ahn, a woman of Korean ancestry in her early thirties and one of the school's two counselors, passes the library door and sees the student from Korea in her usual place at a table by the window. She also sees Ms. Julia Blake, the librarian, sorting books. The images of the quiet sixteen-year-old sophomore with the hyphenated first name and of the librarian turn Ms. Ahn's thoughts to "those Koreans" about whom she is constantly being queried these days. Just that morning, Ms. Blake, an African-American woman about Ms. Ahn's age, told her about the new owners of a small grocery store in the predominantly black neighborhood where Ms. Blake's mother has always lived.

Ten years earlier, the small neighborhood grocery store, owned by Mr. Shapiro for as long as Ms. Blake could remember, had closed. Mr. Shapiro left, discouraged by high insurance premiums and what he perceived as growing crime and violence. Now there is a newcomer from Korea, who, with his wife and assorted relatives as employees, keeps it open sixteen hours a day.

Ms. Blake's mother and her friends wonder how such newcomers, barely able to speak English, can get the money to open a business so soon after coming to the United States. Her mother complains that the owner and the other employees rarely smile, hover around black shoppers, and speak brusquely—some say rudely—to them. They speak in Korean to each other and show little interest in things American. To some of her neighbors, this behavior appears to be both arrogant and racist.

Ms. Ahn looks again at Soon-Young. She also sees a minority female working on her lessons late on a Friday afternoon. Ms. Blake and her mother certainly wouldn't find that behavior foreign. More than once Ms. Blake has told the story of how it was her mother who initiated her lifelong love of books and reading and who still preaches nonstop about education as the way minority women can get a head start. Ms. Ahn continues down the hall. Soon-Young looks briefly out the window and then down at her wristwatch. She still has much work to do before going home.

Three years ago, when she was thirteen years old, Soon-Young's father's business in Korea was doing poorly. To continue supporting both his family and his aging parents, Soon-Young's father decided as a temporary measure to send Soon-Young to live with his younger brother and his wife, who had come to the United States a year earlier. Her parents sent Soon-Young because it was important that her two younger brothers, then aged eleven and twelve, get their education in Korea and thereby be prepared to pass the examinations necessary to enter a good Korean university. Although her parents hoped that Soon-Young would also receive some education after high school, that education was expected to help prepare her to be a good wife to her husband, a good mother to her children, and a devoted daughter-in-law in the same way that Soon-Young's own mother was to her husband's parents.

In Korea, Soon-Young's mother was always the first family member up in the morning in order to prepare a hot breakfast for the family, to pack a fresh and adequate school lunch for the children, and to put out her husband's clothes and see him off to work. She kept their apartment neat and clean, managed the family budget, helped the children with their homework, and kept the accounts for her husband's business. When the children were young, she always found time to play with them and to teach them games and activities that emphasized patience and endurance. She was a source of both encouragement and criticism and believed that there was nothing that could not be accomplished with just more effort.

Soon-Young's uncle and aunt, Mr. and Mrs. Kim, have no children and were happy to take Soon-Young. But they also realize that, as Soon-Young's father's younger brother, Mr. Kim is obligated to help his older brother who, as the eldest son, also supports their parents. Mrs. Kim, who also works, welcomes Soon-Young's extra help with the household chores.

Soon-Young's family in Korea, as well as her aunt and uncle, are committed to the ideal of a peaceful and orderly family—traditionally also the basis for a peaceful and orderly society—advocated by the ancient Chinese philosopher Confucius (Moore, 1949, pp. 3–47). Each family member participates, not as an isolated and individual self, but by finding his or her place in a network of human relationships that stretches from the nuclear family through the extended family into the larger society. This network, governed by tradition and grounded in respect and moral obligation, is defined by the five relationships that Confucius described as the basis for filial piety and fraternal friendships—relationships between father and son, elder brother and younger brother, husband and wife, ruler and subject, and friend and friend (Moore, 1949, p. 28). Individual desires and feelings are always satisfied within the filial context and in a way that does not upset the *kibun,* the sense of well-being of an individual or the group.

Soon-Young's uncle and aunt live in a small but comfortable apartment in a suburban working-class neighborhood outside of a large midwestern metropolis. When Mr. and Mrs. Kim arrived in the United States, they lived for a short time with a cousin of Mr. Kim who came eight years earlier and now acted as their sponsor. There are three other, more recently arrived, Korean families in the same apartment building and other families scattered throughout the neighborhood. Other new arrivals in the same neighborhood are of Filipino, Latino, Chinese, and Vietnamese ancestry.

Mr. Kim speaks better English than his wife but at work continues to be frustrated by his lack of English fluency and by his perception that he is underemployed. His current job is lower in status and responsibility than the one he held in Korea, and he has not been fully able to transfer his previous work experience and skills as quickly as he anticipated (Kim, 1978, p. 186). He has seen Caucasian employees who have been with the company for a shorter time than he has being given more responsible positions. Although his level of spoken English is often the reason given for his not being promoted, he suspects that discrimination is also a factor. However, he is more likely to resign himself to the fact than to make an issue of it (Kim, 1978, pp. 197–198). Mr. Kim eventually would like to open his own business. With a number of other newcomers from Korea, he contributes regularly to a *gae,* an informal system of pooling money in amounts that no single individual could accumulate in the same period of time. Each month, the person willing to pay the highest rate of interest to the others is entitled to take the accumulated savings for his or her own personal use.

Mr. and Mrs. Kim are occasionally homesick for the mountains and countryside of Korea and their relatives and friends; they do not miss the polluted air of Seoul or the continuing political and labor unrest. This does not mean that they are eager to become Americanized. While appreciating the opportunities and freedoms available to them in the United States, Mr.

and Mrs. Kim continue to encourage Soon-Young to be proud of Korea and of being Korean. They speak Korean almost exclusively at home, not only because of the expectation that Soon-Young will return to Korea, but because speaking the language continually reaffirms that they are Korean. Also, English does not contain those honorific forms necessary to maintain essential vertical relationships between people and for promoting and maintaining social propriety (Kim, 1978, p. 81). Social life for the Kims consists of visits with Mr. Kim's cousin's family, and activities centered at the growing nearby Korean Presbyterian Church.

Since her arrival, Soon-Young has been acutely aware of the sacrifices made for her by both her uncle and aunt and her parents. The Kims provide her with food, clothing, and shelter while trying to save enough money to move to a better neighborhood and perhaps start their own business. Her parents, especially her mother, and her brothers have to do without the help that Soon-Young would provide if she were at home. She works hard to be a credit to her uncle and aunt and to her parents.

Early on she gained a working knowledge of English through the school's program for limited English proficiency students and by reading *Anne of Green Gables* using an English–Korean dictionary. At first it was hard for her to adjust to a school so different from the one she attended in Korea. She marvels at the easy relations that exist between boys and girls who have always attended school together. In many Korean intermediate and high schools, boys and girls do not attend school together. She still recalls how, during her first week at school, she furtively watched a boy and girl embracing and kissing while other students passed by unconcerned. She is still not used to the personal freedom that most students exercise as they plan their own academic programs, wear varieties of clothing unhampered by a dress code, and pass rambunctiously down the halls between classes. In Korea, the intermediate and high school students remain in the classroom and the teachers move from class to class.

Soon-Young had anticipated developing close relationships with a class cohort of other girls her age that would result in enduring friendships. Instead, she found that friendship was often individual and competitive, often of short duration, and easily disrupted by the constant preoccupation of her peers with boys and clothes. Even more disappointing and confusing was her need to readjust her perception of her teachers. In Korea a teacher is a teacher, and all of them are expected to serve as role models who not only teach subjects but also act as moral exemplars and caring parents. But teachers here, like the students themselves, stand out less as a category of persons with a common role eliciting common respect and more as individuals with distinct personalities. Even Soon-Young's uncle and aunt, who formerly respected all teachers, now mentally classify them into the categories of "real" and "not real" teachers. In the latter category are teachers who arrive at school as late as possible and leave as early as possible, who give little or no homework, and who view teaching as just another job.

Soon-Young especially likes Ms. Ahn. As a small child, Ms. Ahn came to the United States with her parents from Korea in the early 1960s. Ms. Ahn is a bilingual, a "one and a half" generation American of Korean ancestry who is almost like an aunt to Soon-Young. Soon-Young speaks guardedly to her uncle about Ms. Ahn. Although Mr. Kim appreciates Ms. Ahn's interest in Soon-Young and the academic guidance she has given her, he feels that she is too Americanized and too aggressive for a Korean woman.

Ms. Ahn is proud of her Korean heritage and of Korean culture, but she is not blind to what she considers to be Korea's sexist, male-dominated society (Terry, 1990, p. A21). She is impressed with the quality of Soon-Young's schoolwork and her academic potential, especially in math and science. She thinks that it would be a shame if Soon-Young returned to Korea only to become a traditional wife and mother. She continues to encourage Soon-Young, who, though she misses her family, has become excited by the possibility of staying and attending college in the United States. She dreams of being a science teacher or even a university researcher.

Ms. Ahn recognizes the potential conflict that her encouragement of Soon-Young may create between Soon-Young and her aunt and uncle and between Soon-Young and her parents. Ms. Ahn is occasionally troubled by the thought that perhaps she is preoccupied more with ideological ax-grinding disguised as a concern for Soon-Young's future. She decides, however, that her concern is genuine and that the matter is important enough to Soon-Young's future to risk upsetting the highly valued *kibun* of the family. Perhaps by talking directly with Soon-Young's aunt, she can minimize the disruption of family.

At Soon-Young's urging, her aunt, without consulting her husband, has gone to school and spoken to Ms. Ahn. She agrees with Ms. Ahn's characterization of Korean society as male-dominated, where women have no place in the five valued relationships of Confucius except as wives. Ms. Ahn does not think this is an entirely bad thing. There is status in being a good wife and mother. After all, much that Ms. Ahn admires about Soon-Young and much of Ms. Ahn's own success is owed to a committed Korean mother. Ms. Ahn suggests that the freedom the Kims find so attractive in the United States should be extended to Soon-Young so that she will have the choice of staying in the United States to realize her full potential.

Soon-Young's aunt recalls a close friend from high school who had obtained American master's and doctoral degrees and then returned to Korea and married. For awhile she had tried to hold a teaching position in a small private college that was a three-hour round trip commute from her home.

She worked very hard to be a competent instructor and devoted wife. But her mother-in-law criticized her for not always having dinner ready for her husband, for not keeping the apartment as neat as she felt that her son liked it to be, and for postponing having children, who would bring pleasure to her and her husband as grandparents. Her friend's husband appeared oblivious to her strong desire for a college teaching career and insisted that there was no reason for her to work, because he could comfortably provide for both of them. He also told her that her working was a constant source of friction between himself and his parents. Mrs. Kim remembers with what reluctance her friend gave up her dream of a career. She also knows that this is not an atypical case and that the situation would likely be the same for Soon-Young.

Mrs. Kim would like to support Ms. Ahn and also encourage Soon-Young. However, Mrs. Kim knows that, because her husband wants them to have children of their own, they are in no position financially to support Soon-Young through college. Ms. Ahn assures her that Soon-Young can get sufficient financial aid at the local state college. Mrs. Kim knows her husband's obligation to his brother to abide by his wishes regarding Soon-Young and the expectation that she will return to Korea.

Soon-Young, for her part, feels that to assert her own desires and interests, if they are not shared by her uncle and father, would be to take advantage of her father's business misfortunes, her uncle's obligation to her father that brought her to America, and her aunt's kindness and support during the time she has lived with them. Yet with each passing day, she knows that it will be harder and harder to adapt if she returns to Korea, that she has managed to survive and excel in America, and that she would like to have the opportunity to realize her potential. Where does Soon-Young belong, in the United States or Korea? What life and opportunities does she most deserve? Who should make this decision? What should the decision be?

DANNY KAMAKA'S FUTURE

Romantic stereotypes and myths aside, the islands that compose the State of Hawaii have been a place where many Native Hawaiian people often feel like "strangers in their own land." (McNassor & Hongo, 1972). The ancestors of the present Native Hawaiians migrated from other Pacific islands almost a thousand years before the first European arrived in the Islands (Lind, 1980, p. 19). After that, the native Hawaiian population as a whole experienced a decline in numbers from disease introduced from the outside, lost their sovereign nation through annexation to the United States, were surpassed socioeconomically by later-arriving groups from the U.S. mainland

and Asia, and finally, in the late 1960s and early 1970s, enjoyed a rebirth of interest in Hawaiian culture and of political awareness. Nevertheless, persons of Hawaiian and part-Hawaiian ancestry constitute the largest category of persons who are on welfare or in prison on the island of Oahu, and they suffer disproportionately from poverty-related disease.

Keoki and Betty Kamaka have seen many changes over the years. They remember when Hawaiians were dismissed as lazy and frivolously fun loving. Now they live at a time when having any Hawaiian blood is a source of pride, and when persons of Hawaiian ancestry strive to become a potent political force. Today, on the model of certain mainland U.S. Native American tribes, some Hawaiians demand political sovereignty—the right to control their own land, lives, and destinies.

Mr. and Mrs. Kamaka have four children—a son and two daughters who are still in school and a son who is married. All seven members of the family live in a middle-income subdivision on the windward side of Oahu, the most populous of the islands forming the State of Hawaii. A neighborhood of small frame houses amidst a profusion of trees and flowers, it serves primarily as a bedroom community for persons who take the twenty-to-forty minute drive each day across the island to the state capital, Honolulu, and the surrounding area, where they are employed mainly in the tourist, service, and construction industries.

Mr. and Mrs. Kamaka are entitled to live on Hawaiian Homestead land, set aside for persons with 50% or more Hawaiian blood. But their names have been on a waiting list for ten years, and they are part of a backlog of qualified applicants who despair of receiving such housing in their lifetimes.

Their neighborhood is multiethnic, and the Kamakas' neighbors reflect the generations of people who, over the years, came (sometimes as plantation laborers) to settle in Hawaii from such places as Japan, China, Korea, the Philippines, Portugal, and the U.S. mainland. A large, twin-engine boat that they use for weekend fishing trips occupies most of the Kamaka front yard. Although catching fish is ostensibly the reason for these outings, equally important are the opportunities such activities provide for people to socialize and maintain the bonds of friendship that define them as family. A backyard of bare ground with patches of worn grass testifies to its use as a gathering place for family, extended family, and neighborhood celebrations like baby baptisms, birthdays, anniversaries, and other special occasions. Sometimes a large tent is suspended over the entire yard and a collection of worn folding chairs and tables is arranged for the guests. And for some occasions, a portion of the yard is dug up to create an *imu* for roasting a whole pig underground on heated rocks.

The Kamaka house is well maintained, but not improved in such a way that it stands out from those of their neighbors. Only a bedroom has been added to accommodate their eldest son and his wife. Inside the house, the furniture has a comfortable, worn look, and the friends who gather there feel relaxed and at ease. Neither the Kamakas nor their friends are anxious that small children will break anything or that the furniture will be damaged by occasional spills.

The Kamakas are friendly with all their neighbors and frequently share fruit from their mango and papaya trees, and fish caught on the weekends. Mr. Kamaka often lends his tools and expertise to neighbors, relatives, and friends when they ask him for help. There exists among all of them an easy kind of reciprocity where no one keeps careful track of who owes whom, but each person is always available when needed. A give-and-take relationship that becomes too unbalanced will be noticed, and people will begin to talk. Such sharing also provides opportunities for visiting and the maintenance of neighborly relations.

The Kamaka's second son, Danny, is a high school junior who plays first-string junior varsity football. He is friendly and popular with boys and girls alike and does well in his classes. His explanation for his good grades is that he likes his teachers and the work comes easy to him. He has a kind of joking relationship with his teachers, who find his easy humor infectious. The school counselor, impressed by reports from Danny's junior high teachers and his standardized test scores, persuaded him to enroll in the college pre-paratory curriculum. Danny finds it easy to earn mostly B grades and still play football.

His friends accept Danny's academic success in a good-natured way. He can always be counted on to share his homework with them or help them to find material for a last-minute term paper. When they acknowledge that he is "smart" or "a brain," Danny plays it down by saying that it is "no big thing" and that it is just easy for him (Gallimore & Howard, 1969, p. 12). He emphasizes that he's not smart like "the Japanese and Chinese kids."

Over the years, Danny avoided situations where his academic success might appear to come at the expense of his friends. His teachers learned early on that to praise him publicly and in front of his friends, rather than eliciting greater effort from him, had just the opposite effect. It embarrasses Danny to be singled out because then he must convince his friends that he is still one of them and is not showing off.

Until now, Danny hasn't thought much about making plans for college, but after taking the PSAT he has given it some attention. Most of his closest friends, whom he has known since elementary school, are also of part-Hawaiian ancestry, and he spends much of his free time with them surfing and swimming. Unlike Danny, they are not enrolled in the college preparatory program. Some of them think about attending the local community college, but most plan to go to work after graduation.

Danny, having experienced success in the college preparatory program, now finds it less easy than it might have been to follow the friends for whom higher education is a less compelling option. He also finds that he admires certain adults and is more open to them as role models than are most of his friends. At the same time he is growing more conscious of what it means to be Hawaiian and live Hawaiian.

Mr. Kamaka, a high school graduate, got his start in the construction industry as a pick-and-shovel man through the help of an uncle. Since then, he has become a highly skilled bulldozer and crane operator. After work, he often remains on a construction site or goes to the home of a fellow worker to drink a few beers and "talk story" with fellow workers who may also fish with him on the weekends.

He takes quiet pride in a salary that, as he sometimes points out, is larger than that of most school teachers and many college professors. He has been offered a foreman's position but is reluctant to take it because, to his way of thinking, the additional money won't compensate for having to supervise and give orders to his former peers. Their friendship is based upon an egalitarian relationship and he is concerned that if he accepted the position, his friends would perceive him as thinking he is better than they are and trying to be something he is not (Gallimore & Howard, 1969, pp. 10–16). He spends much of his salary for such things as upgrading his boat and fishing equipment, maintaining his car and truck, gifts for family members, and plenty of food for parties. He easily lends money to friends who ask him and often cosigns loans for them. Several times he has had to repay such loans, but still finds it almost impossible to refuse a friend. He is certain that his friends would do the same for him if the occasion arose.

Mr. Kamaka is a large, powerful man who expects his children to obey immediately and is quick to become angry when they act too slowly. Any anger, however, quickly passes, and the children learn to gauge his moods and to ask him for spending money or other favors only when he is calm and happy.

Mrs. Kamaka completed one year of community college before quitting to get married. She works as a clerk in the admissions office of the state university. She, too, is a generous person who often brings fruit from her yard or store-bought treats to the office. Unlike her husband, who helps out only when there are special needs like Saturday morning work parties, Mrs. Kamaka is active at the nearby United Church of Christ and is always available to cook and serve at luncheons and potlucks and to help out in the nursery on Sunday mornings. She is a less strict disciplinarian than her husband; nevertheless, her children have also learned to assess her mood before asking for favors.

The eldest son, known as Junior, and his wife were married shortly after high school graduation and live with the rest of the family. Mr. Kamaka got Junior started in construction work just as his uncle had gotten him his first job (Gallimore & Howard, 1969, p. 18). Junior's wife is of Japanese ancestry and works as a waitress in a downtown Honolulu coffee shop. Since the wedding, she has become like another daughter to Mr. and Mrs. Kamaka, but her relations with her own family are now minimal.

The Kamakas have two daughters; Jenny is a freshman in high school, and Claire is in eighth grade. They do most of the chores around the house now that the sons are older (Gallimore & Howard, 1969, p. 66). They often grumble about this inequity, but not too loudly. Most of their friends are of part-Hawaiian ancestry, and all of them enjoy hanging out after school at the local shopping mall. Jenny and Claire do make it a point to get home in time to do their chores and help prepare dinner. Mr. Kamaka frowns on their "running wild" with their friends, but if they complete their chores, they can go out with friends on Friday and Saturday nights. On Sunday mornings, they usually help their mother in the church nursery.

Danny's favorite teacher is Mr. Barton, who teaches political science for juniors and seniors. Mr. B, as Danny and the other students call him, is a Caucasian who came to Hawaii ten years earlier and immediately immersed himself in the ongoing Hawaiian Renaissance. Mr. B describes himself as an aging radical, and he and his wife have become deeply interested in things Hawaiian. They are more knowledgeable about Hawaiian music, ancient chants, literature, and language than many persons of Hawaiian ancestry born and raised in the Islands. In addition, they are involved in the Hawaiian sovereignty movement and protest what they view as threats to the natural ecology of the Islands. In particular, they condemn the U.S. military who use the uninhabited but, to Hawaiians, religiously significant island of Kohoo-lawe for ship-to-shore target practice; local, mainland, and foreign investors who build luxury condominiums and resorts that cater to outsiders; and local corporations and politicians who favor developing sources of energy production that threaten the fragile ecosystem of the Islands.

Originally Mr. B's participation in these causes was viewed by locals with some skepticism, but more recently he and his wife increasingly are accepted by some members of the small group of native Hawaiian activists. Others in that group, however, believe that full participation can be achieved only by persons of Hawaiian ancestry, who share that "mystical quality" that binds all native Hawaiians and is related to their "common ancestral origins going back to primeval times." (Kanahele, 1982, p. A19). Increasingly this group avoids making a distinction among Hawaiians based upon specific blood quantum and consider all persons with Hawaiian blood as genuinely Hawaiian.

Mr. B's colleagues, who were all born and raised in Hawaii, are of varying ancestries and include several Hawaiians. Many of these colleagues see his confrontational behavior and politics as antithetical to the spirit of Aloha. To them, a politics of consensus is essential for harmonious living in a multicultural and pluralistic society. They accuse Mr. B of taking an antiestablishment position just to curry favor with some native Hawaiian students who are hard to handle, and of pushing an ideological agenda that is not necessarily in the best interest of the students.

Mr. B tells Danny that, for the Hawaiian people to achieve more political control over their own destiny, they must become politicized under the leadership of a cadre of college educated Hawaiians occupying leadership positions in the state. He stresses that economic development that benefits the tourist industry and wealthy newcomers is robbing locals, especially the Hawaiian people, of their land and the natural beauty of the state.

When Danny discusses Mr. B's ideas at home, his father and brother are critical of them. Although they agree that renewed pride in things Hawaiian is a good thing, they reject Mr. B's criticism of economic development for Hawaii. Mr. Kamaka says that the best thing for Hawaiians is steady, skilled work that enables a person to be a good provider for his family. Mr. Kamaka says Mr. B can afford to play with such ideas because he can count on being paid regardless of the state of the economy and can always go back to the U.S. mainland if things are not to his liking in Hawaii. For Hawaiians, Hawaii is home; they have no other place to return to.

When Danny mentions the possibility of attending a mainland college, his brother says that, of the few Hawaiians he knows who have gone to the mainland for college, most returned after one semester. Junior predicts that Danny will soon miss his land and his people. Both Mr. Kamaka and Junior say that Hawaiians who graduate from the state university or mainland colleges become different; they use fifty-cent words, think they are better than other people, think they know more than their parents, and do not fit in any more because they are more like *Haoles* (Caucasians) than they are like Hawaiians. Such people live in a different world and grow away from their former friends and family. Finally, they say, the college graduates they know usually do not have jobs that pay as well as their jobs in construction do. As an example, they point to one of Danny's cousins who is a teacher, has a hard time making ends meet, married a woman he met on the mainland, and rarely comes to family gatherings and parties any longer. Danny respects and admires both his father and his brother, who is his best friend.

Even if he stays in Hawaii and attends the University of Hawaii or one of the community colleges, Danny knows that he will have to work part-time. That means studying on the weekends and having to forgo time spent with his family and friends. He wonders if it isn't these kinds of shared activities, more than protests and politics, that define him as Hawaiian both to himself and to those he cares most about. On the other hand, he wonders if this way of life will still be available for his children and grandchildren unless the Hawaiian people have the political power and the leadership to maintain and guarantee it. He wishes that he didn't have to make this decision so soon, or that someone else could make it for him. What is the right decision for Danny? Who should make the decision? Who should try to influence it?

REFERENCES

Beyond Desegregation in Taylor City

Banks, J. A. (1983). Multiethnic education and the quest for equality. *Phi Delta Kappan, 64,* 582–585.
Bell, D. (1983). Learning from our losses: Is school desegregation still feasible in the 1980s? *Phi Delta Kappan, 64,* 572–575.
Clark, R. M. (1983). *Family life and school achievement.* Chicago: University of Chicago Press.
Comer, J. P. (1988). *Maggie's American dream.* New York: New American Library.
Gollnick, D. M., & Chinn, P. C. (1990). *Multicultural education in a pluralistic society* (2nd ed.). Columbus, OH: Merrill.
Sheeter, C. E. (1990). Staff development for desegregated schooling. *Phi Delta Kappan, 73,* pp. 33–40.
Wharton, C. R., Jr. (1983, October 29). "Demanding families" and black achievement. *Education Week,* p. 23.

Who Speaks for the Nguyens?

Cannon, A. (1989a, October 31). English-only debate festers. *San Francisco Chronicle,* pp. A8–A9.
Cannon, A. (1989b, October 31). Burgeoning crisis in California schools. *San Francisco Chronicle,* pp. A1, A8.
Fitzgerald, F. (1972). *Fire in the lake: The Vietnamese and the Americans in Vietnam.* Boston: Little, Brown.
Gardner, R. W., Robey, B., & Smith, P. C. (1985). *Asian Americans: Growth, change, and diversity* (Population Bulletin, vol. 40, no. 4). Washington, DC: Population Reference Bureau.
Liem, N. D., & Kehmeier, D. F. (1980). The people of Indochina: The Vietnamese. In J. F. McDermott, W.-S. Tseng, & T. W. Maretzki (Eds.), *Peoples and cultures of Hawaii: A psychocultural profile* (pp. 202–217). Honolulu: John A. Burns School of Medicine and The University Press of Hawaii.
Tran, V. D. (1989, November). Hue: My city, myself. *National Geographic,* pp. 595–603.

A Language or a Thinking Problem?

Glauberman, S. (1991, June 14). Minorities rule still holding true in isles. *Honolulu Advertiser,* p. A1.

Hawaii Department of Education. (1989). *A report on the needs and educational services for Hawaii's limited English proficient students.* Honolulu, HI: Author.

Teodoro, L. V. (1981). *Out of this struggle: The Filipinos in Hawaii.* Honolulu, HI: University Press of Hawaii.

Two Letters of Recommendation

Hsu, F. L. K. (1981). *Americans and Chinese: Passage to differences* (3rd ed.). Honolulu: University Press of Hawaii.

Krauthammer, C. (1990, February 5). Education: Doing bad and feeling good. *Time,* p. 78.

Moore, G. F. (1949). *History of religions.* New York: Scribner's.

Rohner, R. P. (1975). *They love me, they love me not.* New Haven, CT: Hraf Press.

Gloria's Career Decision

Hatt, P. K. (1952). *Background of human fertility in Puerto Rico: A sociological survey.* Princeton, NJ: Princeton University Press.

Rothermund, D., & Simon, J. (Eds.). (1986). *Education and the integration of ethnic minorities.* London: Frances Pinter.

Santiago, I. (1986). The education of Hispanics in the United States: Inadequacies of the American melting pot theory. In D. Rothermund & J. Simon (Eds.), *Education and the integration of ethnic minorities.* London: Frances Pinter.

Soon-Young's Divided Loyalties

Kim, B.-L. C. (1978). *The Asian Americans: Changing patterns, changing needs.* Montclair, NJ: Association of Korean Christian Scholars, Inc.

Moore, G. F. (1949). *History of religions.* New York: Scribner's.

Terry, E. (1990, June 15). Women in Korea are not treated as their men's equal. *Honolulu Star-Bulletin,* p. A21.

Danny Kamaka's Future

Gallimore, R., & Howard, A. (Eds.). (1969). *Studies in a Hawaiian community: Na makamaka o Nanakuli.* Honolulu, HI: Bernice P. Bishop Museum.

Kanahele, G. S. (1982, March 26). Update: Hawaiian Renaissance revisited. *Honolulu Advertiser,* p. A19.

Lind, A. W. (1980). *Hawaii's people* (4th ed.). Honolulu: University Press of Hawaii.

McNassor, D., & Hongo, R. (1972). *Strangers in their own land: Self-disparagement in ethnic Hawaiian youth.* Claremont, CA: The Claremont Reading Conference.

INDEX

ABOUT THE
AUTHORS

Index